ACCESS TO ACADEMICS FOR ALL STUDENTS

Critical Approaches to Inclusive Curriculum, Instruction, and Policy

ACCESS TO ACADEMICS FOR ALL STUDENTS

Critical Approaches to Inclusive Curriculum, Instruction, and Policy

Edited by

Paula Kluth
Diana M. Straut
Douglas P. Biklen
Syracuse University

LAWRENCE ERLBUAM ASSOCIATES, PUBLISHERS
2003 Mahwah, New Jersey London

Lawrence Erlbaum Associates, Inc., Publishers
10 Industrial Avenue
Mahwah, New Jersey 07430

Cover design by Kathryn Houghtaling Lacey

Library of Congress Cataloging-in-Publication Data

Kluth, Paula.
Access to academics for all students: Critical approaches to inclusive curriculum, instruction, and policy / Paula Kluth, Diana M. Straut, Douglas P. Biklen.
p. cm.
Includes bibliographical references and index.
ISBN 0-8058-4166-0 (pbk. : alk. paper)
1. Inclusive education. 2. Educational equalization. I. Straut, Diana M. II. Biklen, Douglas. III. Title.

LC1200 .K58 2003
371.9'046—dc21

2002029482

Books published by Lawrence Erlbaum Associates are printed on acid-free paper, and their bindings are chosen for strength and durability.

Printed in the United States of America
10 9 8 7 6 5 4 3 2

Contents

Preface

In this text we join with a growing number of voices in suggesting that teachers in diverse, inclusive schools move beyond participation and consider ways to intellectually engage all learners. It is critical to stress that this book is not just about disability. *Access to Academics for All Students* is designed to examine the perceptions teachers hold about students with disabilities, students who are racially and ethnically diverse, students using English as a second language, students labeled at risk, students placed in both high and low academic tracks, and students in urban schools. The chapters are designed to highlight how students who traditionally have been denied access to challenging work and educational opportunities can be supported to participate in academic instruction.

Early texts on inclusive education suggested that teachers find opportunities for students with disabilities to meaningfully participate in class activities. They did not typically propose, however, that the participation be linked to content directly or that it meets any standards of complexity or rigor; this is especially true for students with significant disabilities. In fact, many of the texts on inclusive schooling in the 1980s and 1990s were focused on including students socially in schools and classrooms and on facilitating the participation of students with disabilities in lessons and classroom activities. In the past few years, however, educators and researchers have become increasingly interested in the ways in which students with disabilities are intellectually and academically engaged in the classroom (Bottge, 2001; Crossley, 1997; Falvey, Blair, Dingle, & Franklin, 2000; Fisher, Sax, & Pumpian, 1999; Jorgensen, 1998; Kliewer, 1998; Kliewer & Biklen, 2001; Kluth, 1998; Kluth & Straut, 2001; Udvari-Solner, 1996; Udvari-Solner, Villa, & Thousand, 2002).

As we began generating ideas for this book, we explored ways in which many different populations of students are underchallenged in our schools. Students may not receive the education they need because of teacher or community expectations, school culture, mismatch between a teacher's teaching style and a student's learning style, inappropriate curriculum, lackluster instruction, or inadequate resources. *Access to Academics for All Students* examines these issues and offers both a progressive ideology and practical suggestions for those struggling to provide appropriate educational experiences for the diverse population of learners in schools today.

One of the primary reasons we decided to assemble this text was to promote a broad definition of inclusive education that incorporates and attends to all learners. Inclusive schooling, we feel, can be a catalyst for critically examining the education of all students, for interrogating the perceptions and assumptions we have about different types of learners, and for exploring ways to offer a meaningful and appropriately rigorous curriculum to every learner.

In sum, *Access to Academics for All Students:*

- views inclusion broadly and highlights issues related to the education of students with disabilities, students who are racially and ethnically diverse, students using English as a second language, students labeled at risk, students placed in both high and low academic tracks, and students in urban schools;
- critiques schooling as we know it and proposes new ways to view and teach students in our diverse schools;
- presumes that diverse students can participate in academic instruction if appropriately and creatively supported;
- identifies frameworks, approaches, and strategies that foster access to academic curricula;
- includes authors with expertise in general and special education curriculum, instruction, and programming. Some of the authors also have experience teaching and researching issues in multicultural-ism;

In contrast, many traditional texts on inclusive education:

- view inclusion as an issue related primarily or solely to students with disabilities;
- propose ideas for implementing inclusive practices without examining the political and cultural aspects of schooling;
- highlight primarily the voices of researchers and writers from the special education community.

This volume provides ideas for recognizing and challenging inequities. It also offers a framework for school leaders and teachers to foster access to academics for students with a range of strengths and needs. Drawing on classroom and school observations, current research, and stories from teachers and students, the authors explore pragmatic ways of increasing academic access for all learners in our schools.

Each chapter is concerned with an academic content area (e.g., science, reading) or general school issue (e.g., standards, family participation) and provides examples of how (and, in some cases, why) different types of learners have been denied opportunities to learn, succeed, and use the unique talents, gifts, skills, and abilities they possess. Some of the chapters show how students have been included, but still not valued as academic learners. We also include examples throughout this text of how students *can* be seen and appreciated as academic learners.

In *Access to Academics for All Students,* we offer a unique text that is hopeful and optimistic. The book provides concrete examples of how to conduct instruction in today's diverse schools, highlighting the difference in approaching schooling from an access-to-academics approach for all learners and an approach that presumes some students will have access and others will not.

The audience for this volume includes elementary and secondary preservice and in-service teachers. Because the chapters focus on both general schooling issues and content area information, the book could be used for methods courses (e.g., Introductory Social Studies Methods, Reading in the Content Areas) and foundations courses focused on school politics, social issues, and critiques of curriculum and instruction.

Additionally, the book can serve as a resource for teachers, parents, and school and district administrators. The focus on school issues such as standards, tracking, and family issues are critical and currently popular areas of study for new and veteran educators.

Chapter 1 provides an overview of the tenets upon which *Access to Academics* is built. The chapter challenges educators to evaluate the curriculum provided to all students. Paula Kluth, Doug Biklen, and Diana Straut consider some prevailing perceptions, stereotypes, and beliefs about students as learners. The authors present guidelines for supporting diverse learners and providing motivating, interesting, and challenging curriculum, instruction, and assessment for students with a range of needs and abilities. Specifically the authors provide a description of how an access-to-academics framework is manifested in ideology, school culture, and pedagogy.

Chapter 2 examines the question: Can we standardize *and* make curriculum, instruction, and assessment responsive to differences? In this chapter, Paula Kluth and Diana Straut argue that it is not only possible, but also critically important. The authors debunk myths about standards and suggest that a movement toward standards and outcomes may actually benefit marginalized students.

In chapter 3, Tracy Knight demonstrates, through multiple examples, how educators can take advantage of parent knowledge and experience to ensure success for all students. The chapter builds on the assumption that student success is highly predicated on the degree to which educators understand, accept, and appreciate the divergent school and home cultures of the communities in which they teach.

Chapter 4 examines the assumptions educators hold about literacy and learners. Researchers have begun to document the importance of viewing all students as literate (Allen, 1995; Kliewer, 1998) and recognizing that they possess multiple literacies used in various social contexts (Alvermann & Phelps, 1998). Kelly

Chandler-Olcott presents concerns related to access and suggests ways to support and engage all students as they emerge as readers, speakers, listeners, and writers.

Susana Davidenko and Patricia Tinto draw from a case study of English as a Second Language (ESL) students struggling for access to a challenging mathematics curriculum. Chapter 5 presents rich conversations with ESL students to highlight the distinctions between *including* students in a mathematics classroom, and giving them *access* to a challenging curriculum.

Chapter 6 examines ways that all students can access power through social studies instruction. The chapter opens with an examination of the assumptions and structures of social studies instruction that have long excluded many learners. The authors, Diana Straut and Kevin Colleary, argue that all learners deserve to be viewed as contributing members in a participatory democracy. The chapter explores practical ways that educators can create opportunities that empower students to critically examine the society in which they live and to work for social change (Ladson-Billings, 1994).

Questioning why some students are marked for honors courses and other relegated to the vocational track, John Tillotson and Paula Kluth examine how the structure and demands of the high-school content areas can be problematic for both teachers and students. Throughout chapter 7, the authors use the content area of science to reveal how instructional methods often marginalize the very students who have the highest aptitude for being successful as practicing scientists. Comparing and contrasting the skills and abilities needed in auto mechanics and physics as an illustration of this point, the authors critique academic tracking practices and suggest that teachers may need to study the greater school community, the curriculum, and the organization, politics, and culture of the school in order to give all students opportunities to succeed in science.

Chapter 8 emphasizes music as an academic content area that can provide enriching, meaningful experiences for individual learners, including students with special needs and those with special talents, without sacrificing expectations for their musical potential and growth. Katia Madsen examines the issue of appropriate expectations for learners in the arts, and provides adaptive strategies with practical applications for implementation.

Recognizing that not all academic learning takes place in a classroom, the authors of chapter 9 critique the ways in which students have been excluded from extracurricular activities. Mara Sapon-Shevin and Paula Kluth argue that teachers can no longer afford to view the broader "curriculum" of the school to be outside the realm of inclusive schooling. Students with disabilities, students marginalized because of social class, and students with limited financial resources must be included in extracurricular activities for social reasons but also in order to gain access to challenging academic skill and content.

Chapter 10 examines the importance of deconstructing current under-standings of ability, disability, learning differences, and intelligence while building new models and paradigms for understanding and teaching students in the diverse American classroom. Doug Biklen, Diana Straut, and Paula Kluth revisit the tenets of Access to Academics and issue a call to action for all educators committed to improving American schools.

ACKNOWLEDGMENTS

Were authorship of this book to be properly credited, it would be shared among many. More friends and colleagues than we can mention shared our commitment, accomplishments, and our struggles as we considered what is and what can be in public education. We wish to thank:

- The chapter authors, our Syracuse University colleagues, who wrote intensely and honestly and who never refused our suggestions or requests for edits. It is a privilege to work with you.
- The staff at Lawrence Erlbaum Associates, especially Naomi Silverman and Lori Hawver. Your talents have immensely improved this book and helped us to think more critically and deeply about our ideas.
- Jacqueline Thousand (California State University, San Marcos) and Cheryl M. Jorgensen (University of New Hampshire) for generously reading and re-reading this manuscript. Your input and support was invaluable.
- Our families, who endured the late nights, long phone conversations, and last minute editing blitzes.
- The many families, teachers, and administrators who opened their homes, classrooms, and hearts to us so that we could learn. You have helped us to consider what is possible.
- The students who show up in schools everyday, those who will show up in the future, and those who don't show up because they haven't been afforded access. Thank you for inspiring us to imagine.
- Finally, we wish to thank the educators who will read this book and take the necessary risks to enact an access to education agenda.

REFERENCES

Allen, J. (1995). *It's never too late: Leading adolescents to lifelong literacy.* Portsmouth, NH: Heinemann.

Alvermann, D., & Phelps, S. (1998). *Content reading and literacy: Succeeding in today's diverse classrooms* (2nd ed.). Boston: Allyn & Bacon.

Bottge, B. (2001). Using intriguing problems to improve math skills. *Educational Leadership, 58*(6), 68-72.

Crossley, R. (1997). *Speechless: Facilitating communication for people without voices.* New York: Dutton.

Falvey, M., Blair, M., Dingle, M., & Franklin, N. (2000). Creating a community of learners with varied needs. In R. A. Villa & J. S. Thousand (Eds.), *Restructuring for caring and effective education* (pp. 186-207). Baltimore: Brookes.

Fisher, D., Sax, C., & Pumpian, I. (1999). *Inclusive high schools: Learning from contemporary classrooms.* Baltimore: Brookes.

Jorgensen, C. (1998). *Restructuring high schools for all students.* Baltimore: Brookes.

Kliewer, C. (1998). *Schooling children with Down syndrome.* New York: Teachers College Press.

Kliewer, C., & Biklen, D. (2001). "School's not really a place for reading": A research synthesis of the literate lives of students with severe disabilities. *The Journal of the Association for Persons with Severe Handicaps, 26,* 1-12.

Kluth, P. (1998).*The impact of facilitated communication of the educational lives of students: Three case studies.* Unpublished doctoral dissertation. Madison, WI: University of Wisconsin-Madison, Special Education Department.

Ladson-Billings, G. (1994). The dreamkeepers: Successful teachers of African-American children. San Francisco: Jossey-Bass.

Kluth, P., & Straut, D. (2001). Standards for diverse learners. *Educational Leadership, 59,* 43-46.

Udvari-Solner, A. (1996). Examining teacher thinking: Constructing a process to design curricular adaptations. *Remedial and Special Education, 17,* 245-254.

Udvari-Solner, A., Villa, R., & Thousand, J. (2002). Access to the general education curriculum for all: The universal design process. In J. S. Thousand, R. A. Villa, & I. Nevin (Eds.), *Creativity and collaborative learning* (pp. 85-103). Baltimore: Brookes.

Chapter 1

Access to Academics for All Students

Paula Kluth
Douglas P. Biklen
Diana M. Straut
Syracuse University

Inclusive schooling, the educational movement that paved the way for students with disabilities to enter general education classrooms, has given thousands of students opportunities to participate in "typical" schooling experiences. Since the 1970s, students with disabilities have had increased opportunities to develop a wider range of relationships, to attend general education classes, and to engage in the same educational activities and lessons as their peers without disabilities.

While all of these types of participation are critical to the social, emotional, and intellectual growth of students, we are increasingly interested in examining the next steps in inclusive education. Now that so many students with disabilities have secured access to general education environments, educators are becoming more critical of the curriculum and instruction offered to learners with unique learning characteristics. In our own work as teacher educators, we have seen how those committed to inclusive schooling are moving *beyond participation and considering ways to challenge and intellectually engage learners with disabilities.* Consider the following examples:

> A student with Down syndrome, Isaac, is interested in the popular picture book, *Where the Wild Things Are.* Isaac's teacher, realizing that her young student loves to be dramatic, develops a class play around the story. The class works collaboratively to write the script, learn the lines, and create the scenery and props necessary for the production. Through these activities, Isaac's teachers develop opportunities for students to "engage with literacy and nu-

meracy skills, problem-solving and critical thinking processes, and interpersonal capacities." (Kliewer, 1998, p. 77)

When the special education referrals in one school district begin to skyrocket, one team of educators attempts to fix the curriculum instead of looking to "repair" the students. A special educator, a math teacher, and a technology education teacher join forces to teach a diverse group of students with and without disabilities. The teachers introduce the concept of "measuring and predicting natural world occurrences related to the functions of distance, rate, and time" by setting up a car derby course and letting students crate cars to race on the course. Students calculate the car's straightaway speed during each trial. They also construct a graph to show the relation between the release points on the ramp and the car speeds on the straightaway. A student who has a history of struggling in math, earns a perfect mark on the unit posttests. She whispers to one of her teachers, "Don't tell my parents about this. They will faint." (Bottge, 2001, p. 69)

A 10th-grade social studies teacher designs a unit titled, "Can you be free if you are not treated equally?" She adopts the approach of creating lessons based on a "central idea" so that all students can participate and so they can access the challenging course content:

Some students in my class could answer using information from the reading and by thinking about the progress of Civil Rights in this country. One or two students had to approach this question from their own personal experiences/perspectives. Amro knew he was treated differently from his brothers because of his disability, and he has a strong opinion about that. If we start with his personal experiences, it's a little bit easier for him to make a connection with the civil war. (Onosko & Jorgensen, 1998, pp. 77–78)

Although these three examples certainly illustrate how students with disabilities are accessing academic skill and content in inclusive classrooms, it is equally clear that the curriculum and instruction highlighted in each example would be engaging and appropriate for learners with a variety of needs, skills, gifts, interests, and abilities. In this volume, we suggest that inclusive ideology and practices can serve as a catalyst for creating more challenging and meaningful educational experiences for ALL students including students of color, students who are ethnically diverse, students who use English as a second language, students labeled at risk, students in vocational tracks, and students in both rural and urban schools. Many educators, in fact, are beginning to understand inclusive schooling as a reform or movement that addresses all learners, not just those with disabilities (Jorgensen, 1998; Kluth, Diaz-Greenberg, Thousand, & Nevin, 2002; Oyler, 2001; Sapon-Shevin, 1999).

Some see inclusion as a way of thinking, an orientation, or an ideology. Others view it as a set of practices or a policy. Udvari-Solner (1997) offered a definition that incorporates both pragmatic and philosophic issues:

> [inclusive schooling] propels a critique of contemporary school culture and thus, encourages practitioners to reinvent what can be and should be to realize more humane, just and democratic learning communities. Inequities in treatment and educational opportunity are brought to the forefront, thereby fostering attention to human rights, respect for difference and value of diversity. (p. 142)

Like Udvari-Solner, we define inclusive education as something that supports, impacts, and benefits all learners. We see inclusion as an educational orientation that embraces differences and values diversity. Further, we view inclusion as a revolution, a social action, and a critical political movement. We also see inclusion as a way to boost academic opportunities and successes for all learners in public schools.

Specifically, this text is concerned with one often-ignored aspect of inclusive pedagogy: *access to academics.* We have chosen the term *access to academics* carefully, believing that it captures an important principle for educators, namely that participation or inclusion in schooling is not enough for any learner. All students deserve to be educated in ways that make them struggle, think, work, and grow. Students should have opportunities to tackle "hard work," they should be intellectually stretched.

To that end this volume asks a simple, but specific and important question: How can inclusive schooling and the practices associated with it, help all learners gain academic access? In the following chapters, we explore how educators are finding ways of making academic instruction available to all students, irrespective of social and economic class, gender, ethnicity, language, disability, or other factors often associated with access. In this chapter, we provide the following: (a) a framework for thinking about access-to-academics; and (b) an explanation of how school culture can support access-to-academics and (c) teaching practices that support access-to-academics in inclusive classrooms.

THROUGH A CRITICAL FRAME: WAYS OF THINKING ABOUT ACCESS

The dominant discourse style in education implies that there are right ways and wrong ways of going about education, that best ways can be scientifically determined, and that the work of educators is to employ "most appropriate" and "best" practices. In this book we attempt to navigate a far more tentative course in figuring out what to do or to recommend. While we embrace the notion of using scientific inquiry (in the sense of the social sciences where inquiry follows established or, at least, discussed and negotiated, traditions) at the same time, we attempt to step outside of the dominant discourse which we believe assumes too much certainty and not enough criticism.

We begin by comparing two ways of thinking about education; claiming authority to define reality versus an interpretive, critical stance toward teaching and learning. Although we do not believe there are *only* two ways of thinking about education, we understand that it might be useful to compare these two paradigms so that we may illustrate what type of thinking and beliefs we used in developing our access-to-academics framework; that is, in providing an overview of both paradigms we can illustrate not only the orientation we adopted but what types of thinking we attempt to challenge in this book.

Claiming Authority to Define Reality in Teaching and Learning

At the outset of this discussion, we want to clarify what we mean by the dominant discourse style in education—which we wish to set aside and even challenge. We do so with the full knowledge that embedded in the text of this book may be many contradictions of our own thesis; examples where we have engaged in practices characteristic of the dominant discourse.

Traditionally and currently, much educational research takes the form of experiments designed to establish a truth. Consider, for instance, an example of research on school behavior. In the *Journal of School Psychology*, Henington and colleagues (Henington, Hughes, Cavell, & Thompson, 1998) employed a scale for measuring and assigning classifications of aggression and then of relating gender to aggression. They describe their study and findings:

> (The) procedure allowed for the classification of children into one of four groups: children high on overt aggression only (OA), children high on relational aggression only (RA), children high on both relational aggression and overt aggression (combined aggressive, or CA), and nonaggressive children (NA).
>
> There was a statistically significant relation between gender and aggressive classification. More boys than girls were identified as OA. Furthermore, more boys than girls were identified as CA.

Our critique of this account is not that the authors have deviated from principles of social science, but that such an account, presented authoritatively, implicitly encourages us to embrace the findings as stated, and thus to participate in a process of decontextualizing education and, in this case, student behavior. Further, if we accept such findings more or less uncritically, we participate in a process of creating a discourse about education that is fundamentally undemocratic.

The study decontextualizes student behavior by virtue of the fact that we do not see the moments in which students do one thing or another. We are not informed about how students interpret their own actions. We do not get to see how different ways of being or doing are privileged within student culture but not adult or teacher culture. We do not see how teachers engage students academically and socially and how the culture of a classroom changes the dynamics of students' relationships and ways of interacting with each other. In short, we see too little; we are left with the unmistakable impression that aggression is definable as something specific that belongs to individual people not to circumstances or to particular cultural contexts.

To the extent that participants in education, including teachers, parents, and students, are not heard from in this research, the study encourages an undemocratic way of talking about education. True, no piece of research will completely offer the multiplicity of voices within education, but we feel that this study silences too much; we are troubled that the authors define aggression in a particular way without acknowledging that *they are not reporting on a reality*, but are actually creating a way of thinking about behavior, or what they determine to be aggression. The authoritative voice of the researchers leaves the reader feeling that the behavior is *in* the student and that work must be *done to* the student. The implications of this work are many; this way of writing and theorizing about behavior impacts how policies are written, how students are viewed, and how schools are organized.

Adopting an Interpretive, Tentative, Critical Stance Toward Teaching and Learning

Now, having considered an example from what we have described as the overly authoritative dominant discourse, consider an example from a more interpretive tradition. Dyson (1997), in the book *Writing Superheroes*, studied young children's talk and writing to understand how they construct their understandings of themselves, how they negotiate their relationships with each other, and how they make sense of each other. After two boys, Thomas and Aloyse, have been suspended from school for hitting a girl, Monique, two students have the following conversation (beginning with Holly stating the moral of the classroom story):

Holly: You're not supposed to slap girls, 'cause girls are not that strong, like boys.

Tina: HUH! The yellow girls are. Like you. You just don't know. You can use your strength. But you just don't know you can. I used it before.

(Tina is African American; Holly is biracdial—African American and European American—"yellow," in Tina's terms.)

Holly: I can beat up Aloyse. You saw me beat up Aloy—you saw me slap Aloyse twice.

Tina: You saw me beat that boy *up*. Right here. *(Tina points to the upper part of her arm, bent at the elbow.)* That's your strength, Right there . . .

Holly: I know. I slapped Lawrence.

Tina: I slapped him and air punched him. *(Tina acts out her swift moves.)*

Holly: I slapped him five times and punched him six times.

Tina: You must really *like* him. If you punch him and slap him, that means you like him.

Holly: I *hate* him! *(distressed)* I was just joking. (Dyson, 1997, p. 12)

As Dyson then explained, this story has multiple levels. At one level, it is a moral tale: Boys shouldn't use their "superior strength and hit a girl" (p. 12). But then it's far more complicated for it is also "open to interpretation and reinterpretation as the two children struggled with their own desires to be seen by each other as both tough and female, desires complicated by ideologies of gender, strength, love, and, in less explicit ways, race, and class . . . (and) a serious punch . . . may become a teasing 'love tap' in children's cultures" (p. 12).

We find Dyson's interpretive style of inquiry especially appealing, in part because the analysis is forever shifting, but also because it focuses on understanding the meanings that students make of their worlds, including the educational context. We cannot imagine addressing the agenda of access-to-academics without also having a strong commitment to understanding the complexity of school culture, of a variety of ideological perspectives that manifest themselves in school culture as well as in discourses about schooling, and intimate understandings of how students as well as teachers construct their worlds. We use this example and the discussion that follows to identify five tenets of a critical stance toward teaching and learning.

Multiple, Often Conflicting, Frames or Viewpoints Exist in the World. In Dyson, in this book, and in many recent narrative-style, interpretive accounts of education (Kliewer, 1998; Maran, 2000; Meier, 1997; Michie, 1999; Moses & Cobb, 2001; Orenstein, 1994), we can find evidence of the principles underlying critical inquiry. As in the example of the two girls conversing about hitting and what it means, critical inquiry examines multiple points of view. A teacher, using a critical frame, would note or record her own perspectives on a whole range of issues, including for example hitting, but would not treat these as a correct understanding. A teacher as observer, like the researcher, would attempt to be self-conscious about his or her stance in regard to any particular questions. Dyson, for example, did not approach these children or others in the classroom she studied with assumptions about what social rules the children would have or with determined understandings of how students thought about popular culture. Instead, she assumed that she would have to learn about the students' understandings from them and that she would also need to learn more about children's popular culture by studying it herself and then by talking to children about her own analyses. Above all, she assumed that what she would find would not be discrete answers but rather "messy" ones.

We Can and Must Learn From "Local Knowledge" Students Bring to the Classroom. A related characteristic to the notion that critical inquiry involves accounting for multiple viewpoints is the idea that it involves data gathering from the ground up. Glaser and Strauss (1967) called this grounded theory; others have termed it local knowledge (Kliewer & Biklen, 2001); recognition and value is afforded to the knowledge that resides within a study's participants. Again, the example of Holly and Tina's conversation illustrates this, where Dyson reports on a conversation and then attempts, with grounded data or local knowledge (i.e., her classroom conversations and observations), to begin, however tentatively, to construct an understanding of relationships between culture, ideology, immediate events, children's development, self-definition, literacy, and so forth. Were it not for a critical focus on multiple voices or perspectives and the idea of securing grounded data, such analyses would not be possible.

Nothing Can Be Understood Apart From Interpretation. The teacher, in order to understand anything about learning, about teaching, and about making education accessible to all students, needs to know how others make meaning of their worlds—including the "worlds" of the classroom and the school. To refer back to the first principle discussed earlier, the point of hearing multiple voices is to recognize that people make meaning of objects and events and that the work of being critical is to determine what the multiple understandings are and to analyze and interpret them.

Another example may be helpful to illustrate the importance of valuing perspective and being open to different interpretations of situations and events. In *Lucy's Story* (1999), an autobiography of a woman with autism, Lucy Blackman described how her behaviors might be interpreted in a variety of ways and relates how both the behaviors themselves and the ways in which they were interpreted could prove quite confusing to everyone:

> Even in High School, years later, I would behave as a small child if someone tried to treat me as a friend.
>
> This saddened me, but angrily I would play on the situation, or become even less socially competent. The strange thing was that I could see the ridicu-

> lous and comic scenario in my mind's eye, but I could not alter the behavior. As the other person got more and more embarrassed, I became more and more "autistic." Once when I was eighteen I was walking home from school. An elderly lady stood next to me at the pedestrian crossing. I assume she was concerned at my odd movements. She asked me if I were all right. Confused by the fact that she expected me to respond, I started running in a little circle . . . my would-be benefactor was standing aghast, with the attitude of an affable bird mesmerized by a newly hatched snake.
>
> So my weird social overtures (for that is what that behavior was) created inappropriate responses in others. This made it even more difficult for me to respond appropriately in return. I still do not turn and speak or sign when someone speaks to me.
>
> I know that I should say, "Goodbye!" to the speaker after these one-sided conversations, but cannot spontaneously look at someone and speak. Instead I glance sideways and walk off, or wait for someone else to tell me that this is the moment to say farewell.
>
> Occasionally when I am very relaxed and pleased to see someone in a place where I am comfortable, a wonderful flash of enchantment takes over. (pp. 41–42)

In the foregoing account, although we do not have the benefit of the elderly person's perspective, we can well imagine that it might have been one of worry or fright or perhaps just wonderment. At the same time, we can imagine that were we not to have Blackman's insider's account of the incident, *we* might understand her ways of acting quite differently than we do now that we have the benefit of her own explanation. Hence the importance of seeking people's own narratives.

All Practice Is Theorized. We are not suggesting that when a teacher introduces a lesson in a particular way or talks about a student in a certain tone of voice that he or she thinks of these actions as theory-driven, but certainly teachers' actions and ways of talking *are* theorized. A teacher who punishes a student by sending him out of the room is operating on theory as is the teacher who gives a child a gold star for a perfect score on a worksheet. Consider how theory is translated into practice in the following example:

> Recently the second author of this chapter conducted an observation in a second-grade inclusive classroom which included an 8-year-old student with autism who can speak in sentences but often does not respond as other students in group situations. At "circle time" the teacher was working on teaching the students "o" sounds. She drew a large o and small o on a chalkboard. Then she read a story related to seasons of the year where she could demonstrate different o sounds, and asked students to respond to questions and to complete sentences or to fill in blanks where she hesitated: "In the spring we plant

pumpkin seeds and we give them *water* and they get *sun*. And what happens? Then they *grow*. And we get *pumpkin sprouts* and they get *leaves* and grow more and we get *flowers*. And then we get *pumpkins*. First they are small and then they grow into *medium* pumpkins and then they grow into big huge pumpkins. And what do we do after picking them? We *cook* them."

As the teacher read, students raised their hands and tried to guess what the teacher wanted them to say. The student with autism looked away from the teacher, did not raise his hand, and closed his eyes. It was hard to tell whether he was listening or not. A few minutes after the circle time, however, this student, like his classmates, worked at his desk. The teacher asked the students to try and write the letter "o" between two lines, both in upper and lower case. Bob, the student with autism, wrote his Os in uneven form. His capital O was in the shape of an eggplant. After writing it, he turned to me, an observer to whom he had not been introduced, and said, "Look at this." So now I knew he could speak in sentences; at least I had heard a sentence from him. Moments later, his teacher called him over and asked him to identify different letters: "o," "m," "d," and "g." He accomplished this task without any hesitation, pointing to the letters and saying them aloud.

So what theories are operating in this classroom? Clearly the teacher creates multiple (in this case at least two) ways for students to respond, suggesting that she knows or believes that students' responses may take different forms or that performance may vary depending on contextual circumstance. Beyond that, we also get the sense that she sees the student as a learner; this is interesting from a theoretical standpoint, because in many school districts in America the very same child would not be permitted into a regular class and might well not receive an academic program.

In this instance, the teachers' positions are constructivist and democratic. Students are defined as capable and complex, as members of the classroom community who will benefit from exposure to academic curricula. Further, the teachers appear to assume it is their responsibility to develop ways of making competence visible, which is again keeping with a constructivist conception of education.

All Texts—This One Included—Are Rhetorical and Ideally They Should Be Self-Consciously So. Teachers and school leaders, like the writers of this text, are inevitably engaged in a process of making arguments about what we believe, what we care about, and what we observe, discover, and interpret/know. In the process of making our arguments, we are always dependent on strategies of presentation and authorial devices. In this text, for example, we use many descriptive accounts of school practices, drawn from studies in which researchers systematically collected classroom observations. One of the intents of such accounts is to win a level of validity for the arguments—"the argument seems sound because the school observations ring true." Similarly, we rely heavily on references to a broad range of other literature, including various studies of schooling as well as narrative accounts. In addition, teachers speak from years of experience, identify specific lessons drawn from individual students and individual lessons, call upon knowledge of teaching practice and teaching content learned in teacher preparation programs, relate accounts from interactions with other teachers, employ educational terms, as well as using other means of establishing their own authority in educational conversations.

A critical inquiry standpoint for fostering access to academics recognizes, in a self-conscious way, that all arguments about access-to-academics are indeed rhetorical—this is different than claiming they are objectively true. We think such recognition of rhetoric is important inasmuch as arguments and means of arguing about how to fashion access-to-academics will and should shift over time and from context to context. To participate in the shifts, it is necessary to acknowledge their rhetorical qualities.

SCHOOL CULTURE: CREATING A SETTING FOR ACADEMIC ACCESS

Although we believe that inclusive ideology and using a critical frame in thinking about education will help teachers to move students toward a more appropriate and academic education, we also understand that teachers must move *beyond* adopting an inclusive ideology. We believe that philosophy can never be separate from practice or, rather, that practice always reflects ideology or *is* ideological. This idea is illustrated in the story of one school administrator who described how he and his district were attempting to move from a traditional approach where the district educated students with disabilities in special classes to an inclusive model. At the beginning of one school year, the district abandoned disability labels and special education groups. The administrator explained:

> We believe in inclusion, so we have to ask ourselves, how do we manifest that? You have to create the organizational structure for inclusion, or for any belief, otherwise you are constantly finding that you are compromising on your values. (Applying this philosophy to the education of students with disabilities, he explained), you don't create change (i.e., inclusion) by changing special ed (i.e., part of the system). The change process must look at philosophy (of education) overall. (Biklen, 1989, p. 18)

Following this reasoning, we are interested in school climate and school culture that is, at base, committed to social justice, participation, and shared governance. Drawing from the fields of educational foundations and disability studies, we have identified several principles related to school culture that can inform schools as they seek to pursue access to academics. These principles include: developing democratic values; using critical reflection; encouraging community building; learning from the practice of others; and honoring the knowledge of families.

Develop Democratic Values

Democratic values have been at the center of every classic example of schooling where students have succeeded at levels of complexity thought unattainable (Ashton-Warner, 1963; Ladson-Billings, 1994; Matthews, 1988; Meier, 1995; Moses & Cobb, 2001). The teachers involved in these educational experiences held the expectation that all students can learn and identified and implemented practices in order to make this expectation come true. Blatt (1999) articulated this orientation when he wrote: "the job of the clinician is not to make a determination whether people can or cannot change, but to make it come true that people can change" (p. 108).

The core principles of inclusive schooling or what we have re-framed as *access to academics* are all related to the idea of democracy. Teachers using an inclusive pedagogy presume that students with a range of ways or styles of learning do want to learn and that schools exist to involve them in social arrangements where learning is the core focus. Further, in inclusive schools it is the presumption of all stakeholders that students *are* competent, and that it is the educator's task to employ a variety of ways of discovering this. Educators must constantly be scouting for student talents and seeking situations that highlight the abilities and support the needs of diverse learners. Teachers looking for competence and complexity in learners should consider the following questions:

- What gifts/skills/abilities does this student have?
- What does this student value? need? know? want to learn?
- How can I continue to understand this student in new ways?
- In what ways do I see this learner as competent and knowledgeable?
- How does this student learn?
- Under what circumstances does this student thrive?

Perhaps most importantly, teachers and school leaders can be seeking ways to ask themselves and one another: How and what can I learn from this student?

The mission of exploring abilities through learning implies a shared agenda and should call forth, therefore, shared governance; in other words, students, teachers, parents, school administrators, and others in the broader community must share an interest in making sure that schools work. In a school with democratic values, students might be asked to take leadership roles in classrooms; to teach what they know to the teacher and to other students; and to share personal information with classmates. Teachers in these schools will share power with students and will have a voice in school leadership. School administrators will embrace the input of the community, craft inventive ways to use the expertise of families and teachers, and encourage student voice, advocacy, and agency.

Use Critical Reflection

A school pursuing an access-to-academics orientation will ask the following questions related to critical reflection: Are there forums for critical reflection where everyone affected by school culture, especially students, but also teachers, families, and administrators, can have a part in fashioning it? Are there safeguards in the forums for reflection and self-criticism, such that people who traditionally are marginalized within the culture (e.g., girls in relation to boys, students with disabilities in relation to those who do not interpret themselves as having disabilities, students with culturally unfavorable body types, and students who identify as gay and lesbian) can be heard and can enjoy equal authority in defining school culture? Are students' voices involved in critical reflection activities or processes?

Educators must be thoughtful professionals who not only reflect on their experiences and beliefs individually, but approach teaching as a collaborative and dynamic learning experience. Reflective teachers seek opportunities to check their biases, challenge assumptions, question their prejudices, and realize successes. Some schools are now engaging in book clubs, discussion groups, action research projects, journal sharing, and other unique professional development activities that inspire contemplation, growth, and better experiences for students.

Critical reflection also involves evaluating and engaging in change. Seymour Sarason (1997, 1998) has written numerous books about the culture of settings and the struggles associated with change. Central to his understanding of social and organizational cultures is the need of settings to have ways of studying change in order to keep it going. Schools commonly have ways of assessing individual change; it is more rare for a setting to build in ways of studying itself, of fostering self-reflection (Sarason, 1997, 1998). Yet it is hard to imagine any setting, especially one as complex as a school, able to grow and shift as a democratic culture without multiple mechanisms for self-reflection.

A school, like any institution but perhaps more than most institutions, must find ways of creating a culture of self-reflection and change. Presumably this will require multiple strategies, including the creation of forums in which students, especially students who are traditionally marginalized, can help shape school culture. Schools adhering to the idea of fostering critical reflection, would have ways of learning about how individual students experience the world and of hearing those students' ideas about what would make for a supportive, educationally nurturing environment. Teachers might ask students with unique learning characteristics to evaluate their supports and programming; students who are racially and ethnically diverse to critique school climate, and students new to the school to share successful practices from other schools they have attended. Reflective schools would ask all students to collaborate on curriculum planning and help in developing policies and practices.

Encourage Community Building

On April 20, 1999, two high school students in Jefferson County, Colorado, entered their high school and proceeded to kill 13 classmates and injure 21 others. Columbine High School became the site of the most devastating school shooting in U.S. history. Sadly, the situation at Columbine is not unlike others that have occurred nationwide in the past few years. Although tragic incidents like the one that occurred in Colorado inspired many to write, think about, and discuss issues of safety and discipline, we also heard cries from families, teachers, and community members for increasing community-building efforts (Peterson & Skiba, 2001; Poplin, 1999; Raywid & Oshiyama, 2000; Sapphire, 1999) in classrooms and schools.

It is difficult for students to meet high standards and realize their potential when they are scared, frustrated, ignored, or in some way suffering. Thernstrom (1999) reported that 41% of Black high-school students, as compared with 27 percent of Whites, "felt that disruptive students were a 'very serious problem' at their school" (p. 18). Thernstrom (1999) indicated that this statistic is significant for many reasons:

> The disparity is important because, on average, black and Hispanic students are academically far behind whites and Asian. Violence and disorder surely affect the level of learning "Serious and nonserious offenses are negatively related to gains in achievement," a 1998 Educational Testing Service study concluded. Parents and teachers put the matter more simply. "My kid hates the school. She is scared," a mother of a tenth-grader at the overwhelmingly black Dorchester High School in Boston reports. Scared kids who hate school are not likely to learn much. (p. 18)

Helping students to connect with one another, lobbying for smaller classes, connecting students to each other, challenging competitive structures (e.g., homecoming court; spelling bees; cutting students from sports teams), and getting to know more about the personal lives of our students may help communities build more peaceful schools and, therefore, provide better access to instruction and curriculum for all learners.

In her ground-breaking book, *The Dreamkeepers* (1994), Ladson-Billings highlighted the work of one teacher, Pauline Dupree, who keeps community issues at the center of her classroom practice. Dupree fosters unity in her classroom and reports that she expects her classroom to be both a center of serious learning and a place of comfort and community. She sees her classroom as "rigorous and demanding" and a place where "students do lots of reading and writing every day" (p. 72), but Dupree also constantly teaches about cooperation in her classroom and asks students to serve as resources for one another:

> From the day that they walk into my room they know they have to select a buddy. This is their learning partner for the year. A lot of times when a student is having a hard time I'll call the buddy to my desk and really give him or her an earful. "Why are you letting your buddy struggle like this? What kind of partner are you? You're supposed to be the helper." Within a couple of months I begin to see them looking out for one another. One student will hesitate before he turns in his paper and will go check to make sure the buddy is doing okay. Eventually, they begin to check very carefully and they may discover some errors that they themselves have made. (p. 72)

Likewise, students in Kim Rombach's first-grade classroom are asked to take responsibility for managing conflicts (Sapon-Shevin, 1999). Rombach facilitates this process by providing two "talking chairs" that are available to any two students who are engaged in a conflict. Students in this classroom don't go to the teacher to have their recess scuffle or lunch time disagreement assessed, instead they secure permission from the teacher to use the talking chairs. In the chairs they discuss their issues and try to find a solution or explain their feelings. One boy explained the purpose of the chairs this way: "Sometimes it takes us a long time, but we try to get to be friends again" (Sapon-Shevin, 1999, p. 139).

As Pauline Dupree and Kim Rombach illustrate with their practices, cultivating community involves more than expectation and hope. The development and sustenance of a school community involves strategies and practices that purposefully encourage and teach sharing, learning, interdependence, and respect. For example, teachers might encourage community through cooperative learning experiences, conflict resolution opportunities, cooperative play and games, class meetings, service learning, social-justice education, cross-age and same-age tutoring and mentoring, and school and classroom celebrations (Sapon-Shevin, 1999).

Teachers who value community can find opportunities to teach to it and about it throughout the school day. Schools that promote community building become cultures in which teachers, parents, administrators, and students, including those students who have traditionally been marginalized within the culture, have multiple opportunities and forums in which to reveal their learning, see how learning occurs within the school setting, and share themselves with others. As a result, schools that promote community in these various ways become cultures where all stakeholders feel welcome, safe, and appreciated.

Learn From the Practice of Others

Schools need ways of bringing learners and teachers together, of becoming cultures in which participants learn from each other. Schools, like any social organizations, must have ways of renewing themselves, of being open to new ideas, and of trying out different strategies and approaches to learning. Teachers and students should be encouraged to view peers as partners and to value the diverse experiences that these partners bring to the classroom and the school.

Teachers may find informal ways of sharing and learning from one another including asking for help with individual students and sharing lesson plans. Educators might also devise more formal ways of learning from and with each other. Teachers might become more knowledgeable and skilled when they teach together, when they write together or otherwise reflect on their practice in collaborative ways, and when they ask colleagues to observe and critique their work.

Another way teachers learn from one another is through the formation of study groups. Karp (1994), for example, described a handful of teachers in Portland, Oregon, who moved from acting as a study group to working together as a team of activists. They moved from small-group discussions to taking initiatives through their union's education reform committee to developing a public school reform document. Likewise, teachers in Milwaukee, Wisconsin, came together to challenge their district's commitment to basal textbook readers. They formed a committee and challenged both the textbook adoption process used in their district and curriculum issues linked to overuse of basal readers. The result? The teachers were successful in garnering support for a whole language alternative for their district and were able to form a Whole Language Teachers Council. Due at least in part to these efforts, the number of teachers using whole language approaches in Milwaukee increased ten-fold.

If we are open to learning from the practice of individuals with expertise and those we respect, then we must look to students for input and ideas, as well. Students are underutilized and incredibly powerful resources for staff development and professional growth. They are also catalysts for change and innovation in teaching and learning. In her article, "The Day Sondra

Took Over," Cynthia Ellwood (1994) described how her classroom was transformed when she capitalized on a spontaneous opportunity to learn from one of her students. A powerful message was communicated to all of the students when Ellwood abandoned her position at the front of the class and swapped roles with one of her teenage students:

> "If you write that big, you're never gonna be able to get them all up there," said Sondra, voicing her third critique of my teaching in five minutes. With that, I deposited the chalk in her hand.
>
> "Take over," I said.
>
> "Oh, my fault, Ms. Ellwood," she apologized.
>
> "No, really, go for it. I want you to."
>
> She looked doubtful, not sure whether she was being admonished.
>
> "Try it. I think you'd be great"
>
> After a minute of this back and forth, Sondra stood up, and I moved to a seat near the back of the room. (p. 98)

Ellwood goes on to describe how Sondra's teaching methods departed from the approaches typically used in the class and, further, how Sondra's pedagogy and her sense of agency positively changed the tone and enhanced learning in the class. Ellwood explains that she never relinquished control over her class, but did make strides in shifting classroom power and inspiring students to become leaders in their own learning. As importantly, Ellwood was able to assess student learning and enhance her own teaching by observing students and their questioning techniques, reactions, and decisions.

Cynthia Ellwood might have been threatened by her student's outbursts and disapproval. She might have reacted to Sondra with anger or sarcasm. Instead, she chose deliberately to learn from her young critic and tap into the expertise of her teenage pupil. She listened and valued what she heard.

Students cannot be invited to serve as experts if we are not willing to honor their input. As Cynthia Ellwood discovered, however, listening to students is not simply a matter of giving attention and providing opportunity. In order to democratize classrooms, educators must respond to student voices even when students present information or ideas that challenge authority or criticize institutional structures.

Honor the Knowledge of Families

In the memorable American novel, *To Kill a Mockingbird* (Lee, 1960), the young and precocious heroine, Scout, is less than enchanted with her first schooling experiences. When she enters the first-grade classroom and exhibits competence in reading and writing, her teacher is shocked and upset:

> [S]he went to the blackboard and printed the alphabet in enormous square capitals, turned to the class and asked, "Does anybody know what these are?" Everybody did; most of the first grade had failed it last year. I suppose she chose me because she knew my name; as I read the alphabet a faint line appeared between her eyebrows, and after making me read most of *My First Reader* and the stock-market quotations from *The Mobile Register* aloud, she discovered that I was literate and looked at me with more than faint distaste. Miss Caroline told me to tell my father not to teach me any more, it would interfere with my reading. (p. 21)

The teacher in this scenario is not only shocked that her young pupil can read, but upset by the notion that she is receiving instruction in her home. Miss Caroline sees teaching as the domain of the school and views parents as potential barriers to her work.

Clearly, we cannot afford to employ teachers with Miss Caroline's attitude or beliefs about teaching and learning—especially regarding families and the incredible knowledge they possess and history they can share. Although it is surely rare to find a teacher who would discourage learning in the home, it is not so uncommon to learn of situations in which family expertise is untapped or worse yet, situations where the knowledge of the families is unrecognized or seen as unimportant. Harry (1992) suggested that teachers constantly ask the question ". . . Do we assume that professional efforts constitute the only legitimate source of opinion, and that the role of parents is to give permission for professional activities and automatic approval to professional decisions?" If the answer to the question is "yes," then changes are essential as a true partnership with families cannot grow from such a belief system.

In their study of poor, urban families, Taylor and Dorsey-Gaines (1988) discovered that parents were not only able to influence and support their children as they learned to read, but that, as importantly, they were able to model the skills necessary to understand the literacies in the neighborhood. For example, the families often had to navigate the policies, rules, and "codes" of social agencies. They had to master several different types of literacies in order to be successful in locating and receiving services for themselves and for their families.

Families in the same study also encouraged literacy through sociohistorical reading which the authors define as "reading to explore one's personal identity and the social, political, and economic circumstances of one's everyday life" (p. 173). Sociohistorical documents included *Ebony* magazine, school year books that were read and re-read by family members, writings done by family members or friends, and newspaper clippings related to the family or the community. One mother wrote pieces of her life story to share with her daughter, thus creating a text prompting togetherness and resulting in a historical record of family life. A teacher who honors the knowledge of families would seek opportunities to teach from these materials and learn from the strategies used in these homes.

Teachers who do not connect with families and do not seek expertise or concrete strategies from families, may miss all of the rich opportunities for building on the skills that are already acquired and fail to capitalize on the important links that can be developed between parents, communities, schools, and students (Taylor & Dorsey-Gaines, 1988). Through families, teachers can learn about materials that are familiar and valued; strategies that are effective; situations that prompt learning; topics of conversation and discussion that spur discovery and interest; and activities and issues that are relevant and have meaning in students' lives.

IN THE CLASSROOM: TEACHING PRACTICES THAT ENCOURAGE ACADEMIC ACCESS

In our work as teacher educators, our university students often remind us that teachers who think about teaching and learning critically and use this thinking to build democratic schools and a welcoming school climate still need to know what to do in the classroom on Monday morning. While we believe that teaching is a dynamic process and that it is difficult if not impossible to provide a prescription for how teachers should "do business" in the classroom, we do offer here a set of *general* practices that can be used as a guide for planning lessons and developing instructional strategies in inclusive schools. Many of these practices are described in more detail in other chapters. In general, teachers who wish to give students access-to-academics should appreciate and teach to learning differences; consider lesson authenticity and relevance; share "what works"; encourage voice and dialogue; and appreciate the multiple literacies that students bring to the classroom.

Appreciate and Teach To Learning Differences

A popular teaching mantra in diverse classrooms is "If they can't learn the way we teach them, let's teach them the way they learn." This philosophy is especially important for today's inclusive classrooms. Teaching students the way they learn may involve observing and interacting with students to uncover their learning strengths, idiosyncrasies, and preferences.

Vivian Paley, a kindergarten teacher who is well known for narrative accounts of her own teaching, recognizes the unique needs and approaches of all her students and both realizes and cherishes their learning differences. In one of her books, *The Boy Who Would Be a Helicopter*, Paley (1990) shared an account of how she profits from interacting with her diverse group of students. Jason, a child with unique learning characteristics, prompts her to grow as an artist and scientist—as a teacher. Jason speaks only of "helicopters and broken blades" and seems "indifferent to the play and stories":

> He has his own design for learning and, so far, it seems different from everyone else's. This makes Jason a valuable class member and an important character in a book about teaching, for one does not teach in the abstract. A style of teaching is best illuminated by those who do not meet the teacher's expectations. (p. 11)

Paley's refusal to boil Jason's personality, quirks, idiosyncrasies, and talents down to a label or characterization is precisely the reason we are attracted to her work. We admire Paley as practioner and ideologue and agree enthusiastically with her assertion that children who "shed the strongest light on the classroom" are those who "do not meet the teacher's expectations." We believe, in fact, that those who do "not meet the teacher's expectations" in some way are actually the best catalysts for change and innovation in the diverse classroom.

The idea that students learn in different ways or different styles is now widely accepted within the literature, if not uniformly implemented in practice (Armstrong, 1987, 1994; Gardner, 1983, 1993; Ladson-Billings, 1994; Kliewer, 1998; Nieto, 2000; Paley, 1990; Taylor & Dorsey-Gaines, 1988; Smith & Strick, 1997; Udvari-Solner, 1996). The "myth of the average learner" has been shattered and teachers are recognizing the need to individualize and honor the unique profiles of all students. Inclusive schooling has been a vehicle for such a model and has prompted educators to differentiate instruction and attend to diverse learning styles in the planning of curriculum, instruction, and assessment. Few students are exclusively one kind of learner.

Unfortunately, the positivist tradition prevalent in education continues to influence educators' impressions of learners. In some instances, IQ scores are still being used as a determining factors in deciding who goes where (Hallahan & Kaufmann, 1994) and what type of instruction should be provided. Proponents of inclusive schooling, however, have moved away from these traditional means of assessing and classifying students. Many have found the multiple intelligences theory, developed by Howard Gardner (1983), to be a better and more helpful way of assessing abilities. In *Frames of Mind*, Gardner challenged the practice of stressing the assessment of only two forms of symbol use: linguistic symbolization and logical-mathematical symbolization. Gardner believes that intelligence includes a much larger range of skills and abilities than schools and society have respected or validated in the past. Through his research, Gardner identified seven intelligences: verbal/linguistic intelligence, logical/mathematical intelligence, visual/spatial intelligence, body/kinesthetic intelligence, musical/rhythmic intelligence, interpersonal intelligence, and intrapersonal intelligence. An eighth intelligence, naturalist, has recently been added to the theory (Checkley, 1997).

Teachers who subscribe to the multiple intelligences theory appear more likely to meet the needs of a greater variety of learners. Classrooms that honor this theory typically provide a differentiated curriculum, offer a wide range of activities, allow students to express knowledge and expertise through multiple modes, and respect a variety of learning styles (Udvari-Solner & Thousand, 1996). For these reasons, many of those promoting inclusive education suggest the use of the multiple intelligences theory as a framework for curriculum, instruction, and assessment (Falvey, Givner & Kimm, 1995; Udvari-Solner & Thousand, 1996).

The multiple intelligences theory also fits into a multicultural curriculum not only because it reaches a variety of learners, but also because it is sensitive to cross-cultural interpretations of intelligence. Different cultures may place extreme value on some of the "less traditional" intelligences incorporated in Gardner's model. Smerechansky-Metzger (1995) enforced this point: "Individual differences, as well as problem-solving and product-making are valued in particular cultural settings . . . As educators we must increase the opportunities to maximize the individual potential of every student in all social and cultural settings" (p. 14).

Consider Lesson Authenticity and Relevance

- In 1992, at Crenshaw High School in Los Angeles, students in biology classes start gardening as part of their coursework. Within months "Food From the 'Hood" is created, a student group that grows and sells produce. Initially students made a few hundred dollars a year (which went toward college scholarships for participants). By the late 1990s, the students had started a small company, expanded the garden activities, and have increased profits to $100,000 per year. (Lopez, 1999)
- Students in Boston take a ride on the subway (the "T"), construct models and draw pictures of the trip, discuss and write about the experience (this part of the lesson may include personal stories). Teachers then mathematize the trip by asking student about directionality and distance (e.g., In what direction and how many stops is Park Street Station from Central Square?) (Moses & Cobb, 2001).

- A teacher needing some books-on-tape for his middle school classroom, asks a handful of girls to dramatically read *The House on Mango Street,* the story of a young Mexican-American girl growing up in Chicago, into a tape recorder. The students become completely spellbound by the project and learn about issues of culture and identity through their storytelling experiences. Their inventive teacher is so impressed with their reading that he takes them to a professional sound studio to record the final version of the audiotapes. Enthusiastically, the girls write to Sandra Cisneros, the book's author, to invite her to the school. The students are delighted when Cisneros responds to them, visits the school, and conducts a special question/answer meeting with the "Mango Girls." (Michie, 1999)

What do all of these lessons have in common?

- They engage students in real-world problem solving or connect them to authentic work;
- They ask students to participate actively in their own education;
- They allow students to come to answers, gain understanding, and participate in many different ways; and
- They are challenging, interesting, meaningful, and relevant to students lives.

When planning a lesson or unit for a diverse, inclusive classroom, the first and perhaps the most important aspect is to choose content that is motivating and available to all. How do teachers learn what is relevant to students? One critical educator suggests that we ask the stakeholders who matter most:

> Relevance is in the eye of the beholder. That means that students decide what is relevant to them. I read in education texts, and hear teachers talk, about "making the material relevant to students." None of us can make anything relevant to others. We search for relevance together. Teachers guide that search. Students join the search by being willing to stretch themselves to give authentic work a try. (Smith, 1999, p. 27)

There is perhaps no better way to make sure that curriculum resonates with students than to include them formally or informally in the planning process. Even students in preschool and kindergarten can participate in curriculum design by making choices about what they want to learn and bringing questions into the classroom. They may want to further develop their gifts and strengths (e.g., fishing, making tamales, scrapbooking, dancing, writing poetry, drumming). They may also want to tackle curriculum that gives them answers or makes them feel useful (e.g., learning about homeless problems in our neighborhood, studying the nutritional value of school lunch, researching quality daycare in the city).

Cultural relevance must also be a focus of curriculum and instruction (Banks, 1995; Ladson-Billings, 1994). Ladson-Billings (1994) defined culturally relevant teaching as "... a pedagogy that empowers students intellectually, socially, emotionally, and politically by using cultural referents to impart knowledge, skills and attitudes" (p. 18). Culturally relevant pedagogy calls for teachers to support learners in making connections between the student's knowledge and discourse and the school's knowledge and discourse. In lessons designed around culturally relevant pedagogy, students can explicitly see and understand the connections between what they know and have experienced and what the teacher is asking them to learn.

For example, a teacher working with many Native American students may teach them how to write a compelling story by reading and discussing various legends. Students might study the practices of famous Native American storytellers, bring their families to come to the classroom and tell their favorite legends, and develop their own stories and legends to share with each other.

The power of this pedagogy is that it has important implications for all students, not just students of color or students who are linguistically or ethnically diverse. According to Reagan (1988), culture contains a set of beliefs and social behaviors, a history, and a language that is unique to an identified group of people. A culture may also share art, humor, and a common narrative or identification. It can be argued that the deaf culture contains all of these elements, though it is mentioned little in the multicultural literature. Therefore, a teacher using culturally relevant pedagogy might encourage a student who is hard of hearing to study Deaf humor in a language arts course.

Share "What Works"

In the book we reference earlier in this chapter, *Lucy's Story*, Lucy Blackman (1999) described how her teachers and teaching assistants, as well as fellow students, responded to her autism, and how she and they learned that she could succeed educationally. The book includes numerous examples of how she learned to be an ever more competent learner. For example, she details how her mother painstakingly taught her to read for content, running her finger over the page, and across lines, and doing so in a progressive, line-by-line, paragraph-by-paragraph, page-by-page progression until she saw that this was indeed an efficient way of getting the content of stories, as opposed to skipping about and picking up odd bits of information, which had been her way.

At the end of one school year, in preparation for whoever would work with her the next school year, the teaching assistant sat down and wrote out a statement about how Lucy performed in class and how best to support her. Among the points of advice were that instructors and assistants might "find it difficult" to reconcile her "doing 'strange' things" with her thoughts and intentions. For example, "If she sings 'Happy Birthday,' 'Tie Me Kangaroo Down Sport,' or 'He's Got the Whole World in His Hands' you will know she is upset about something. She may also bite her hands. Laughing and clapping generally mean she is pleased about something." The teaching assistant warned that Lucy might not look at the person with whom she is speaking, though she does try to maintain eye contact, and she may appear not to be listening to someone speaking to her, even though she *is* listening. The assistant points out that in reading, "If clarifying a particular passage, she will run her finger along under the line, but the actual line she is reading is *two lines up* from her finger" (Blackman, 1999, pp. 137–138). And in her writing she likes to "play" with words and phrases in an imaginative, if unconventional way, with the effect that her phrasing is "strange" seeming (Blackman, 1999, p. 137).

Too often, this critical information related to student learning needs and the technology and art of teaching is lost in the shuffle of files and records that occurs between teachers, between classrooms, and between school years. Students clearly lose academic access when each teacher and support person in the school needs to re-learn "what works" for every learner, every year.

There are many ways in which teachers might share this knowledge. Perhaps the most important element involved in sharing ideas is related to collaboration and cooperation; in order to share "what works" effectively, teachers and teaching teams must be *open* to learning and giving and getting critical feedback. We maintain that "professionalism" can have a negative impact on the collaborative process if it is translated to mean that some team members have expertise that is valued absolutely over the experiences or ideas of others. In the example from *Lucy's Story* shared earlier, the "expertise" needed to understand Lucy's learning style and to help her succeed comes from Lucy and her teaching assistant. If these members of the educational team are not valued or if the classroom teacher, school psychologist, or speech therapist is always viewed as knowing more than other members, it will be impossible for stakeholders to take advantage of collective expertise and to give the learner the best education possible.

Knowledge might also be shared through documents or other materials. Teachers and students might work together to create traveling personal portfolios that move from grade to grade and classroom to classroom. Students can be invited to fill portfolios with work samples and any other artifacts or data they feel communicates who they are and how they learn. For instance, a student might include pictures of her dance recital, with captions that communicate her need for movement in the classroom. Expertise and successes can also be shared and communicated across teachers, students, and even families through the Internet and e-mail (e.g., web pages, list serves), videotaped lessons, audiotaped reflections, and short journal or "log book" entries that highlight successful practices.

Encourage Voice and Dialogue

Many educators speak of all good education as dialogical (Ashton-Warner, 1963; Freire, 1970; Ladson-Billings, 1994). Applied to the education of students classified as retarded, Blatt said education could never succeed if it was not truly dialogical:

> It's not enough to create something—even something good and decent—for people. Eventually, there must be the element of participation. Eventually, there must be something there that represents accomplishment by retarded persons themselves. . . . because we can learn from them, but moreover because they can help themselves in ways that other people cannot. (Taylor & Blatt, 1999, p. 156)

The idea of learning as dialogue is of course what Freire (1970) meant by the term "concientizao" or education as consciousness-raising as opposed to a nondialogical or banking concept of instruction; in the banking approach, the teacher deposits information in an empty vessel, the student. The banking approach stifles creativity, promotes passivity, encourages compliance, rejects the notion of student or teacher reflection, and disallows real communication. Students voices are absent from the educational process. Freire dismissed banking education as dehumanizing and called for a different kind of learning. He promoted instead a student-centered and relevant curriculum, a multicultural, democratic, and dynamic pedagogy, and a safe, tolerant, sensitive, and active learning environment. In Freire's mode of teaching reading through consciousness-raising, the learner must engage with the material and bring his or her own life into the material, otherwise there is not connection and therefore no real learning; at some point the learner must come to believe that education has a transformative potential for the individual's life.

Freire also specifically challenged the knowledge that is presented in schools and in other learning environments. He insisted that learners do not enter into the process of learning by memorizing facts, but by constructing their reality in engaging, dialoging, and problem solving with others (Freire, 1970; Gadotti, 1994). In other words, knowledge is continually created and recreated through reflection and action. It is not neutral or static.

In order to give students access to academics, Bob Peterson (1994), a fifth-grade teacher in Milwaukee purposefully makes dialogue a central focus of his classroom. He prompts students to interact by presenting songs, stories, news items, literature, and cartoons. He asks students to engage in conversation and uses the interactions to hook students into academic lessons. During one lesson, for example, he showed his young students a *New York Times* photograph of homeless people sleeping on benches near the White House. The picture drew a range of passionate responses from the students. According to Peterson, the discussion ranged from "their own experiences seeing homeless people in the community to suggestions of what should be done by the President" (p. 33). The discussion not only engaged students in a critical dialogue, but coaxed them into content. One student wrote a poem about the conversation and all learners gained access to content related to civics, government, and sociology.

Another example of dialogue teaching comes from the work of Erin Gruwell (Freedom Writers & Gruwell, 1999), a teacher who taught in a Pasedena, California, high school and helped to assemble the social justice group called *The Freedom Writers.* Gruwell, who believes it is not truly possible to challenge students without integrating their voices and ideas into classroom practices and politics, built her entire curriculum around students, their experiences, their concerns, and their ideas. She supported their interrogation and critique of institutions and authorities in their communities. Gruwell's students thrived on the discourse of social justice she cultivated in her classroom. Students in *The Freedom Writers* became involved in community service, political action, and critical literacy. They raised money to bring Miep Gies, a friend of Anne Frank's, to visit their school; they held a peace demonstration; they co-taught a college class on diversity; they visited the Holocaust Museum in Washington D.C.; they conducted a candlelight vigil honoring friends and family lost to violence; they mentored local elementary students; and they collectively wrote a book about their experiences.

Students' voices must be central to work in the classroom. They must take part in shaping school structures and policies, providing leadership, constructing curriculum, and designing instruction. In addition, they must be provided opportunities to construct learning experiences on their own—they must have opportunities to teach peers, to talk, to move, and to share. This includes having a voice in offering criticisms about schools and schooling. Along these lines, one 13-year-old with disabilities recently shared with us his ideas about how to improve education. We offer his ideas not as a definitive plan, but rather as an example of content that could be available if students had a forum to talk about school and how schools should or could be. He offers recommendations for the school environment, teacher attitudes, and pedagogy:

> A school of good soft seats and desks that held wonderful books. . . . Kids would need to behave in most kind manner and teasing would be a detention time. Everyone would be asked to join all clubs if desired and pleasing music would play everywhere.
>
> The lunch would be a time for peaceful eating and not loud talking and annoying bells and whistles which split my ears as a sword. . . .
>
> Dear parents are welcomed to meet really good all dear teachers to tell of kids powers.
>
> (Teachers) must realize that their dreams are not ours. Ask us what we will need to be an independent person later in our life. Teach good skills in a respectful way. Conversation with me will tell u if I'm happy. (J. Burke, personal communication, April 15, 2001)

Value and Build On the Literacies Students Bring to the Classroom

When teachers speak of students being literate, they are often referring to a learner's ability to read and write. In order to serve all students effectively, we must expand this definition of literacy. When teachers can identify ALL of the ways in which students are literate, they can then build on these strengths to develop new skills and abilities. If a student's interest in designing comic books is not seen as literacy-related, it is unlikely that her teacher will use this experience to teach the learner new vocabulary or literary devices that she can use to make her books more interesting and complex.

This expanded vision of literacy must include valuing engagement in conversations; performances; reading and writing; interpreting context; and listening actively or carefully. Students who are fantastic storytellers, those who improvise their own rap songs, those who love to page through texts, those who navigate a new environment with ease, those who communicate needs without words, and those who come to understand the codes and policies of institutions are demonstrating literacies. Edwards, Heron, and Francis (2000), provide this broader definition of literacy:

> An ideological model of literacy expands the definition of literacy from the ability to read and write to the practice of construing meaning using all avaliable signs within a culture, including visual, auditory, and sensory signs (Neilson, 1998; Gee, 1996; Eisner, 1991). To become literate, then, students must develop a critical awareness of multiple texts and contexts (Neilson, 1998; Gee, 1996). This involves an ability to understand how social and cul-

tural ways of being and understanding affect how meaning is construed and conveyed (Gee, 1996; Brown, 1991; Eisner, 1991). (p. 1)

We must value the literacy-related skills and abilities students bring to the classroom—especially those that have not traditionally been valued. Students who speak English as a second language, for example, have not always been encouraged to share and further develop their first language, even though first language preservation and development has been documented as beneficial in a number of ways. Preserving and valuing a student's native language can boost pride in one's identity (Cummins as cited in Diaz Soto, 1998) and help learners become more divergent thinkers (Hakuta, 1986). Diaz Soto (1998) believes that teachers need to be more "courageous than ever" in this age of "conservative English-only and bilingual education abolitionists" (p. 165). She asks that educators not only value multiple literacies, but that we use the richness of bilingual and bicultural classrooms to teach to and about equity and social justice.

Critical literacy must also be considered when interpreting literacy broadly. The advancement of critical literacy is one way to liberate and empower students who have been uninvolved in their own educational and life decisions for too long. Students engaged in critical literacy need to be exposed to a variety of materials and experiences. They need to listen and speak to peers and educators alike. They also need to be provided with experiences that support reading and writing.

Critical literacy involves much more than decoding, fluency, and phonetic exercises and extends beyond the promotion of reading and the identification of "good literature." Critical literacy does inspire reading, thinking, and speaking development, but it also encourages the questioning of historical products and knowledge discovered through literacy experiences. In this model of literacy, teaching and learning become forms of research and experimentation (Shor, 1987). Students and teachers discuss and scrutinize language and the society in which language and meanings are created. In fact, critical literacy involves both the reading of the "word and of the world." (Friere, 1970)

Critical literacy "empowers individuals to analyze and synthesize the culture of the school and their own particular cultural circumstances. . . . Critical literacy also allows teachers to connect classroom text to student experience" (Kampol, 1994, pp. 54–55). For students with disabilities, critical literacy may involve reading autobiographies of individuals involved with disability-rights. It may also entail introducing students to the ideas of "dominant culture" and "identity politics." Likewise, gay and lesbian students might learn to deconstruct heterosexism in their schools by reviewing course materials and suggesting ways to make them more inclusive. For example, students might read documents and stories about how the Nazis arrested, imprisoned, and even executed gay and lesbian people. They might then put together a lesson to teach during a history class.

CONCLUSIONS

How can teachers be sure to challenge all learners? We suggest that teachers interested in moving all students toward more challenging and motivating educational experiences might draw on the inclusive schooling movement for answers. The inclusive schooling movement, as interpreted and outlined in this chapter, asks teachers to respond to ALL of the diversities that learners bring to their schooling experience. It also asks teachers to provide supports and build experiences in ways that *inspire student learning*. By adopting democratic and critical ways of thinking about teaching and learning; considering ways to build safe, peaceful, and supportive school culture; and using classroom practices that allow for the active participation and academic engagement of all, educators can create a context that allows every student to grow intellectually and find academic success.

In this chapter, we have provided the basic framework for an access-to-academics agenda in inclusive schools. Throughout this book, you will find examples of how this model can be implemented in schools. You will find not only strategies, but stories too. You will find information and ideas, but also questions. It is our hope that throughout the book, we not only offer practical tips for evolving classrooms, but that we are offering a broader definition of inclusive schooling for the new century—a definition that inspires educators to transform policies and adopt new paradigms for supporting, teaching, learning from, collaborating with, and academically "seeing" and challenging ALL students.

For Discussion and Reflection

1. Inclusive schooling has traditionally been a term people associate with students with disabilities. What is *your* definition of inclusive schooling? How can a broad, ideological definition of inclusion support a more rigorous, challenging, and appropriate education for *all* students?

2. What can individual teachers do to promote an access-to-academics framework in their schools and districts?

3. What prevents educators from broadening their vision of inclusive schooling? What are barriers, fears, uncertainties, and assumptions that get in the way?

In the Field

1. How would implementing an access-to-academics framework impact the look, feel, and "business" of schools? Consider policies, scheduling, relationships with families, assessment and reporting on student performance, materials, classroom environments, faculty responsibilities, discipline procedures, classes offered, etc.?

2. The authors suggest five ways schools can cultivate an inclusive climate (development of democratic values; use of critical reflection; encouragement of community building; learning from the practice of others; and honoring the knowledge of families). Select one of these elements and describe how you have seen it manifested in your school. Devise a professional development plan around each element; how could you enhance each of these in your school right now?

3. Five practices related to teaching and learning using an access-to-academics framework are also included in the chapter (teach to student differences; consider lesson authenticity and relevance; share "what works," encourage voice and dialogue, and appreciate multiple literacies). Select one of these elements and describe how you have seen it manifested in your school. Devise a professional development plan around each element; how could you enhance each of these in your own teaching right now?

REFERENCES

Armstrong, T. (1987). *In their own way.* Los Angeles: Tarcher.

Armstrong, T. (1994). *Multiple intelligences in the classroom.* Alexandria, VA: Association for Supervision and Curriculum Development.

Ashton-Warner, S. (1963). *Teacher.* New York: Simon & Schuster.

Banks, J. (1995). The historical reconstruction of knowledge about race: Implications for transformative teaching. *Educational Researcher, 24,* 15–25.

Biklen, D. (1989). Redefining schools. In D. Biklen, D. Ferguson, & A. Ford (Eds.), *Schooling and disability* (pp. 1–24). Chicago: NSSE.

Blackman, L. (1999). *Lucy's story: Autism and other adventures.* Brisbane, AU: Book in Hand.

Blatt, B. (1999). The controversies. In S. J. Taylor & S. Blatt (Eds.), *In search of the promised land* (pp. 108–119). Washington, DC: American Association on Mental Retardation.

Bottge, B. (2001). Using intriguing problems to improve math skills. *Educational Leadership, 58*(6), 68–72.

Checkley, K. (1997). The first seven . . . and the eighth: A conversation with Howard Gardner. *Educational Leadership, 55,* 8–13.

Diaz Soto, L. (1998). Bilingual education in America: In search of equity and social justice. In J. L. Kincheloe & S. R. Steinberg (Eds.), *Unauthorized methods: Strategies for critical teaching* (pp. 153–172). New York: Routledge.

Dyson, A. (1997). *Writing superheroes: Contemporary childhood, popular culture, and classroom literacy.* New York: Teachers College Press.

Edwards, E., Heron, A., & Francis, M. (2000). *Toward an ideological definition of literacy: How critical pedagogy shaped the literacy development of students in a fifth-grade social studies class.* Paper presented at the meeting of the American Educational Research Association, New Orleans, LA.

Ellwood, C. (1994). The day Sondra took over. In B. Bigelow, L. Christensen, S. Karp, B. Miner, & B. Peterson (Eds.), *Rethinking our classrooms: Teaching for equity and justice* (pp. 98–101). Milwaukee, WI: Rethinking Schools, Ltd.

Falvey, M., Givner, C., & Kimm, C. (1995). What is an inclusive school? In R. Villa & J. Thousand (Eds.), *Creating an inclusive school* (pp. 1–12). Alexandria, VA: Association for Supervision and Curriculum Development.

Freedom Writers, The & Gruwell, E. (1999). *The freedom writers diary.* New York: Doubleday.

Freire, P. (1970). *Pedagogy of the oppressed.* New York: Herder and Herder.

Gadotti, M. (1994). *Reading Paulo Freire: His life and work.* Albany, NY: State University of New York.

Gardner, H. (1983). *Frames of mind: The theory of multiple intelligences.* New York: Basic Books.

Gardner, H. (1993). *Multiple intelligences.* New York: Basic Books.

Glaser, B., & Strauss, A. L. (1967). *The discovery of grounded theory: Strategies for qualitative research.* Chicago: Aldine.

Hakuta, K. (1986). *Mirror of language: The debate of bilingualism.* New York: Basic Books.

Hallahan D., & Kaufmann, J. (1994). Toward a culture of disability in the aftermath of Deno and Dunn. *The Journal of Special Education, 27,* 496–507.

Harry, B. (1992). Restructuring the participation of African-American parents in special education. *Exceptional Children, 59*(2), 123–131.

Henington, C., Hughes, J. N., Cavell, T. A., & Thompson, B. (1998). The role of relational aggression in identifying aggressive boys and girls. *Journal of School Psychology, 36*(4), 457–477.

Jorgensen, C. (1998). *Restructuring high schools for all students.* Baltimore: Brookes.

Kampol, B. (1994). *Critical pedagogy: An introduction.* Westport, CN: Bergin & Garvey.

Karp, S. (1994). Why we need to go beyond the classroom. In B. Bigelow, L. Christensen, S. Karp, B. Miner, & B. Peterson (Eds.), *Rethinking our classrooms* (pp. 162–166). Milwaukee, WI: Rethinking Schools.

Kliewer, C. (1998). *Schooling children with Down syndrome.* New York: Teachers College Press.

Kliewer, C., & Biklen, D. (2001). "School's not really a place for reading": A research synthesis of the literate lives of students with severe disabilities. *The Journal of the Association for Persons with Severe Handicaps, 26,* 1–12.

Kluth, P., Diaz-Greenberg, R., Thousand, J., & Nevin, A. (2002). Liberatory theory in the classroom. In R. Villa, J. Thousand, & A. Nevin (Eds.), *Creativity and collaborative learning* (pp. 71–83). Baltimore: Brookes.

Ladson-Billings, G. (1994). *The dreamkeepers.* San Francisco: Jossey-Bass.

Lee, H. (1960). *To kill a mockingbird.* Philadelphia: Lippincott.

Lopez, C. (1999). What food from the 'hood has done. In J. C. McDermott (Ed.), *Beyond silence: Listening for democracy* (pp. 37–38).

Maran, M. (2000). *Class dismissed.* New York: St. Martin's Press.

Matthews, J. (1988). *Escalante: The best teacher in America.* New York: Holt.

Meier, D. (1995). *The power of their ideas: Lessons from a small school in Harlem.*

Meier, D. (1997). Learning in small moments: Life in an urban classroom. New York: Teachers College Press.

Michie, G. (1999). *Holler if you hear me.* New York: Teachers College Press.

Moses, R. P., & Cobb, C. E. (2001). *Radical equations: Math literacy and civil rights.* Boston: Beacon Press.

Nieto, S. (2000). *Affirming diversity.* New York: Longman.

Onosko, J., & Jorgensen, C. (1998). Unit and lesson planning in the inclusive classroom: Maximizing learning opportunities for all students. In C. Jorgensen (Ed.), *Restructuring high schools for all students* (pp. 71–105). Baltimore: Brookes.

Orenstein, P. (1994). *School Girls: Young women, self-esteem, and the confidence gap.* New York: Doubleday.

Oyler, C. (2001). Democratic classrooms and accessible instruction. *Democracy & Education, 14,* 28–31.

Paley, V. (1990). *The boy who would be a helicopter.* Cambridge, MA: Harvard University Press.

Peterson, B. (1994). Teaching for social justice: One teacher's journey. In B. Bigelow, L. Christensen, S. Karp, B. Miner, & B. Peterson (Eds.), *Rethinking our classrooms: Teaching for equity and justice* (pp. 30–33). Milwaukee, WI: Rethinking Schools, Ltd.

Peterson, R. L., & Skiba, R. (2001). Creating school climates that prevent school violence. *The Clearing House, 74,* 155–163.

Poplin, M. S. (1999). The global classroom of the 21st century: Lessons from Mother Teresa and imperatives from Columbine. *Educational Horizons, 78,* 30–38.

Raywid, M., & Oshiyama, L. (2000). Musings in the wake of Columbine: What can schools do? *Phi Delta Kappan, 81,* 444–446, 448–449.

Reagan, T. (1988). Multiculturalism and the deaf: An educational manifesto. *Journal of Research and Development in Education, 22,* 1–6.

Sapphire, P. (1999). Know all your students to reduce violence. *The Education Digest, 65,* 4–5.

Sapon-Shevin, M. (1999). *Because we can change the world: A practical guide to building cooperative, inclusive classroom communities.* Boston: Allyn & Bacon.

Sarason, S. (1997). *Crossing boundaries: Collaboration, coordination and making the most of limited resources.* San Francisco, CA: Jossey-Bass.

Sarason, S. (1998). *Political leadership and educational failure.* San Francisco, CA: Jossey-Bass.

Shor, I. (1987). *Friere for the classroom: A sourcebook for liberatory teaching.* Portsmouth, NH: Heinemann.

Smerechansky-Metzger, J. (1995). The quest for multiple intelligences. *Gifted Child Today,* 12–15.

Smith, C., & Strick, L. (1997). *Learning disabilities: A to Z.* New York: Fireside.

Smith, H. (1999). To teachers and their students: The question is "How can we learn?," not "what are we going to do today?". In J. C. McDermott (Ed.), *Beyond silence: Listening for democracy* (pp. 37–38).

Taylor, S. J., & Blatt, S. D. (Eds). (1999). *In search of the promised land: The collected papers of Burton Blatt.* Washington, DC: American Association on Mental Deficiency.

Taylor, D., & Dorsey-Gaines, C. (1988). *Growing up literate: Learning from inner-city families.* Portsmouth, NH: Heinemann.

Thernstrom, A. M. (1999). Courting disorder in the schools. *The Public Interest, 136,* 18–34.

Udvari-Solner, A. (1996). Examining teacher thinking: Constructing a process to design curricular adaptations. *Remedial and Special Education, 17,* 245–254.

Udvari-Solner, A. (1997). Inclusive education. In C. A. Grant & G. Ladson-Billings (Eds.), *Dictionary of multicultural education* (pp. 141–144). Phoenix, AZ: Oryx Press.

Udvari-Solner, A., & Thousand, J. (1996). Creating a responsive curriculum for inclusive schools. *Remedial and Special Education, 17,* 182–192.

Chapter 2

Toward Standards for Diverse Learners: Examining Assumptions

Paula Kluth
Diana M. Straut
Syracuse University

Stakeholders in American education—political leaders, families, and educators alike—have recently been focused on the movement toward educational standards in America (Elmore, 1997; Hill & Crevola, 1999; Popham, 1999; Schmoker & Marzano, 1999; Wright, 1998). The idea of holding students to high standards and seeking measurable outcomes in learning is not new, however. According to Hill and Crevola (1999), what *is* new about standards "is (1) the degree of focus and commitment to the goal of ensuring that all students achieve defined and challenging standards of performance, (2) the coherence and depth of the beliefs and understandings that underpin the response, and (3) the rigor and sophistication with which every aspect of schools and school systems is examined, redesigned, and managed to ensure that high standards are achieved" (p. 117).

In addition, stakeholders are increasingly concerned about what the standards movement means for the pluralistic American classroom. Today's classroom includes students with disabilities, students who use English as a second language, students considered at risk, students with a range of gifts and abilities, and students who are culturally and ethnically diverse. Children, in fact, "are the most diverse segment of American society" (Marlowe & Page, 1999, p. 19). What kind of diversity do America's children represent? Every kind. How diverse are this nation's classrooms? Incredibly. Consider the following profile of students in today's schools:

- Students can no longer be categorized as Catholic, Jew, or Protestant, in fact, the fastest growing religion in America is Islam (Hodgkinson, 1998);
- Most of the 5.3 million U.S. students with disabilities spend some part of their day in classes with nondisabled students, with 40% of those students spending at least four fifths of their day in inclusive environments (Kaye, 1997);
- By 1995, two-way bilingual programs were operating in nearly 200 schools nationwide. Languages such as Korean, Chinese, Arabic, French, Japanese, Russian, and Navajo are represented in these programs (Rethinking Schools, 1998).
- At least a third of school-aged population today is non-White (Marlowe & Page, 1999);
- 43 million people move every year in this country (Hodgkinson, 1998) creating an increasingly mobile student population.

In addition, trends such as multicultural education, antitracking pedagogy, inclusive education, dual bilingual programs, busing for racial balance, and multiage classrooms are contributing to the richness and difference represented in schools today.

The standards movement will have little meaning if it cannot respond to this range of students. Can we standardize *and* make curriculum, instruction, and assessment responsive to differences? We argue that it is not only possible, but vitally important. As we talk to teachers, we are finding that many are confused or frustrated with standards documents and initiatives, but not opposed to the standards themselves. In most cases, teachers want better information, ideas for implementation, and clarification on the purpose and possibilities of using standards. We have also found that many teachers, administrators, families, and students are operating on erroneous assumptions about the standards movement.

EXAMINING ASSUMPTIONS

In this chapter, we examine the standards movement and its relationship to diversity in the American student body. In doing so, we outline and challenge six common assumptions made about the standards. We also provide a rationale for using the standards to teach all students.

Assumption #1: High Standards Equal High Stakes Testing

Many have criticized the standards movement because of the link professional literature and the popular media often imply between standards and testing. Standards and testing are *not* one in the same, however. The assumed link between them must be realized and challenged. We suggest that rather than assume high-stakes testing to be an accomplice in the move toward high standards, educators should separate testing from the standards in collegial conversations, in the design of curriculum, and in classroom instruction.

Most high-stakes assessments are, in fact, harmful and exclusive (Kohn, 2000; Sacks, 2000). Under the guise of accountability, U.S. states and some individual school districts have proposed or implemented models of evaluating students and teachers that rely only on standardized tests. These tests serve to sort, eliminate, or stratify students from Kindergarten through 12th grade and provide little, if any, useful information about learners and their needs.

When students do achieve higher test scores, we do not necessarily know that they have learned more, learned better, or become more skilled or knowledgeable. These tests, as a rule, do not provide information about how students solve and analyze problems or approach questions. They do not help teachers understand how students think or what they understand. In addition, these tests do not provide much information about whether or not students have met the standards—although they may provide plenty of information about how skilled students are at taking standardized tests on a given day. Interestingly, test scores may provide more information about students' families and backgrounds than their academic ability. As Sacks (2000) pointed out, standardized tests, while providing little data related to student abilities and learning, do "tend to correlate exceedingly well with the income and education of one's parents" (p. 3). Sacks calls this phenomenon the "Volvo Effect" and claims that "the data is so strong in this regard that one could make a good guess about a child's standardized test scores by simply looking at how many degrees her parents have and what kind of car they drive" (p. 3).

When standardized tests become the focus for planning and instruction, teachers may teach to the test, focus on isolated aspects of the curriculum, limit their instructional techniques to drill and practice, or use inappropriate amounts of class time to teach test-taking skills and behaviors. None of these outcomes can be positive for student learning, self-esteem, or motivation.

Standards clearly need to be connected to some type of consistent and comprehensive assessment system, however. As Wright (1998) emphasized, "standards by themselves won't change education" (p. 10). Used as a tool, the standards may help us realize that we need to move beyond traditional assessment in order to collect reliable information about what students know and are able to do.

Kentucky is one state that has resisted high-stakes testing and has moved beyond such models in order to include all students in the formal assessment process (Kearns, Kleinert, & Clayton, 1998; Kearns, Kleinert, & Kennedy, 1999). Most students in Kentucky participate in a system that includes both traditional and alternative measures of assessment. Students with significant disabilities also engage in the statewide system through participation in an alternative portfolio that is tailored to the needs and strengths of each particular child. The Kentucky system was based on a belief in the participation and engagement of all learners in inclusive classrooms. Educators and other leaders in Kentucky constructed a system that is heavily performance-based and contains several different assessment tools. This system was designed because many students struggle with traditional assessments and, perhaps more importantly, because a reliance on such assessments does not reflect a rich or meaningful snapshot of any child's abilities, skills, or progress.

Teachers are most likely to know how to teach and meet the needs of learners when they have the best information about what students already know and can do. The most effective way to gather this information is to use a wide range of data collection strategies and assessment tools including curriculum-based tests, projects and exhibitions, portfolios, interviews, observations, anecdotal records, error analysis, self-evaluation questionnaires, journals, learning logs, and document analysis (Lopez-Reyna & Bay, 1997; Pike & Salend, 1995). A student charged with "explaining the ideas embodied in the Declaration of Independence" could, for example, demonstrate her understanding through an individual interview, a group skit with class members, or a short essay on the topic. A student who needs to communicate his knowledge of the characteristics and uses of computer hardware and operating systems can do so by creating a new user's manual for his school's laptops, by giving a PowerPoint presentation to his classmates, or by teaching a peer how to use different programs on the classroom computers.

In contrast to standardized measures, authentic assessments offer a fuller picture of student learning in that they are linked directly to what students are learning, are continuous and cumulative, are collaborative, are easily communicated to all stakeholders, and occur during real learning experiences (Pike, Compain, & Mumper, 1994; Pike & Salend, 1995; Valencia, 1990). Perhaps most importantly, authentic assessments are student centered. That is, students engaged in authentic assessments often evaluate themselves, have choices in how to be evaluated, and participate in designing criteria and assessment materials.

Clearly, high-stakes standardized testing cannot be an assessment centerpiece of the standards movement. Ultimately, we do not want students to become the best test takers they can be; we want them to become the best citizens, creators, problem solvers, workers, collaborators, leaders, parents, and community members possible. Standards ask students to perform a range of competencies; thus we will need a wide range of assessment procedures to measure the learning of these competencies. Good standards paired with a reliable, meaningful, and carefully constructed assessment system can provide all students access to appropriate academic opportunities.

Assumption #2: The Standards Are a "One Size Fits All" Approach to Education

Although many have conceptualized the standards as a way to make learning uniform, many others have viewed this movement as a tool for customizing curriculum and instruction. Reigeluth (1997) warned against standards-based programs that do not allow for such individualization:

> Uniform standards may be appropriate for business—a manufacturer wants all microwave ovens to meet specified standards of quality. That's good. But to what extent do we want all students to be alike? Of course, there are certain skills we want all students to master, but should all students be required or expected to attain them at exactly the same age or grade level? To use a travel analogy, standards for manufacturing are comparable to a single destination for all travelers to reach, whereas standards for education are more like milestones on many never-ending journeys whereby different travelers may go to many different places. We must be careful not to overgeneralize what works well for business. (p. 204)

Unfortunately it seems schools *have* overgeneralized principles from the business world. We have expected students to act, learn, behave, respond, react, and understand in the same ways. We have encouraged teachers to "teach to the middle," asked them to draw curriculum primarily from content area textbooks, and expected them to work with 20 to 40 students at any given time. Similarly, many students in U.S. schools have passively "participated" in countless lectures and presentations, sat in rows and columns in the same ways in different rooms, and completed the same tasks and activities as their same-age peers.

Sheldon and Biddle (1998) agreed that we have historically provided a standardized education to students. The authors claim that we ask learners in American classrooms to perform similarly and then "condemn or punish those who do not fit this expected mold" (p. 178). This faulty cloning approach to teaching and learning has undoubtedly frustrated and confused both students and teachers.

A student cannot and should not be expected to know and do exactly the same things as his or her peers at the end of a school year. For this reason, the standards must be viewed as developmental and flexible. This orientation to the standards provides different students in the same classrooms with opportunities to work on a range of concepts and skills, based on individual abilities, needs, and interests (Natriello, 1996; Reigeluth, 1997).

Geenen and Ysseldyke (1997) endorsed this personalized approach and suggest that the standards do "allow a range of acceptable performance" in that "all students may continue to work toward student-outcome goals such as numeracy or literacy, but within each goal area knowledge and skill standards may vary based on student-ability levels" (p. 222). For example, students may address the math standard, "explain to others how to solve a numerical problem," in dozens of different ways. Some may use augmentative communication devices to show understanding, other students may be able to explain in a written paragraph, still others may best express their knowledge through drawings. In addition, students in the same classroom may be expected to focus on problems that range in complexity with some students describing the process for reducing fractions and others designing and explaining radical equations.

Standards-based does not mean standardized. Teachers can use the standards as a curricular guide but retain multilevel and student-centered instruction. In fact, the standards should *inspire* teachers to use more varied and active approaches to learning. Teachers will need as many different approaches as there are students in their classes in order to move all learners closer to a complex curriculum and high educational standards. The standards should be an invitation to use a wide range of approaches including classroom games, debates, skits, dance, drama, movement exercises, work experiences, lab work, project-based instruction, mentorships, cooperative learning, group investigation, and community-based instruction.

In order to effectively teach to the standards in a diverse classroom, educators may also need to create curricular adaptations to meet the individual needs of learners. For instance, teachers may need to make alternatives available for instructional materials (Udvari-Solner, 1996). Children might study obtuse and acute angles through the use of a protractor and compass or by interacting with a geometry computer software program. Likewise, students might write a story using a typewriter, a pencil and paper, a tape recorder, rubber alphabet stamps, or pictures from magazines.

A teacher in a standards-based classroom might also need to mix-up the lesson formats to reach all learners (Udvari-Solner, 1996). Projects that encourage vocalizing and movement might be implemented to meet the needs of active students who like to get out of their seats, investigate problems, and manipulate materials. Students who are very social might excel in a cooperative learning structure, whereas those who are more reserved might appreciate working with one partner on a small individual project. Changing student groupings and lesson structures continuously ensures that all students will have some opportunity to learn in his or her most preferred way at some point.

Some teachers may be apprehensive about designing and implementing adaptations in a standards-based classroom due to a belief that this type of support will diminish curriculum and instruction. In contrast, the creative and effective use of adaptations and modifications allow teachers to make curriculum relevant, better connect the instructor's teaching style to the student's learning style, and make abstract concepts concrete (Udvari-Solner, 1996). The following lesson illustrates how rich, interesting, and challenging standards-based lessons can be when they incorporate strategies and approaches appropriate for students with various learning needs and strengths:

> Mr. Lee drafted daily lessons based on the standards he was teaching. For example, Mr. Lee decided to read every other chapter of [a historical novel] aloud to the students. They would read the opposite chapters in partners. He also decided to use learning centers with cooperative groups. Each center focused on an aspect of World War II and engaged students via one of the multiple learning styles. For example, one of the centers involved journal writing, based on actual diaries from the Holocaust. Another center focused on geography and involved mapping the progress of war based on listening to actual radio broadcasts recorded during World War II. (Fisher & Roach, 1999, p. 18)

Mr. Lee's careful planning and conscientious up-front designing of curriculum and instruction clearly invites all learners to both participate in interesting, age-appropriate curriculum, but also allows for individualization and responds to a variety of learning styles or intelligences (see Gardner, 1983). In Mr. Lee's classroom, "one size" is not expected to fit all students. This teacher obviously assumes that students are incredibly diverse and that they need a multitude of approaches to reach the standards. He uses the standards to frame lessons and learning outcomes, but expects that students will learn in different ways and in their own time.

Assumption #3: In the Absence of Standards, Students Get Equitable Access to Meaningful Content

There is ample evidence that what we currently offer students in terms of curriculum is not necessarily engaging or relevant. There is no common structure in place that helps educators to be mindful of a challenging curriculum when they plan learning experiences for students. Take, for example, social studies instruction in elementary schools. In many school districts, social studies instruction is reduced to a celebration of holidays—Thanksgiving, Christmas, maybe Hanukah, and occasionally Veterans Day. Perhaps with a set of learning standards to guide planning, instruction, and assessment, teachers can plan activities—even those activities that are holiday centered—to teach important historical, civic, or geographic content.

In other words, the standards may push teachers to move beyond recognizing Columbus Day and give them a structure for planning rich lessons about issues related to Christopher Columbus, such as exploration and discovery, oppression, and culture.

Another example of the potential of standards to give diverse learners access to content comes from a classroom we visited. Reese, a student with significant disabilities, was working in his "inclusive" general education fourth-grade classroom when we were first introduced to him. Whereas general education students worked in small groups to explore fossils, Reese sat in the corner of the classroom and completed a color-by-number worksheet with a paraprofessional. Some students in the class examined specimens from a fossil collection. Another group studied detailed photographs of excavation sites and generated hypotheses about how scientists determine the age of fossils. Still another group of learners built models of the sea floor spreading.

Had Reese been expected to participate in a standards-based curriculum, perhaps there would have been more creativity and challenge in his curriculum and instruction. The National Council for Teachers of Mathematics (NCTM) has among its "Data Analysis and Probability" standards that "students will develop and evaluate inferences and predictions that are based on data" (*www.nctm.org*). The National Science Standards (1995) stress that engaging students in inquiry helps them develop "understanding of science concepts" and "skills necessary to become inquirers about the natural world" (p. 105). It seems reasonable to expect that Reese could be meeting his Individualized Education Program[1] (IEP) goals of "interacting appropriately with peers" and "classifying objects by at least three different characteristics" while participating in the curriculum that addressed the aforementioned math and science standards. While working on individual objectives, Reese could have been provided with an opportunity to use interesting materials, work with same-age peers, and learn about geography and history. Making guesses about fossil origins or building a scientific model with a cooperative group would have been both more meaningful and content-based than filling in a worksheet that did not relate to science and failed to facilitate Reese's participation in the classroom community.

If there were some alternative to the standards, which ensured that all students—regardless of learning profile, race, ethnicity, or proficiency in English—across school districts, cities, and states had access to rigorous academic content, then perhaps we could dismiss the standards movement. The truth is, we have not done a good job giving all students—particularly

---

[1]An Individualized Education Program (IEP) is a document developed for students identified as having disabilities. The IEP outlines the student's educational program.

those students with unique learning characteristics—access to a rich curriculum. A set of standards, articulated across the state or a district, can give parents, teachers, students, and administrators a common language for talking about student goals and progress. Attention to a common framework might also serve as a challenge to view students as capable and to respect them with a consistent and appropriately rigorous curriculum.

Assumption #4: Teaching the Standards Is Another Job for the Classroom Teacher

With so many reforms being discussed and implemented in schools today, educators may feel weary about another "thing to do" when asked to address standards in their classrooms. Standards, however, do not need to be a task or set of activities in which educators engage. Instead, they can become a useful structure or framework for teachers as they plan curriculum, develop lessons, and evaluate student learning.

Gennen and Ysseldyke (1997) proposed that standards may actually be a tool to free teachers from external demands on their time and creativity. These authors argue that the standards movement reflects a shift from a focus on the process to a focus on outcomes in education. This philosophical swing has the power to free teachers from providing instruction in prescribed ways. The standards outline what students should learn, *but they do not put parameters on how teachers should teach.* In other words, a focus on the standards does not preclude educators from instructing, collaborating, inventing, and creating as they have in the past. In fact, teachers should view the standards as a catalyst for innovation. Teachers may, in fact, find that the standards movement drives them to work with new people, try new techniques, and reflect on their practice in novel ways.

Further, teachers must realize that they can and should address the standards movement as part of a collaborative team. For example, general and special education co-teaching is becoming increasingly popular in inclusive schools (Cook & Friend, 1995). Students will potentially have more opportunities to address the standards and practice related skills when they have access to a range of professionals who can assess and teach them in different ways. Students with and without disabilities may benefit from the different teaching approaches, varied instructional styles, and different perspectives offered by two or more different educators working within the same classroom day after day.

Special area teachers can also be powerful partners in standards-based education. Although physical education, art, and music educators have their own learning standards for students, many are open to supporting the curriculum of classroom teachers. Of course, classroom teachers must also be open to supporting the curriculum of the special area teachers, and ideally in planning and teaching across curricular areas. One physical education teacher we met at a conference shared how his students benefited from the impromptu planning of his collaborative team. When teachers shared their lessons with him, he incorporated related concepts into his teaching. One kindergarten teacher told him that her students needed to recognize and categorize objects by shape, so during his daily lesson he was able to review the classroom teacher's curriculum by indicating shapes of different objects in the gymnasium. This creative instructor asked students to name the shapes of tumbling mats, hula-hoops, and floor scooters. Therefore, while students played and learned new skills like hopping, galloping, and following rules, they were also engaged in a cross-curricular, standards-based lesson with just a moment or two of informal planning between two inventive professionals.

Classroom teachers, however, are not the only adults who can support a standards-based curriculum. Teachers should also consider sharing selected standards with the school secretary, classroom volunteers, recess monitor, lunchroom aides, teaching assistants, and family visitors. In one school we visited, we observed a custodian who was practicing spelling words with students as they waited in line for lunch. Imagine the benefit of this fun, low-risk exchange over time. This custodian should serve as a reminder that educators should ask all adults in the building (and in the community, when possible) to reinforce learning and to support them in teaching critical content to every student every day.

Similarly, the standards concern students, but they are the least informed group when it comes to learning about and implementing them. Students can become aware of standards in many ways, and, consequently can act as allies in their own learning. For instance, Strong, Silver, and Perini (1999) suggested that teachers post standards in the classroom, as students are more likely to hit a target when they can see it. Further, teachers might deconstruct and interrogate standards documents with students, asking learners – "Do these goals make sense for the students in this classroom?"; "How can we learn about these issues/skills?"; and "What questions or concerns do you have about these standards?" Similarly, students can be asked to develop personal strategies for meeting standards. Older students can even assist in developing lessons that are standards based.

School communities must work together to support student learning and to integrate the standards into other goals and activities that support and challenge learners and improve schools. The standards movement is part of a bigger vision of school restructuring in this country. Standards are a visioning tool—not another task for individual teachers to accomplish. All educators, families, and community members can and should participate in standards-based teaching and learning.

Assumption #5: Standards Are Not Appropriate for Truly Diverse Classrooms

All students benefit from a classroom that recognizes and appreciates diversity. Therefore, teachers are being asked to design curriculum and instruction and to engineer classroom activities that are personally and culturally responsive, engaging for a range of learning styles, and appropriate for learners with various strengths and needs. Less attention has been paid, however, to giving diverse learners appropriately demanding academic work.

We, as teachers, often make assumptions about what our students can and cannot achieve based on our perceptions of them. Unfortunately, however, educators are often wrong about the abilities of their students. For example, throughout history we have assumed that several different populations of people who behaved differently had cognitive disabilities including people with cerebral palsy, people with autism, and the Deaf (Crossley, 1997). Historically, educators have also made dangerous negative assumptions about the learning potential of girls, students of color, students from urban and rural areas, and students who use English as a second language.

Perhaps the only thing that can be done to remedy a history of poor judgment and inaccurate assessment is to stop making harmful assumptions about students' abilities and potential. All students will be better served if teachers expected the best from learners and provided interesting, motivating, and significant experiences for them.

These lessons are pertinent for all educators and they apply to students with a variety of different learning experiences and needs. Teachers make assumptions about students daily and act on them in a variety of ways, some of which are harmful. Through our assumptions, we decide who is college bound and who is not, who benefits from extra support and who does not, who shows promise and who is "unmotivated," and who can meet standards and who cannot. Though the decisions seem innocuous individually, an educational life filled with them undoubtedly impacts students' current and future experiences in a variety of ways. Therefore, teachers must internally monitor their assumptions about students and maintain high expectations for every learner in the classroom.

Standards can be a useful tool in helping teachers to interrogate their beliefs about student abilities. During busy classroom days, filled with distractions and seemingly endless tasks, it becomes difficult to learn about students in deep and holistic ways. Therefore, we may make dangerous assumptions about learners who do not learn or behave in the most conventional ways. Kliewer (1998) provided one illustration of how we can shortchange students if we rely on perceptions and partial pictures of their performance and abilities:

> Lee Larson, a 9-year-old with Down syndrome in a second grade classroom, was completing a workbook page for a language arts lesson. He squeezed his glue bottle but applied too much pressure, resulting in a glob of glue spread across his desk. He looked surprised, then apprehensive, as he glanced toward an assistant teacher helping a classmate nearby. Lee attempted to scoop the puddle of glue back toward the middle of the desk, drenching his fingers as he did. He promptly stuck his hand into his mouth, resulting in an audible expression of distaste that caught the assistant teacher's attention. Looking over she cried out, 'That is not to eat!' Several classmates laughed. One wrinkled her nose and said, 'Oh gross!' Lee, who did not speak, was unable to explain the situation. Though he had been working diligently on the assignment, his effort resulted only in a drenched worksheet, an angry adult, a bunch of disgusted classmates, and glue dribbling down his chin. (p. 67)

The assistant teacher in the aforementioned scenario is not ignorant or uncaring. She is most likely caught in the middle of a busy moment and distracted by a classroom full of active youngsters. It is important to consider, however, that this educator may also have been reacting more to societal and cultural understandings of Down syndrome than to Lee as a worker, a student, a creator, or a learner.

L. C. Clark (1994), a teacher of many students labeled "at risk," has also noticed the perils of stereotypes and assumptions in the classroom. In an article entitled, "Expectations and 'At Risk' Children," Clark shared the story of a young man named Jamie who seemed disengaged and listless during class activities. When Clark approached the building principal for support, it became clear that some in the educational system viewed Jamie's troubles as a rationale for lowering expectations for him:

> [the principal] stood in silence for a moment and then proceeded to tell me that it was possible that Jamie has had difficulty in class because of an incident which had occurred in his home last evening that required police involvement. I acknowledged his comment and waited for his input regarding alternatives for assisting Jamie with his learning. Neither of us spoke, and it dawned on me that what he had said about the previous evening was his response to mine (and Jamie's) dilemma. . . . I decided that the time had come for the issue of expectations to be addressed. . . . It is my firm belief that when children, teachers, and administrators continually turn away from [teaching and learning], the children, particularly those already deemed "at-risk," are placed in a cycle, the continuance of which is clearly detrimental to their individual lives and, in time, the society . . . by adhering to a relativistic philosophy, educators in effect lock those considered to be "disadvantaged" or "at-risk" into the very situations from which education should free them. Intended acts of compassion result in outcomes which promote subtle racism. (p. 127)

Research has shown that teachers treat "low expectation" students differently that other students (Haertel, 1997). They wait less time for them to answer questions, they demand less from them, and they pay less attention to them (Hilliard, 1994). Likewise, Brophy and Evertson (1981) found that teacher expectations were tied very closely to student achievement. Specifically, they learned that a teacher's assumption that students will learn curriculum is positively related to student achievement.

Most teachers understand this connection and realize instinctively that their expectations and attitudes impact students in many ways. Many educators engage in constant reflection and interrogation of their biases so they may see a more complete and complex picture of their students. The standards, used critically, can be another tool used in the evaluation of both student learning and teacher perception.

As teachers review the standards and use them to plan lessons, they might consider how they can teach them in ways that *all learners* can comprehend. Educators might challenge themselves to reject the notion that some students are not capable of meeting certain standards and instead to focus on giving every learner access to standards-based lessons. In the best situations, the standards will have a positive impact on school communities and will inspire teachers to seek and find promise in every child in their classroom. The standards, therefore, are not only appropriate for the diverse American classroom—they are essential.

Assumption #6: Standards Are the Answer to Educational Excellence

This assumption may be the most dangerous of all. Many hope that this singular initiative will respond to a wide range of educational and societal ills and some proponents of standards are marketing them as the savior of public education. Without question, standards can be a useful component of a comprehensive educational portrait, but they will not make an impact on students unless schools have caring learning communities, skilled and responsive teachers, adequate financial, human, and material resources, effective partnerships with families, and concerned and visionary leadership.

To impose standards on a system that is in need of improvements such as those listed earlier, is little more than putting old wine in a new bottle. A significant contribution that state and local standards can make is that they can start the discussion about what schools must look like if students are going to achieve high standards. For example, if students are expected to "show that matter may exist as a liquid" or "recognize situations in which estimation is appropriate," how must we reconfigure and improve the delivery of instruction? The scheduling of the school day? Relationships with families? Partnerships with community organizations? Staff development opportunities?

The standards won't make our other educational woes go away, but they may help us to identify and address the most pressing and critical issues that stand in the way of students and a quality educational experience. Perhaps the standards will even motivate political leaders to attend to the need for more social supports in schools (e.g., counseling, family liaisons), better staff development opportunities, increased teacher planning time, more computers and other types of technology, increased funding, and smaller class sizes. If we are committed to standards-based schools, we must consider the range of issues connected to such a lofty and important goal (Duke, 1998). Clearly, standards are not the answer to educational excellence, but they may help us find it in our schools.

CONCLUSIONS

Some of those involved in the standards debate "seem to assume that problems in American schools occur because educators are not sufficiently focused on the bottom-line issue of student performance" (Sheldon & Biddle, 1998, p. 164). We believe that educators are *very* concerned about both students and their learning, but that the standards have confused and frustrated teachers who are committed to truly reaching and teaching all learners in their diverse American classrooms. When we consider the assumptions outlined in this chapter, we may find new ways to both view and implement standards.

Due to these assumptions about the standards there is a backlash forming in communities and in the larger nation. We fear that this backlash will encourage educators to discount the valuable aspects of having learning standards for all students. This is unfortunate since there are so many benefits to be realized for our diverse American classrooms if educators can remain focused on the purpose and promise of standards. If teachers use the standards critically and wisely, they can serve as a compass for crafting a rich curriculum and appropriate instruction. In addition, they will provide new opportunities and set high expectations for the students in American classrooms.

For Discussion and Reflection

1. The authors suggest that "If teachers use the standards critically and wisely, they can serve as a compass for crafting a rich curriculum and appropriate instruction." What does "critical and wise" use of the standards mean to you?

2. The authors identify six commonly held assumptions about standards. Can you think of additional assumptions held by teachers? Parents? Principals and other administrators? Policymakers? Students?

3. What are the skills and dispositions required of a teacher who gives all learners access to a standards-based curriculum?

4. As an educator, how will you protect your students from (or minimize the impact of) the potentially harmful effects of high-stakes testing?

5. Do you feel that teachers, families, and community members are informed about alternatives to standardized testing? How can teachers educate themselves and others about what types of assessments could be used in place of standardized tests?

In the Field

1. Interview teachers and parents in your school to find out what they know about the standards. Ask teachers to describe how the standards have influenced their practice. Ask parents to describe their reaction to the standards movement.

2. Standards exist at the National, State, and Local Level. Do a parallel review of a standards document for a content area of your choice and a student IEP (Individualized Education Plan). Look for IEP goals and objectives that could be met through an academic standard. Propose a lesson that gives a student access to standards-based curriculum and embeds at least one IEP goal.

REFERENCES

Brophy, J., & Evertson, C. (1981). *Student characteristics and teaching.* New York: Longman.

Clark, L. C. (1994). Expectations and 'at risk' children: One teacher's perspective. In B. Bigelow, L. Christensen, S. Carp, B. Miner, & B. Peterson (Eds.), *Rethinking our classrooms: Teaching for equity and justice* (pp. 126–128). Milwaukee, WI: Rethinking Schools Limited.

Cook, L., & Friend, M. (1995). Co-Teaching: Guidelines for creating effective practices. *Focus on Exceptional Children, 28,* 1–15.

Crossley, R. (1997). *Speechless: Facilitating communication for people without voices.* New York: Dutton.

Duke, D. (1998). Challenges of designing the next generation of America's schools. *Phi Delta Kappan, 79,* 688–693.

Elmore, R. (1997). The politics of education reform. *Issues in Science and Technology, 14,* 41–49.

Fisher, D., & Roach, V. (1999). *Opening doors: Connecting students to curriculum, classmates, and learning.* PEAK Parent Center.

Gardner, H. (1983). *Frames of mind: The theory of multiple intelligences.* New York: Basic Books.

Geenen, K., & Ysseldyke, J. E. (1997). Educational standards and students with disabilities. *The Educational Forum, 61,* 220–229.

Haertel, G. D. (1997). Creating school and classroom cultures that value learning: The role of national standards. *Educational Horizons, 75,* 143–138.

Hill, P. W., & Crevola, C. A. (1999). The role of standards in educational reform for the 21st century. *Yearbook, Association For Supervision and Curriculum Development, 1999,* 117–142.

Hilliard, A. G. (1994). Teachers and cultural styles. In B. Bigelow, L. Christensen, S. Carp, B. Miner, & B. Peterson (Eds.), *Rethinking our classrooms: Teaching for equity and justice* (p. 127). Milwaukee, WI: Rethinking Schools Limited.

Hodgkinson, H. L. (1998). Demographics of diversity for the 21st century. *The Education Digest, 64,* 4–7.

Kaye, H. S. (1997). Education of children with disabilities. [on-line]. Abstract 19. San Francisco, CA: Disability Statistics Center.

Kearns, J. F., Kleinert, H. L., & Clayton, J. (1998). Principal supports for inclusive assessment: A Kentucky story. *Teaching Exceptional Children, 31,* 16–23.

Kearns, J. F., Kleinert, H. L., & Kennedy, S. (1999). We need not exclude anyone. *Educational Leadership, 56,* 33–38.

Kliewer, C. (1998). *Schooling children with Down syndrome.* Teachers College Press.

Kohn, A. (2000). *The case against standardized testing: Raising the scores, ruining the schools.* Portsmouth, NH: Heinemann.

Lopez-Reyna, N. A., & Bay, M. (1997). Enriching assessment: Using varied assessments for diverse learners. *Teaching Exceptional Children, 29,* 33–37.

Marlowe, B. A., & Page, M. L. (1999). Making the most of the classroom mosaic: A constructivist perspective. *Multicultural Education, 6,* 19–21.

National Science Standards. (1995). National Academy Press, Washington, DC.

Natriello, G. (1996). Diverting attention from conditions in American schools. *Educational Researcher, 25,* 7.

Pike, K., Compain, R., & Mumper, J. (1994). *New connections: An integrated approach to literacy.* New York: Harper Collins.

Pike, K., & Salend, S. J. (1995). Authentic assessment strategies: Alternatives to norm-reference testing, *28,* 15–20.

Popham, W. J. (1999). Why standardized tests don't measure educational quality. *Educational Leadership, 56,* 8–15.

Reigeluth, C. M. (1997). Educational standards: To standardize or to customize learning? *Phi Delta Kappan, 79,* 202–206.

Rethinking Schools (1998). Number of language-minority students skyrockets. *Rethinking Schools Online, 12.* http://www.rethinkingschools.org Milwaukee, WI: Rethinking Schools.

Sacks, P. (2000). *Standardized minds: The high price of America's testing culture and what we can do to change it.* Cambridge, MA: Perseus Books.

Schmoker, M., & Marzano, R. J. (1999). Realizing the promise of standards-based education. *Educational Leadership, 56,* 17–21.

Sheldon, K., & Biddle, B. (1998). Standards, accountability, and school reform: Perils and pitfalls. *Teachers College Record, 100,* 164–180.

Strong, R., Silver, H., & Perini, M. (1999). Keeping it simple and deep. *Educational Leadership, 56,* 22–24.

Udvari-Solner, A. (1996). Examining teacher thinking: Constructing a process to design curricular adaptations. *Remedial and Special Education, 17,* 245–254.

Valencia, S. (1990). A portfolio approach to classroom reading assessment: The why, whats, and hows. *The Reading Teacher, 43,* 338–340.

Wright, E. F. (1998). Connecting teaching and testing. *Thrust for Educational Leadership, 27,* 10–12.

Chapter 3

Academic Access and the Family

Tracy Knight
Syracuse University

I believe that our own experience instructs us that the secret of education is respecting the pupil.

—Ralph Waldo Emerson (1903)

There is little argument, that in the broadest sense, a central goal of education is to foster comprehensive human development. If this goal is to be realized, teachers must seek to understand, accept, and appreciate all children and all that is *of* children. A myriad of factors serve to encourage or hinder intellectual, physical, social, and psychological growth. Chief among these factors are families, which are prolific and enduring forces in the lives of children. The influence of family organization, adaptability, functioning patterns, and resources on educational reform and service delivery efforts, is well documented (Esposito, 1999; Jackson & Sedehi, 1998; Liu, 1996). Thus, a foremost necessity for providing equitable access to education to all students is a working knowledge of contemporary familial permutations and the ensuing needs and strengths of families today.[1]

The need to examine the diverse nature of families is especially important in urban areas where the students' experiences, culture, and social circumstances are often very different from the teachers'. Consider the disparity between the cultural orientation of the student population and that of the current teaching force (Burstein & Cabello, 1989). As of 1992, the sta-

[1]The terms *parents* and *families* are used interchangeably in this chapter.

tistical composition of the U.S. teaching force was approximately 87% White, 8% Black, and 3% Hispanic (National Education Association, 1992). Almost 10 years later the teaching force continues to be dominated by middle-class, English speaking, heterosexual, White women (Gomez, 1996; Olmedo, 1997). In contrast, the U.S. populace, and hence the student population, is consistently becoming more ethnically diverse (Hernandez, 1989; Hodgkinson, 1985). According to most demographic profiles, one in every three school children is from an ethnic, racial, or linguistic minority group (Perkins, 2000).

Social, racial, and cultural mismatches between teachers and students are problematic; all students (including White students) would undoubtedly benefit from having more teachers of color. White teachers, however, *can* be effective teachers of students of color, but they must be willing to learn about and become familiar with the lives of their students (Ladson-Billings, 1994). There are grave implications when children and their families are misunderstood, marginalized, and gauged by foreign and subjective standards (Harry & Anderson, 1994; Hilliard, 1987). For many inner-city students, in particular, school will pose the first occasion for their private lives to become public and for them to be exposed to societal standards of what is acceptable, good, or bad (Hulsebosch & Logan, 1999).

Children do not come to school barren and ready to adapt values, attitudes, and behaviors that may differ from those they have learned from their family; they all enter classrooms with a plethora of forces, frames of reference, and understandings operating in their lives. In every culture, families explicitly and implicitly teach their children skills of immense variety and power; a curriculum of far greater complexity than anything that can be created within classrooms (Tharp & Gallimore, 1988). This is particularly true of children being reared in modern urban communities by nontraditional families that necessitate the command of unique survival strategies. Consider the roles and responsibilities of children raised in single-parent homes. Children raised by single parents are more likely to take on adult roles of household management, decision making, and child rearing, particularly for younger siblings. With these adult responsibilities, come adult concerns and behaviors that will surface in academic and nonacademic settings.

Because such arrangements exist, an intimate familiarity with students that extends across environments must be established. This chapter provides strategies that educators can employ to ensure the inclusion of all families in varied aspects of schooling. In each case, the information presented is in regard to urban families whose participation in the education process, is limited, implicitly or explicitly, due to gender, ethnicity, race, age, marital status, sexual orientation, language, educational and economic standing.

Despite this urban focus each of these strategies should also be considered appropriate for any school, any student, and any family. Some of the characteristics of urban schools such as mismatches between student and teacher culture, significant lack of appropriate resources, and teacher shortages, happen in rural and suburban schools as well. Therefore, teachers in any type of school setting should be able to relate to and learn from the strategies outlined in the following pages.

A LOOK AT URBAN AMERICA

Urban areas house a matrix of activities that together comprise one of the largest and most complex forms of social organization (Flanagan, 1999). More than three fourths of the U.S. population reside in urban areas (Kleniewski, 1997). Most metropolitan cities are dichotomies of poverty and wealth. Urban areas are rich in resources, as they remain the center of substantive activities and businesses, including but not limited to, major hotels, restaurants, large corporations, reputable educational institutions, cultural outlets, museums, athletic franchises, government facilities, and transportation system headquarters. Ironically, many neighborhoods and citizens are excluded from accessing these opportunities despite their close proximity for reasons ranging from lack of skills in getting to these resources to prejudice (Hacker, 1992; Judd & Swanstrom, 1994).

Wilson (1996) defined social organization as the extent to which residents of a community are able to sustain effective social control and realize their common goals. Numerous urban community problems—crime, gang violence, drug trafficking, welfare recipiency, deterioration of family structures, high birth rates—undermine social organization (Casserley & Kober, 1990; Hodgkinson, 1989; Peng, Wang, & Walberg, 1992; Wilson, 1996). These community dilemmas outlined above are parallel to those seen in urban schools (Anyon, 1997). The majority of teaching shortages in the United States persist in large urban areas (Howey & Zimpher, 1991) and the qualifications of individuals who do teach in urban schools are questionable. More than one third of inner-city teachers are unlicensed, underlicensed, and ill-equipped for teaching in urban classrooms (Quality Counts, 1998). A host of reasons, ranging from inadequate working conditions to school violence, make teaching assignments in urban settings unattractive for qualified applicants—even for teachers of color and for those who have lived in urban settings. Furthermore, recruitment and retention of qualified teachers from minority populations has been and continues to be a daunting task for urban schools (Gursky, 2000).

Many students exit urban schools unprepared for the world of work, with minimal academic skills, limited independent living competencies, restricted social lives and minuscule supports in place to facilitate continuing education and development. Additionally, many public urban schools are plagued by unimaginative curricula, overcrowded classrooms, inadequate facilities, high levels of stress, overburgeoning special education populations, and depleted levels of motivation among students and teachers (Flake, 1999; Reed & Davis, 1999; Wilson, 1996).

The urban school crisis has not been ignored. Major cities, such as Chicago, have taken over the failing urban school systems (Lewis, 1996). Deregulation efforts have been instituted to foster greater autonomy and collective governance over school policy and practice (Newmann & Wehlage, 1995). In addition, urban education issues are continually being incorporated into preservice teacher education program curricula (Burstein, & Cabello, 1989). Although laudable, these attempts to support urban schools offer no panacea; efforts must continually be broadened, synthesized, and renewed. Goodlad (1994) contends that renewal involves continuous individual, cultural, and structural change in which all stakeholders critically examine current practices and engage in ongoing innovation.

At the crux of most education renewal and reform efforts are teachers who must strive to personally foster affirmative change within their respective classrooms; global reforms require local action. If change is to take place, educators must gain command of content knowledge and relevant pedagogical methods. Most importantly, educators must question personal frameworks for understanding urban children and their families.

WORKING WITH FAMILIES: MOVING TOWARDS PARADIGMS OF INCLUSION AND UNDERSTANDING

Paradigms embody a constellation of sanctioned beliefs, values, and procedures (Kuhn, 1970). Teachers' beliefs are manifested in their professional conduct. Embedded in the challenge of teaching in diverse schools must lie the commitment to evaluate, challenge, reconstruct, assimilate, and, in some cases, relinquish entrenched teaching and learning paradigms. That is to say, urban educators cannot afford to embrace myopic conceptualizations of teaching and learning. Educators must be willing to extend teaching beyond the classroom to every individual who is central to the academic and personal development of children. I suggest five ways teachers can move toward more respectful and effective partnerships with families. In order to work in concert with families and ultimately in order to give students access to a rigorous academic education, teachers must: understand different connotations of family; expand definitions of involvement; recognize colleagues in unlikely places; connect with the community; and broaden the parameters of teaching.

Understanding the Different Connotations of Family

I have two grandsons that are my daughter's. She went to jail and I kept the children.
—A grandparent on parenting[2]

Families are hailed as the most pivotal social conduits for conveying cultural beliefs and behaviors, traditions, and reasoning strategies from one generation to the next (Henry, 2000; McCubbin, McCubbin, Thompson, & Thompson, 1998). Some researchers surmise that the family is the most powerful factor in determining the potential, level of interest, and degree of learning for children (Marjoriebanks, 1996). There is little debate that families play a central role in child development or teaching and learning. Yet a major question remains: What is a family?

The concept of family is both tangible and elusive. This universal social institution has been altered by the multitude of changes that society has undergone. Nuclear and extended structures are the prototypes that have historically been used to authenticate a family unit. Father–mother–child arrangements are no longer the norm. It has been reported that 30% to 60% of students attending urban schools live with caregivers other than their biological parents (Hampton, Rak, & Mumford, 1997). Nontraditional family structures, such as same-gender and single-parent families, are becoming conventional due in part to a movement toward gender equality, advanced childbearing technological procedures, and personal preferences (*UN Chronicle,* 1994). Furthermore, shifting social, demographic, and economic trends necessitate family transformations. A prime example of this type of transformation is the evolving role of senior family members. Traditionally, grandparents have provided supplemental parent-like support; serving as the nucleus of an extended family. With soaring rates of teenage pregnancy, substance abuse, and family dysfunction in urban communities, many grandparents are emerging as *primary* caregivers.

The number of grandparents raising grandchildren increased by 40% from 1980 to 1990 (National Center for Health Statistics, 1998). In 1996 the NCHS reported that one million American children, lived in a grandparent's home without a parent present. This arrangement presents a unique set of demands. For example, surrogate grandparents are likely to contend with exacerbated financial dilemmas, social isolation, and mental and physical health conditions. These challenges can be compounded by variables

---

[2]Quotations in this chapter are taken from several sources including personal accounts of my own teaching and the teaching journals of novice, veteran, and preservice teachers. Information was also based on observation and personal accounts of urban families who have participated in workshops and parent support groups. Both educators and families provided permission for their words and perceptions to be used. All excerpts have been edited to ensure anonymity of students, educators, and families involved.

such as a disability on part of the child. For example, Shore and Hayslip (1994) suggested that grandparents caring for children with behavioral needs frequently seek treatment for the children, while neglecting to seek assistance for themselves. Another fundamental point of concern for custodial grandparents is the generation gap; there is a significant difference between the needs, ideas, and experiences of grandparents and their grandchildren. The following comment by grandmother of a middle school child with a learning disability is an illustration:

> My child is slow. She can do the work but it takes time . . . and I want to help her but I don't know the homework she brings home. We didn't have that kind of math when I was in school and there are no examples to go by.

The novelty of grandparents raising their children's children does not belie the validity of the arrangement as a legitimate family unit. With this in mind, teachers must honor all family arrangements by crafting a code of etiquette that fosters dignified and respectful interactions, communications, and portrayals of familial differences in classroom curricula. Put another way, teachers must develop an expansive concept of family. This concept of family should include all individuals and groups significant within the lives of children. "Family members" may include person(s), organization(s), and/or institution(s). In order to understand how family is defined for any given child, a teacher might ask: How does the child obtain food, shelter, love, physical safety, financial resources, and guidance?

Because families are critical to the success of students, we must acknowledge all arrangements despite their degree of deviation from our personal views of the "ideal." Family friends, community advocates, neighbors, and older siblings, are just a few examples of individuals who can play a pivotal role in the education process. As such, they should be recognized and included as part of the school community. Classroom pedagogy, home–school communications, organization of classroom and school events, and environmental imagery/decor must embrace and pay homage to all families. For example, "Feature Father Week" could become "Caring Person Week" and "Parent–Teacher" conferences can become "Family–Teacher Conferences." Such a simple play on language would serve to accommodate, as opposed to exclude, those children who have concerned individuals in their lives other than fathers or parents.

Expanding Definitions of Involvement

> *She has my number and calls me whenever she wants when she is having problems with my child. But I work during the day and can't always talk to her. I asked if I could call*

her at home in the evenings when I get off and she said no because that is her family time. What am I supposed to do?

—*One parent's view on reciprocity*

Have you ever walked into a teachers' lounge and heard: "We invite them and they don't come" or "Parents can always take off of work and run to the school for a few minutes." Consider the requisite conditions for the former statements. At the very least, a parent must have reliable transportation and a flexible employment situation (and the teacher must have an inviting environment that welcomes parents). These conditions are not a reality for some families. Consider parents who are concerned with basic issues of survival and are not at liberty to forgo even a miniscule cut in pay. Those same parents may perceive their efforts to provide a clean quiet homework environment as comparable to a school visit and as an alternative form of involvement. They are correct in this assertion if the outcome of both activities, a school visit and preparation of a home learning environment, result in children gaining access to academic dividends.

Teachers must expand their definition of involvement in order to better understand families, to enhance their own teaching, and to boost learning for students in their classes. Type, purpose, and degree are descriptive dimensions of involvement that merit professional scrutiny.

Type of Involvement. Three rudiments of productive parental involvement include acclimation, home-based, and school-based activities. Clarification of purpose and direction is a major element of, and precursor to, productive involvement. Families must be *acclimated* to the importance of their involvement and some may need to acquire the academic and nonacademic skills essential to active participation in various school activities. Parenting classes, adult education courses, conflict resolution workshops, English-literacy classes and substance-abuse counseling are but a few activities and tools that will establish the groundwork for different and more meaningful forms of involvement. Consider the following journal reflection from my first year of teaching:

> Semeko's diagnosis was Fetal Alcohol Syndrome but I was thinking more along the lines of mental retardation and behavior disordered depending on the day. That day she would not behave and kept getting mouthy. I threatened to call her mother three times and finally I did it . . . about twenty minutes passed and I smelled her before I saw her. She bypassed the office and came straight to the class. She was drunk at 10:00 in the morning, Semeko was embarrassed and I was sorry that I had called her. I know she wanted to help but . . .

Obviously, the parent in the vignette had the desire to be involved and expressed concern for her child. Yet, her physical and mental state precluded her from doing so in an acceptable and productive manner. In this case, an appropriate acclimation activity for this parent could have involved a referral to a substance abuse program or an orientation on etiquette when visiting her child's class and school. Another example of an acclimation activity is teaching families how to create *learning* environments within their *living* environments to support their children as students.

Home-based activities are actions that can exist and operate independent, or in conjunction, with school support. In either case, home-based activities should be considered a viable form of parental involvement because they serve to proactively establish, reinforce, and enhance academic performance standards and goals for children. They can entail organizing and monitoring the child's use of time, assistance with homework, guidance or advice on school-related topics, discussing career goals, reading to children, utilization of after-school and tutoring programs, providing school supplies, support of home visits, initiation of home–school communication, and responding to school communications (Arroyo, Rhoad, & Drew, 1999; Finn, 1998).

School-based activities are those characterized by mutually beneficial, child-centered interactions taking place within academic settings. Predictably, school-based activities are among the most recognized and acceptable forms of involvement. They can entail parent–child, parent–teacher, parent–administrator, and parent–parent arrangements. Classroom visits, service on committees and site-based management teams, parent–teacher conferences, attending sporting events, and volunteering in classrooms are just a few examples of school-based involvement.

The types of involvement presented should be considered in concert because power emanates from choice. Furthermore, different types of involvement should be considered as equal especially when these different courses of action lead to the same outcomes. A continuum of acclimation, home-based, and school-based activities will empower families to be involved how, when, and where their circumstances allow.

Purpose of Involvement. Another issue worth considering involves the divergent perspectives on the value and purpose of parental involvement. Studies show that a teacher's expectations of a child are related to adult family members' involvement in school activities (Wiseman, Cooner, & Knight, 1999). This position is troubling in a pluralistic society. Consider the participation of recently immigrated families of Asian descent in special education activities. In the United States, parental involvement is a defining hallmark and prized entitlement of special education. However, many Asian Pacific Islanders perceive education professionals to be absolute authorities. As such, they are likely to view invitations for family involvement as interference in the schooling process or incompetence on the behalf of teachers (Sileo & Prater, 1998). Unfortunately, their reluctance to become involved is likely to be viewed as indifference by school personnel.

In order to enhance involvement by families, teachers need to broaden their perspectives on family values, expectations, and practices that correlate with school success. Books, colleagues, refugee and community service organizations are a few resources that can assist teachers in developing a greater understanding of a community and its people. Although a broad understanding is necessary and invaluable, we must always be mindful that families can differ in the degree to which they identify with their cultural origins and the broader culture in which they are required to function (Barnwell & Day, 1996). Thus, the need to also seek to understand families on an individual basis. Each family must be seen as unique and different from all other families. A working knowledge of family differences (structure, functioning, resources, strengths, and needs) can be translated into appropriate involvement activities and can help both families and teachers gain a common understanding of the purpose of school involvement.

Degree of Involvement. Families occupy a central role in children's learning, yet educators and parents continue to grapple with setting parameters (DuFour, 2000). How much involvement is too much? When does involvement become interference? Take into account the paradox of involvement for poor parents from minority backgrounds. Often teachers negatively view their noninvolvement, while simultaneously responding negatively when the same parents challenge the status quo and begin to assert themselves in a manner similar to that of socioeconomically empowered families (Shannon, 1996). This inability or reluctance to view involvement as a multifaceted occurrence amounts to a "damned if I do and damned if I don't" scenario for many families. As a general rule of thumb families should be empowered to do what they can, when they can, where they can and how they can.

Teachers must also take cues from families who are involved to various degrees and whose children are achieving. In a society where the failures of urban children are hailed as significant and newsworthy, while examples of success are viewed as coincidence, the characteristics leading to success are often disregarded or overlooked. Understanding the processes through which families and communities contribute to risk and resiliency is critical to prevention of school failure among urban children (Henry, 2000). In order to fully comprehend determinants of risk and resiliency we should explore the multitude of urban families and schools that manage to foster competency in youth and help them to flourish in spite of dire social and economic adversity. In schools across the United States, there are students in urban areas who are achieving. In many cases, these students have actively involved, education-minded, concerned parents (even though some may never have set foot in their child's school).

Recognizing Colleagues in Unlikely Places

No matter where you teach, always make friends with the secretary and the janitor.
—Professional advice from my mother

I am the one with the degree! Echoed in classrooms, teacher-education programs, boardrooms, and teacher's lounges across the nation, this statement can best be described as the mantra of the educated expert. Upon graduating from institutions of higher education, many of us assume that our personal and academic experiences have equipped us with the intellectual prowess to understand and appreciate the various situations we are likely to encounter in our respective professions. This narrow perspective is common among well-meaning educators in urban classrooms. Hulsebosh and Logan (1999) suggested that even teachers from minority populations who grew up in urban areas tend to lose focus of community resources and familial knowledge as they are socialized into the teaching profession.

Urban families are most often viewed from the deficit perspective, particularly those from poor minority backgrounds. The widely held perception of urban families as uninvolved and economically and socially disadvantaged often causes teachers to dismiss the wisdom of families. Efforts to promote academic achievement and involvement are usually provided *for* children and their families and not in conjunction with them.

Socioeconomic success, advanced degrees of education, and standard use of language are among the most ambiguous, and culturally sanctioned, markers of respect and knowledge in the United States. Therefore, teachers needing help and insight are likely to consult with individuals with respected communication styles and education levels. More often than not, that means other teachers or education professionals. Unfortunately, this tendency to rely on "experts" is incredibly limiting and, perhaps, detrimental to students.

It is crucial for educators who work with diverse populations to have the ability and willingness to distinguish between a person's circumstance or job title and his worth as an education partner. Any individual in the school or community milieu that can provide support, information, and resources, should be considered a potential colleague. Teachers can capitalize upon the knowledge and support of such colleagues by reconceptualizing the roles, responsibilities, and relationships of families, community institutions, and school support staff. The following reflection from my first year of teaching exemplifies the need to expand professional circles:

> Some days he would come in and be an angel. Other days he would come in and call me a fucking bitch. I would sometimes get physically ill before school. When Alex was not there it was a good day. The kids in the school were scared

> of him and I guess I was too. I documented his behavior, talked to other teachers, called administration downtown and begged them to come and observe Alex in my class. I didn't know what to do with him. People in the school could see that I was floundering. It was the custodian who told me that his father was in prison for killing his mother . . . that he lived in a three bedroom apartment in the projects with his grandmother, two young aunts who boosted for a living, their six or seven children and his four siblings. I still didn't know what to do with him, but I understood him more.

Families as Colleagues. In order to become certified, teachers are required to engage in a number of experiences under the guidance of authorities that have, in essence, "been there and done that." Following formal schooling, in-service training and professional development opportunities are extended to perpetuate professional growth. How often do teacher need to listen to families as part of their professional development?

Numerous conclusions are drawn about parents' roles as caregivers, relationships with schools, levels of involvement, and value systems. Sadly, most of these conclusions have been drawn without the input of families. When attempting to ascertain information on a child's physical, social, emotional, cultural, and cognitive characteristics, who better to consult than parents, who serve as their child's first teachers? Families and their children have worked and played together for at least 5 years before that first day of kindergarten (Wiseman et al., 1999).

When wondering how we can get more families involved, why don't we go to the source? The consumers of a service are the best informants for evaluating service provision; if we want to know more about families and their involvement in schools, we should ask families in our schools about involvement! Empowered families can be instrumental in establishing and facilitating family support groups; functioning as liaisons between schools and hard-to-reach families; and engaging in mentoring activities for other families.

Support Staff as Colleagues. Support staff such as secretaries, janitors, hall monitors, lunch workers, and paraprofessionals, often reside within the urban communities where they work. Paraprofessionals, in particular, are proving to be crucial in staffing urban classrooms. Paraprofessionals—also known as education or instructional assistants, teacher's aids, and paraeducators—are paid classroom assistants who perform instructional and support duties under the supervision of a teacher. Their value as education partners is evidenced in the growing number of training, professional development, and advanced degree opportunities being offered across the United States.

Gursky (2000) described paraprofessionals as a considerable and highly promising group of potential teachers. Paraprofessionals often have extensive classroom experience, familiarity with school curriculum, and, more importantly, community roots and connections. Not only can paraprofessionals, and other support staff provide information about individual students, they can serve as school–family liaisons as families tend to trust individuals who are their neighbors. In seeking expert advice about families and communities, teachers need not look further than their colleagues who shop in the same stores, attend the same worship services, and speak the same language as their students and their families.

Community Organizations and Resources as Colleagues. Finally, in an effort to foster family involvement we must familiarize ourselves with services, policies, and procedures of organizations that have a history of successfully meeting the needs of urban families. Youth, cultural, and community centers, food banks, domestic violence and homeless shelters, libraries, and community colleges are just a few of the organizations and resources that might be open to developing more intimate relationships with schools.

Churches should be also be viewed as potential partners. Churches and other religious institutions often bear the unique distinction of remaining viable organizations in communities, particularly in urban ones, that have often lost all other institutional underpinnings (Vidal, 1995). Despite issues associated with the separation of church and state, they can offer tried-and-true methods for facilitating involvement.

Churches and other faith-based organizations have historically served as the nucleus of urban entrepreneurial ventures, political and social activism, and educational reform. Because faith-based organizations pose little threat of judgment, inner-city dwellers are more apt to seek assistance and solace there. In addition, people tend to participate and flourish when and where they feel valued, welcomed, and appreciated. Childcare assistance, food, transportation, counseling, and individualized care are just a few common practices utilized in faith communities that can be replicated in urban classrooms and schools. Further, church leaders are often held in high esteem and considered to be extended family members (Wiseman et al., 1999). It is not unusual for church leaders to serve as family counselors, spokespersons, and advocates in academic and nonacademic settings. In view of the historic role of the church as a dominant source of support for urban children and their families, it stands to reason that their expertise can also be of immense value to teachers.

Connecting With the Community

> *They are trying to teach my child stuff that she already knows. I have tried to tell them what she does at home and they don't listen. Their expectations are wrong.*
>
> —A mother's perspective on curriculum

The most valuable and personally fulfilling educational experiences for students and families are those that endorse and encourage the retention of cultural integrity. It is argued that the majority of urban youth with poor attendance, achievement, and graduation rates tend to be skeptical of the applicability of schooling to their real life situations or environments and future status in society (Fine, 1991; Natriello, McDill, & Pallas, 1990). To add to the problem, few urban school teachers live within the communities in which they teach and consequently, are at a loss for understanding the characteristics, strengths, and needs of urban students (Fleishner & Van Acker, 1990). Just as students and their families must see the purpose in teaching, learning, and involvement, so must teachers.

Children tend to value, and families tend to support, activities in which they have a vested interest. Boykin and Bailey (2000) examined the manner in which preceding home cultural factors and cultural socialization experiences of low-income African-American children impinged upon their ensuing cultural orientation and preferences for learning. It was concluded that children preferred teaching and learning approaches, strategies, and contexts consistent with their familial values and routines.

Teachers are more apt to set appropriate goals, relate to and provide support for students who are culturally, racially and ethnically similar to themselves (Cochran-Smith, 1995). It is not unusual for teachers encountering an incongruous student population to resort to teaching autobiographically by employing the use of the familiar techniques that were used in *their* own learning (Lortie, 1975). In addition, teachers are less likely to utilize culturally sensitive curriculum, instructional practices, and family involvement policies when they feel disconnected from their students and perceive those differences in a negative or deficient manner. Consider the following reflection:

> It was a culture shock to teach at a school where students were Black, White, Latino and Asian. Even though I felt like a competent teacher I went through some changes because the children were different. Mia and Dou were both my students and one year apart in age. Mai would come to school tired, inadequately dressed, with dirty hair . . . while her brother was always rested, neat and clean. I knew about gender differences in Asian cultures but I was thinking, "When in Rome do as the Romans do." I lost it—got so angry—when she came to school on a snowy day with a T-shirt, shoes with holes in the bottom and without the coat I had gotten for her from a local charity. I asked where her coat was and she said that her mother had given it to her sister. I called and sent notes home but received no word back. I felt they were neglecting this child. Finally, the school social worker, a translator and I made a home visit. In the end, I was wrong . . . the mother was newly immigrated, did not speak English, was very concerned about both of her children, respected the expertise of teachers, and needed some help getting acclimated to a new

world where her cultural practices were easily construed as abuse. (A novice teacher's experience)

Educational outreach activities should be grounded in the daily lives of students, including problems and characteristics unique to their respective communities (Chadsey-Rusch, Rusch, & O'Rielly, 1991). Further, teachers should be allowed to retain their cultural integrity and identity. It had been suggested that this delicate balance is achieved, in part, when educators become active members of the communities in which they teach. Attitudinal changes emanate from exposure, knowledge acquisition, and experience. Without direct interaction, in school and community environments, inherent distortions and distrust are bound to persist on the part of families and teachers. This lack of positive interaction and communication is reflected in the following comment:

> They only call when he done something wrong. I know it before I answer the phone and I just don't feel like hearing it. I know he ain't perfect but I feel like she just waits for him to something or aggravates him on purpose.

Although some teachers may express care and concern in the classroom, many hesitate to move beyond school walls in order to connect with students and their families. Professionals, particularly those from middle-class backgrounds, are reluctant to visit homes situated in poverty-stricken urban neighborhoods (Jackson & Sedehi, 1998). In turn, families do not always feel comfortable or welcomed in schools, which as social institutions, pose the threat of loss, criticism, and oppression. For example, many parents have had unpleasant school experiences. Although viewing their children's education as important, they continue to view schools and teachers as intimidating and uninviting figures. Fortunately, there are a number of environments and contexts that represent safe spaces for teachers and families such as community centers, museums, local churches or synagogues, sporting events, local shopping centers, and area restaurants. Why not hold school functions at one of these locations? Kozol (1997) eloquently illustrated the gravity of becoming a part of the community in which one teaches:

> I wish that we could do away with the notion of the school as a fortress against the community and think of it as a bridge into the community. The best way to cross that bridge is not by slogans or rhetoric, but by getting out there in the street ourselves, walking a few blocks and knocking at that door, walking up five floors, sitting down, having a meal, having a drink, and letting them discover that we're human. (pp. 5–6)

Broadening the Parameters of Teaching

> *My daughter's birthday is coming up and I need to move. If I move I can't afford to give her a birthday party and all that, I feel like that may affect her later. What am I supposed to do?*
>
> —Dilemma posed to a parent support group

At one time or another all teachers ask themselves where does it end? Is it my responsibility? What is my job? Children are the products of an interrelated system of societies, communities, and family units that are not mutually exclusive and that, consequently, cannot exist independent of one another. In other words, they must be the recipients of diversified intervention efforts. Teachers cannot feed every hungry student, house every homeless family, eradicate poverty, or guarantee that each student will finish high school. In sum, teachers are limited in the services that they can render to students and their families. But they can, and must, orchestrate and organize services in order to support students and mitigate their social problems.

Schools that respect the values, self-determination, and priorities of families and translate their needs and desires into appropriate resources, supports, and services are effective learning communities (Roberts & Magrab, 1999). National efforts such as school-sponsored vision and hearing screenings, free and reduced priced meals, and physical examinations can help teachers expand teaching parameters. In the following passage a veteran teacher describes how she broadened her teaching responsibilities to meet some of the basic nonacademic needs of students.

> When I was teaching I kept soap, toothpaste, combs and wash rags in my room. I would clean the kids up as best I could and then we would get to work. Some people don't feel comfortable with doing stuff like that, but I always say you will do it if you care about your children. When they look better they feel better.

Some high school teachers make coffee and tea available for students who work substantial hours, while others allow 10 minutes of "down time" for students who need to make the transition from difficult home situations to "learning mode." Accommodations such as these are oftentimes useful for facilitating working relationships with families.

Teachers may also need to accept the responsibility for reasonably supporting, in some way, individuals critical to the personal and intellectual well being of a student. For example, a child living in the home with a violent sibling may begin to exhibit antisocial behavior in the classroom. Reasonable support for this student might mean identifying programs and services that assist families in developing strategies that will empower them in supporting both of their children.

Virtually every American community encompasses a basic cluster of viable health, education, welfare, community conscience business groups, and social service organizations (Kagan, 1997). These agencies can be utilized to create a network of services that will address the complex needs of urban youth and their families. Teachers can gain access to families by amassing an arsenal of nonschool support systems and services. In other words, teachers must ask and answer the question, "If I can't ______, who can? It is preferable that teachers cultivate relationships with individuals from a variety of agencies, but at the very least, we should be able to refer families to appropriate sources of support and vice versa. Every teacher should have an inventory with the contact information for every local service agency that can provide services to children and their families.

In expanding the parameters of teaching, educators may experience stress and encounter struggles. Angry parents, student mortality, overcrowded classrooms are just a few unfavorable circumstances that contribute to the high levels of stress, burnout and turnover among urban teachers. Put simply, teachers must take care of themselves in order to be effective by developing a number positive self-help practices and strategies. Teachers might join or establish a support group for urban teachers or engage in correspondence with teachers who can provide insight into teaching challenges. Others may adopt positive coping practices such as singing, sewing, walking, writing poems, journaling, or exercising.

CONCLUSIONS

Many of our students' communities are in constant flux as they are arenas of industry and crucibles of social, cultural, and political changes. The convergence of these amount to substantial challenges for families, communities, and schools (Knox, 1994). The significance of family involvement on achievement is indisputable, and yet it continues to serve as a dilemma across a continuum of professional groups. Granted, families bear a responsibility to their children but teachers are also charged with undertaking risks and responsibilities in hopes of garnering greater educational returns. As with many social reform efforts, teachers are unofficially in leadership positions. Despite administrative regulations, political bureaucracy, and other hurdles that often limit professional autonomy, teachers have the capacity to make a difference for every student in their classroom. By connecting effectively and sensitively with families, teachers can help students access an academic education. Teachers who adopt attitudes, behaviors, and practices that allow them to honor and include all families in the education process will not only be fostering a more respectful school community, but will be helping all students to learn and succeed.

For Discussion and Reflection

1. How can teachers actively demonstrate that they value cultural differences *and* individual family differences?
2. What can teachers in rural or suburban schools learn from this chapter?
3. Specifically, how can teachers use urban environments and all of the resources within them to provide a better education for all students?
4. Think about a time when someone made an assumption about you or your family that proved to be false. How did you feel? How did your react?
5. Discuss an instance when you made an assumption about a family or person that proved to be false. What did you learn from that experience?
6. Discuss views that you will need to challenge in order to honor all families, particularly those which greatly deviate from your ideal of what a family should be and do.

In the Field

1. Teachers often ask one another, "How can we get families more involved in our schools?" This is an important question, but educators might also look at how they can take a proactive role in promoting that involvement. Consider the following question and contrast it with the previous question: "How can you make your school more welcoming and accessible to families?"
2. What affirming organizations, activities, or individuals do students and families in your school gravitate towards? Discuss the attractiveness of such entities. Identify ways of exploring and involving such entities in your teaching.
3. If teachers or schools want to enhance relationships with parents, how might they inform or educate parents about this desire? What first steps can educators take?
4. List all of the ways in which families are involved in your school. Brainstorm ways in which these roles might be expanded or enhanced. For example, could classroom volunteers become co-teachers during certain lessons? How might you learn about and capitalize on the expertise that families bring to your school?

REFERENCES

Anyon, J. (1997). Ghetto schooling: *A political economy of urban educational reform.* New York: Teachers College Press.

Arroyo, A. A., Rhoad, R., & Drew, P. (1999). Meeting diverse student needs in urban schools: Research-based recommendations for school personnel. *Preventing School Failure, 43,* 145–153.

Barnwell, D. A., & Day, M. (1996). Providing support to diverse families. In P. J. Beckman (Ed.), *Strategies for working with families of young children with disabilities* (pp. 47–68). Baltimore: Brookes.

Boykin, A. W., & Bailey, C. T. (2000). *The role of cultural factors in school relevant cognitive functioning: Description of home environmental factors, cultural orientations, and learning preferences* (Rep. No. 43). Washington, DC: Center for Research on the Education of Students Placed at Risk.

Burstein, N. D., & Cabello, B. (1989). Preparing teachers to work with culturally diverse students: A teacher education model. *Journal of Teacher Education, 40,* 9–16.

Casserley, M., & Kober, N. M. (1990). *Results 2000: Progress in meeting urban educational goals.* Washington DC: Council of the Great City Schools.

Chadsey-Rusch, J., Rusch, F. R., & O'Reilly, M. (1991). Transition from school to integrated communities. *Remedial and Special Education, 12,* 23–33.

Cochran-Smith, M. (1995). Uncertain allies: Understanding the boundaries of race and teaching. *Harvard Educational Review, 4,* 541–569.

DuFour, R. (2000). Clear connections. *Journal of Staff Development, 21,* 59–60.

Emerson, R. W. (1903). *The complete works of Ralph Waldo Emerson (Centenary Edition).* Boston: Houghton, Mifflin.

Esposito, C. (1999). Learning in urban blight: School climate and its effect on the school performance of urban, minority, low-income children. *The School Psychology Review, 28,* 365–377.

Fine, M. (1991). *Framing dropouts: Notes on the politics of urban public high school.* New York: State University of New York Press.

Finn, J. D. (1998). Parental engagement that makes a difference. *Educational Leadership, 55,* 20–24.

Flake, F. (1999). No excuses for failing our children. *Policy Review, 93,* 48.

Flanagan, W. G. (1999). *Urban sociology: Images and structure.* Needham Heights, MA: Allyn & Bacon.

Fleischner, J. E., & Van Acker, R. (1990). Changes in the urban school population: Challenges in meeting the need for special education leadership and teacher preparation personnel. In L. M. Bullock & R. L. Simpson (Eds.), *Critical issues in special education: Implications for personnel preparation* (pp. 73–92). Denton, TX: University of North Texas.

Gomez, M. L. (1996). Prospective teachers' perspectives on teaching "other people's" children. In K. Zeichner, S. Melnick, & M. L. Gomez (Eds.), *Current reforms in preservice teacher education* (pp. 109–132). New York: Teachers College Press.

Goodlad, J. I. (1994). *Educational renewal: Better teachers, better schools.* San Francisco, CA: Jossey-Bass.

Gursky, D. (2000). From para to teacher. *American Teacher, 84,* 8.

Hacker, A. (1992). *Two nations: Black and white, separate, hostile, unequal.* New York: Ballantine Books.

Hampton, F. M., Rak, C., & Mumford, D. A. (1997). Children's literature reflecting diverse family structures: Social and academic benefits for early reading programs. *ERS Spectrum, 15,* 10–15.

Harry, B., & Anderson, M. G. (1994). The disproportionate placement of African American males in special education programs: A critique of the process. *Journal of Negro Education, 63,* 602–619.

Henry, D. B. (2000). Peer groups, families, and school failure among urban children: Elements of risk and successful interventions. *Preventing School Failure, 44,* 97–104.

Hernandez, H. (1989). *Multicultural education.* Columbus, OH: Merrill.

Hilliard, A. G., III. (1987). Testing African American students. *The Negro Educational Reviews, 38,* 135–208.

Hodgkinson, H. L. (1985). *All one system: Demographics of education and service delivery system.* Washington, DC: Institute of educational Leadership, Center for Demographic Leadership.

Hodgkinson, H. L. (1989). *The same client: The demographics of education and service delivery systems.* Washington, DC: Institute for Educational Leadership.

Howey, K. R., & Zimpher, N. L. (1991). *Restructuring the education of teachers.* Reston, VA: Association of Teacher Educators.

Hulsebosch, P., & Logan, L. (1999). Inner-city parents co-construct better schooling. *The Education Digest, 64,* 33–39.

Jackson, A. P., & Sedehi, J. (1998). Homevisiting: Teaching direct practice skills through a research project. *Journal of Social Work Education, 43,* 283–290.

Judd, D. R., & Swanstrom, T. (1994). *City politics: Private power and public policy.* New York: Harper Collins.

Kagan, S. L. (1997). Support systems for children, youths, families, and schools in inner-city situations. *Education and Urban Society, 29,* 277–295.

Kleniewski, N. (1997). *Cities, change and conflict: A political economy of urban life.* Belmont, CA: Wadsworth.

Knox, P. L. (1994). *Urbanization: An introduction to urban geography.* Englewood Cliffs, NJ: Prentice-Hall.

Kozol, J. (1997). Reflections on resiliency. *Principal, 77,* 5–6.

Kuhn, T. S. (1970). *The structure of scientific revolutions.* Chicago: University of Chicago Press.

Ladson-Billings, G. (1994). *The dreamkeepers: Successful teachers of African-American children.* San Francisco: Jossey-Bass.

Lewis, A. C. (1996). A modest proposal for urban schools. *Phi Delta Kappan, 78,* 5–6.

Liu, P. (1996). Limited English proficient children's literacy acquisition and parental involvement: A tutoring/family literacy model. *Reading Horizons, 37,* 60–74.

Lortie, D. (1975). *School teacher: A sociological perspective.* Chicago, IL: University of Chicago Press.

Marjoribanks, K. (1996). Family learning environments and student's outcomes: A review. *Journal of Comparative Family Studies, 27,* 373–394.

McCubbin, H. I., McCubbin, M. A., Thompson, A. I., & Thompson, E. A. (1998). Resiliency in ethnic families: A conceptual framework for predicting family adjustment and adaptation. In H. I. McCubbin, E. A. Thompson, A. I. Thompson, & J. E. Fromer (Eds.) *Resiliency in Native American and immigrant families* (pp. 3–48). Thousand Oaks, CA: Sage.

National Center For Health Statistics (1998). Available online at http://www.cdc.gov/nchs

National Education Association (1992). *Status of the American public school teacher.* New Haven, CT: National Education Association.

Natriello, G., McDill, E. L., & Pallas, A. M. (1990). *Schooling disadvantaged children: Racing against catastrophe.* New York: Teachers College Press.

Newmann, F. M., & Wehlage, G. G. (1995). *Successful school restructuring: A report to the public and educators.* University of Wisconsin-Madison: Center on Organization and Restructuring of Schools.

Olmedo, I. M. (1997). Challenging old assumptions: Preparing teachers for inner city schools. *Teaching & Teacher Education, 13,* 245–258.

Peng, S. S., Wang, M. C., & Walberg, H. J. (1992). Demographic disparities in inner city eighth graders. *Urban Education, 26,* 441–459.

Perkins, L. M., (2000). The new immigrants in education: Challenges and issues. *Educational Horizons, 78,* 67–71.

Quality Counts 1998: Report on urban education in the 50 states. Bethsheda, MD: Editorial Projects in Education.

Reed, D. F., & Davis, M. D. (1999). Social reconstruction for urban students. *The Clearing House, 72,* 291–294.

Roberts, R. N., & Magrab, R. P. (1999). *Where children live: Solutions for serving young children and their families.* Stamford, CT: Ablex.

Shannon, S. M. (1996). Minority parental involvement: A mexican mother's experience and a teacher's interpretation. *Education and Urban Society, 29,* 71–84.

Shore, R. J., & Hayslip, B. (1994). Custodial grandparenting: Implications for children's development. In A. Gottfried & A. Gottfried (Eds.), *Redefining families: Implications for children's development.* New York: Plenum.

Sileo, T. W., & Prater, M. A. (1998). Creating classroom environments that address the linguistic and cultural backgrounds of students with disabilities: An Asian Pacific American perspective. *Remedial and Special Education, 19,* 323–327.

Tharp, R., & Gallimore, R. (1988). *Rousing minds to life.* Cambridge, England: Cambridge University Press.

UN Chronicle (1994 March), *v. 31,* 46–47.

Vidal, A. C. (1995). Reintegrating disadvantaged communities into the fabric of urban life: The role of community development. *Housing Policy Debate, 6,* 169–230.

Wilson, W. J. (1996). *When work disappears.* New York: Alfred A. Knopf.

Wiseman, D., Cooner, D., & Knight S. (1999). *Becoming a teacher in a field-based setting.* Belmont, CA: Wadsworth.

Zimmerman, S. L. (1995). *Understanding family policy: Theories and applications* (2nd ed.). Thousand Oaks, CA: Sage.

Chapter 4

Seeing All Students as Literate

Kelly Chandler-Olcott
Syracuse University

In *Adaline Falling Star* (2000), novelist Mary Pope Osborne wrote a fictionalized account of Adaline, the real-life daughter of scout Kit Carson and his Arapaho wife. When her father takes on an expedition after her mother's death, Adaline stays with relatives who treat her poorly because of her mixed heritage. Admonished by her father to hold her tongue and keep out of trouble, she takes his advice one step further, refusing to speak at all. Her cousin, a teacher, introduces her as the schoolhouse's new servant, saying, "She's a mute, and none too smart, and I'm sorry to say she has the devilish mix of white and Indian blood" (p. 5). Although her relatives can't see it, Adaline *is* smart, possessing book-learning as well as practical knowledge, and she thinks about how she might demonstrate her literacy if given the opportunity:

> No one knows I can read or write. They think . . . all I'm good for is sweeping floors and fetching wood and water. They never ask me to join in the spelling matches or guessing games or to recite the Lord's Prayer. . . . Somebody invite me to do just one of these things, and I might break my silence. (p. 4)

More than 130 years after Kit Carson's death, American education has moved beyond excluding children from formal schooling on the basis of classifications such as race or ethnicity. Court decisions such as *Brown vs. Board of Education* (1954), legislative acts such as P.L. 94-142 (1975), and activism on the part of parents, teachers, and community organizations have resulted in public school enrollments more diverse than ever before in our nation's history. Commitments to inclusion (Biklen, 1992; Jorgensen, 1998; Stainback & Stainback, 1996) and bilingual education (Crawford, 1989; Freeman & Freeman, 1994) mean that students with disabilities and students who are learning English are frequently educated in settings with their nondisabled or English-speaking peers. Consequently, many children are being "invited," as Adaline Carson puts it, to join a range of classroom activities from which they would have been excluded in the past.

Despite these significant gains, access to high-quality literacy instruction remains elusive for numerous students (Allington, 1998; Shapiro-Barnard, 1998; Kliewer, 1998). Although many teachers accept the premise that work in truly heterogeneous groups often results in social benefits, it seems harder for some to recognize that such learning environments can also lead to gains in reading and writing. Nowhere is this more evident than in the case of children with severe disabilities, according to Erickson and Koppenhaver (1995):

> It's not easy trying to learn to read and write if you're a child with severe disabilities in U.S. public schools today. . . . Your preschool teachers are unlikely to be aware of emergent literacy research or to include written language activities in your early intervention program (Coleman, 1991). Many of the teachers you encounter across your public school career do not view you as being capable of reading and writing and consequently provide you with few opportunities to learn written language (Light & McNaughton, 1993). Even if you are fortunate enough to have teachers who view you as a capable learner and see literacy as a part of your instructional program, you are likely to engage largely in word-level skill-and-drill activities, seldom reading or listening to text, and even more rarely composing text (Koppenhaver & Yoder, 1993). (p. 676)

Just as Adaline Carson's relatives assumed she was not a reader and could not become one, assumptions are still made, inside and outside education, about the appropriateness—even the necessity—of literacy instruction for some students. Keefe (1996), for example, documented several visits she made to classrooms where students eagerly composed stories and responded to literature—the same students whose low I.Q. scores previously prompted experts to speculate that they might never learn to read or write. Kliewer's (1998) book is peppered with examples of adults who failed to see or explained away evidence that children with Down syndrome already knew how to read or exhibited emergent reading behaviors. In one notable episode, an otherwise well-meaning teacher interrupted a student's physical struggle to page through a book, "inadvertently dismissing," as Kliewer described it, "what might otherwise have been interpreted as rather sophisticated literacy skills" for his age (p. 66). In each of these cases, children were capable of attaining higher levels of literacy than their adult caregivers or evaluators acknowledged.

But the cost is rising, both to individual students and to society, for assumptions that interfere with our ability to see all students as literate. According to a report by the Educational Testing Service, literacy is the "economic key for the new millennium" because of globalization and rapidly changing technologies (cited in Alvermann & Phelps, 1998, p. 11). The standards movement has led to more frequent and more rigorous testing in numerous states; success on such examinations generally demands strong literacy skills in addition to discipline-specific knowledge. The increasing influence of electronic technologies requires people to compose, scan, and digest information-packed digital texts at home and at work. To help students, including those with disabilities, keep pace with such trends, we need to examine our attitudes as educators. Unless—until—we can see all kids as potentially literate, it is unlikely that we will be able to help them develop the competencies necessary in these arenas.

SEEING STUDENTS AS LEARNERS ISN'T THE SAME AS SEEING THEM AS LITERATE

I know from personal experience that our (mis)perceptions can sometimes create blind spots for us when teaching literacy to students with disabilities. After graduating from a progressive teacher education program that espoused inclusion, I began searching for a position where I could work with diverse groups of kids. I found just such a job at a Maine high school whose recent restructuring efforts included the adoption of block scheduling, interdisciplinary teaming, and heterogeneous grouping. The 80 students in my four sections of sophomore English included a dozen or so who had been identified with learning disabilities, behavioral disorders, autism, or Down syndrome. Although I knew very little about any of those conditions, I was eager to learn about them and was convinced—as I still am—that heterogeneous grouping was the most effective and democratic way to educate students.

And in many ways, the system worked well, both for me and the members of my classes. In particular, reform offered my special education students access to academic content they would undoubtedly have been denied had they attended the school just 5 years earlier. Instead of segregated classes with skill-focused curriculum, they participated in courses organized around key concepts and habits of mind (Meier, 1995). For example, my history-teaching teammate and I designed an integrated humanities unit on America's antebellum period that asked students to consider the factors that led to the eruption of civil war. All students, regardless of whether they were labeled or not, worked in pairs to research, write, and perform a conversation between two historical figures of that period (e.g., Confederacy president Jefferson Davis and abolitionist Sojourner Truth). In order to provide extra assistance for students who needed it, Betsey, my special education teammate, consulted with me on assignment modifications, "pushed into" my classes during worktime, and coached students in our drop-in learning center. I invited students to attend extra class sessions that met during their study halls and to confer with me during our newly expanded, 40-minute lunch periods. These additional supports paid off, as nearly all students prepared their scripts carefully, presented their conversations enthusiastically, and appraised the experience positively in end-of-the-year evaluations.

When I reflect on the project's specific opportunities for *literacy* learning, however, particularly for my special education students, I wince a little. I did expect Roy, a student with a severe learning disability, and Brian, a student labeled as "educably mentally retarded," to benefit from and contribute to class discussions about the debates on slavery depicted in *Uncle Tom's Cabin.* I did expect them to plan and perform dialogues that would push their thinking and offer valuable perspectives to other students. But my expectations for their written literacy development were far less explicit and far less ambitious. Mostly concerned with how to provide them with content information with the least amount of independent reading (something I wasn't sure they were capable of), I asked myself questions like the following:

- When would students listen to the audiotapes I had made of myself reading *Narrative of the Life of Frederick Douglass*?
- Would Betsey be able to skim through their primary sources with them in the Learning Center?
- Would they glean enough from an in-class discussion of the Fugitive Slave Act to avoid plowing through the description of it in the textbook?

Unfortunately, I wasn't also asking myself questions about students' facility (or lack thereof) with comprehension strategies, decoding, or spelling. I made few provisions for formal teaching in any of these areas. In hindsight, I realize that I saw my special education students as learners and members of the classroom community, to be sure, but not necessarily as readers and writers in formal ways.

My shortcomings were partially attributable to a lack of knowledge and experience. Having had only one course in writing instruction and none in reading, I was ill-equipped to identify Brian and Roy's literacy strengths or to provide the kinds of teaching that would have moved them forward. I knew a lot more about literary devices and genre than I did about developmental literacy and diagnosis. I'm convinced, however, that at the time, I lacked something even more important: an explicit appreciation of the kinds of literacy growth *all* learners might achieve under my care. My perceptions of students' disabilities limited my ability to see their potential literacy development; my stance was similar to, although perhaps more subtle than, the doubting professionals described by Keefe (1996) and Kliewer (1998).

BROADENING OUR VISION OF STUDENTS' LITERACY

Fortunately for me, although too late for my former students, the 7 years since I left the secondary classroom have brought numerous opportunities to work with colleagues, both K–12 teachers and professors, who have scaffolded my learning about teaching literacy, particularly reading, to students with diverse needs. I know more about reading processes, developmental literacy continua, and intervention strategies than I did during those first years of teaching. If I were Roy and Brian's teacher now, I don't guarantee I would do a perfect job, but I am sure that my foci for instruction would include specific aspects of literacy development in addition to the acquisition of more generic knowledge or thinking skills.

Where learners' diverse needs are concerned, the most important concept I encountered didn't come from a course in literacy education, however, but rather from one in qualitative research. During our sessions, we spent a good deal of time discussing the fact that what a researcher or teacher can see in a classroom depends, to a significant degree, on what she is *expecting* to see. From the readings for that class, I learned that beliefs, prior knowledge, and personal experiences make an enormous difference in our perceptions of learners (Fine, 1992; Lather, 1991). This led me to reassess not only the research I was conducting at the time but also my previous teaching, and to consider what lenses I'd been using to view my work with students. Now, as I work with preservice teachers destined for diverse classrooms, I draw on that insight frequently, and I've had the opportunity to think through its implications for practice. I believe the following four approaches can help us to broaden our vision, making us better able to see all students as potentially literate and therefore better able to meet their needs as learners:

1. Employ "Elastic" Instructional Frameworks

How we structure literacy curriculum and instruction has a profound impact on what we perceive when we work with students. If we organize our classrooms in what Brooks and Brooks (1993) called the "transmission model," with the textbook at the center, the lecture as a primary method of content delivery, and all students moving through the same series of assignments at the same pace, then we are almost guaranteed to see some students as more literate than others. Learners who speak first and finish quickly will be viewed as more competent, both by the teacher and their peers, than those who need to rehearse their thinking and/or require more processing time. In effect, such one-size-fits-all instructional frameworks construct failure for a substantial number of learners who might be perceived quite differently if the learning environment itself were different. Fortunately, other models exist that allow us to see more.

A number of educators (Allen, 1995; Henry, 1995; Oberlin & Shugarman, 1989; Roller, 1996) advocate reading–writing workshops to meet the needs of learners with differing levels of literacy development and experience. During workshops as they are most commonly conceived, students read from self-selected books, write about their responses, participate in small-group discussions, and confer on a regular basis with peers and their teacher. Students initiate and complete texts and related projects at different times. In a multiyear study of a residential summer program for struggling readers, many of whom had been labeled with a variety of disabilities, Roller (1996) proposed that the workshop structure "works because it assumes that children's abilities vary":

> Because children are variable the classroom accommodates variability. Choice is the mechanism for accommodation. When children choose their activities within a structured environment, they are able to choose tasks consistent with their abilities and interests. Thus, there is no need for them to be "disabled." Rather than view children as capable or disabled, workshop classrooms assume that children are different, that each child is unique and has unique interests and abilities, and that difference is normal. (p. 7)

In the third-grade bilingual classroom described by Kucer, Silva, and Delgado-Larocco (1995), the "inquiry-based and process-oriented" curriculum (p. 15) was organized around thematic units. For example, as part of a unit entitled "Getting to Know About You, Me, and Others/*Tu, Yo, y Otres,*" students read, wrote, and talked about a variety of English and Spanish texts that explored the generalization, "Being true to yourself may have negative as well as positive consequences." The curriculum and instruction accommodated the heterogeneity of the class:

> [W]e noticed how a thematic approach allowed all students, regardless of their linguistic, cultural, and intellectual differences, to share in the curriculum. . . . Because students shared some basic concepts and experiences, they were willing to focus on the meaning their classmates were attempting to convey rather than on the language forms. Students were more at ease knowing

> that they could develop a general understanding even though they might not grasp all the details. (pp. 15–16)

Similarly, instructional sequences organized around an essential question (Sizer, 1992) or central issue (Onosko & Jorgensen, 1998) have also been proposed as structures that accommodate diversity in literacy learners' needs. These frameworks allow heterogeneous classes to be united in their exploration of a common set of concepts, while permitting students to explore different subtopics of interest and receive different kinds of assistance from their instructors. As Onosko and Jorgensen (1998) explained, such units "maximize opportunities for higher-order thinking, in-depth understanding, and cohesive (i.e., nonfragmented) learning" (p. 78). Like workshops, these instructional frameworks are "elastic": they stretch to accommodate literacy learners at either end of a developmental continuum, without requiring these students to be labeled or segregated from each other.

2. Use Multiple Texts

One-size-fits-all materials are just as detrimental to the needs of diverse learners as monolithic instructional frameworks. When all students are expected to learn to read exclusively from the same text, whether it is a content-area textbook, a basal reader, or a class novel, we can't be surprised when some kids seem more successful than others. Such instruction is reminiscent of asking all children in the neighborhood, despite their differences in size, to learn to ride bicycles whose seats are adjusted to the same height. In contrast, multiple-text approaches (Short, Harste, & Burke, 1996) support the needs of diverse learners because they allow individual children to choose—or, alternatively, teachers to assign—texts that are at students' instructional level. As numerous literacy educators have pointed out (Fountas & Pinnell, 1996; Hart-Hewins & Wells, 1999), learners become better readers from transactions with texts they can mostly understand—not from slogging through material that is too difficult or flying through material that is too easy. In addition, multiple-text approaches raise varied perspectives on a topic (Levstik, 1993), and each text in a set provides information relevant to the ones that are read subsequently. The latter is an especially important point for struggling readers, whose lack of background knowledge on a topic often impedes them as much as or more than their lack of decoding facility (Vacca & Vacca, 1999).

Informational study groups, a multiple-text approach described by Harvey and Goudvis (2000), bring students together around a common area of interest (e.g., the rainforest, flight, or the Harlem Renaissance). Under the "umbrella" of the common topic, students choose texts that may otherwise vary considerably; some may be short and simple treatments of the topic, whereas others may be lengthier and more complex. In a study of the Holocaust, for example, one child might be reading a picture book biography of Anne Frank while others read a collection of poetry written by survivors or a nonfiction account of Gentiles' interventions on behalf of Danish Jews. Students read their selections independently, gathering periodically to report to their peers on what they have learned. Their personal meaning-making is scaffolded by the questions about the topic that group members develop together, therefore setting a purpose for the reading, and by their group discussions, during which students help each other to clear up confusion and synthesize material. Because each member is reading a text at his or her instructional level, students see themselves and each other as competent and capable of contributing to the group.

When the Gulf War began in 1991, bilingual elementary teacher Caryl Crowell decided to develop a text set of various picture books on war and peace because of her dissatisfaction with media coverage of the conflict:

> To my dismay, most of the articles in the local paper concern the technological nature of the Persian Gulf war . . . and the superiority of American and allied forces. There is little to give my students a picture of the harsh realities that accompany war, the devastation and death on both sides of the battle lines. The [text set] . . . provides children with a humane, historically accurate look at war over time, particularly related to U.S. history, to help them answer their questions and to counter the distorted view of war they are receiving from mass media. (Whitmore & Crowell, 1994, p. 132)

The eight students who selected the war and peace text set from among several other choices were committed to the theme and interested in current events. The chance to choose increased their motivation for literacy-related activities. They also made choices about how to proceed as a literature study group. For example, instead of selecting texts to match their individual reading levels and interests (as was most often the case with text sets in this classroom), the students negotiated which books from the set to read and discuss together. Their group meetings, particularly because they provided a space to ask questions of peers, helped scaffold learning for those children who might have found it difficult to read the books independently. The transcript excerpts that Whitmore and Crowell include in their book suggest that the children's collaboration led to a "high level of intellectual expectation" for everyone involved (p. 147).

In addition to published sources like picture books, many teachers have found student-generated texts to be powerful resources in revealing previously undetected strengths in struggling readers and writers. Routman's (1994) portrait of Paul, a student with learning disabilities who was basically a nonreader in fourth grade, demonstrates the power of this approach, commonly known as language experience. The core activity of Routman's tutoring sessions with Paul involved her scribing as he talked to create small stapled books. After illustrating these stories, Paul would reread them repeatedly for practice. Eventually, he was able to read these familiar texts fluently, with expression and varied pacing. Over time, he took over more of the responsibility for writing, as well as for choosing books written by adult authors. Five months after Routman's intervention, he was reading and writing independently—a feat that would probably have been impossible had he and his teacher not identified his strengths as a literacy learner in the context of his predictable self-generated texts.

3. Tap the Power of Technology

In the texts I read about educating students with disabilities, technology is most often mentioned in the context of adaptations and accommodations. Students who struggle to speak use boards with preselected symbols to communicate their choices; students with cerebral palsy use specially designed keyboards to ameliorate their motor difficulties; students who are deaf or hard of hearing wear aids connected to a microphone worn by their teacher. Although these devices are tremendously important, opening new possibilities for communication in a variety of contexts, they don't reflect the only ways that various technologies are shifting literacy instruction for all students, including those with identified disabilities.

A number of studies have demonstrated that students with diverse learning needs benefit from literacy teaching that incorporates technology, whether they use a word-processing program to revise, edit, and publish their writing (Kinzer et al., 1998); participate in e-mail partnerships with students from other schools (Pirrone, 1998); or develop comprehension skills using electronic books (McNabb, 1998). Different kinds of software and/or Internet access can help students create more legible and conventional texts (important for those with poor penmanship and spelling), as well as provide links to human resources to guide their research (helpful for those who struggle with reading).

One of the finest examples I know of technology changing adults' perceptions of students' potential literacy, as well as students' perceptions of themselves, comes from Wilhelm and Friedemann's (1998) study of middle schoolers' use of the software program HyperCard. Early in their book, Wilhelm, a reading/language arts teacher, and Friedemann, a social studies teacher, described the context in which they worked:

> We taught in the "house" (or "school within a school") that served all of our district's labeled students at the seventh-grade level. Any student with initials behind his name like LD (learning disabled), ED (emotionally disturbed),

> ADHD (attention deficit-hyperactivity disorder), or ESL (English as a Second Language) was in our "house." . . . We used to joke that our students' real problem was that they were "severely labeled" and that school is "teacher disabled." By that we meant that the structures and strictures of school often worked against our attempts to innovate teaching responsive to our students' needs. (pp. 8–9)

The authors were able to overcome some of these challenges when they taught students to design "stacks"—nonlinearly-linked screens including written, audio, video, and graphic texts—to communicate findings from a series of inquiry-based humanities projects. According to Wilhelm and Friedemann, the results were amazing, particularly for kids who hadn't always been well-served by their schooling experiences: "When we put our students, including the 'severely labeled' ones, into this kind of learning situation, all of them shined. And those who were labeled or considered at risk seemed to thrive the most" (p. 9). As is often the case with technology-enhanced compositions, the software supported the needs of visual, spatial, and aural learners while motivating students to improve the quality of their work for a real audience.

Similarly, Lissi and Schallert (1999) found that weekly computer-mediated communication with peers and their reading teacher provided valuable language exposure for students who were deaf and learning English to supplement their signing. The electronic conversations, which took place in the school's computer lab, helped students to develop greater facility with a variety of literacy strategies, including "addressing questions posed by the teacher, posing their own questions to the teacher or other students, reacting to other participants' messages, sharing information, and generally having fun" (p. 373). According to the authors, several students were more active participants in the networked conversations than they were in regular classroom activities, suggesting that learners' interactions with technology may provide additional data about their literacy competence that might otherwise not be available.

4. Assess Students Using Multiple Tools, in Multiple Contexts

In assessing student learning, our goal should always be to perceive the child's growth as clearly as possible. Ultimately, we need to create portraits of individual learners that are sharply focused and finely grained. The title of Mary Jane Drummond's (1994) book on assessment—*Learning to See*—acknowledges this principle. Without assessment strategies that are sensitive to diversity, we run the risk of seeing students inaccurately, even when we use instructional tools (e.g., literacy workshops, multiple-text approaches, and technology) meant to improve our vision.

Overreliance on one method of assessment—particularly a norm-referenced test which, by its very nature, constructs failure for some kids—can often present a distorted picture of children's literacy learning. My favorite example of this comes from *Jamie: A Literacy Story*, Diane Parker's (1997) case study of a student whom she taught for 3 years in a Hawaiian primary school. Because a physical disability (spinal muscular atrophy) classified her for special education services, Jamie was scheduled for formal testing on a regular basis, in accordance with federal law. Strong-willed and cognitively quite unimpaired (!), Jamie saw the examinations as an unwelcome intrusion. "Jamie resisted those tests fiercely during her preschool years, often refusing to respond to the examiners," Parker wrote:

> This exasperated [her parents] Laurie and Lambert, who wanted the testers to know Jamie's capabilities, but they couldn't budge Jamie. They'd ask her, "Why don't you answer? You know that," and she'd whisper, "Because I know they're testing me." (p. 4)

Anyone who took Jamie's performance in these situations as the full measure of her abilities would have been gravely mistaken, as her literacy skills in meaningful contexts were among the most sophisticated in her class. In order to see Jamie's true capacity for learning, Parker needed to gather data using a variety of tools, including observational note taking, one-on-one conferences, and analysis of entries in a reading response journal.

The context for assessment can make just as much difference as the method. Sometimes, students display strengths in their out-of-school lives that are less apparent during formal school activities, as the following anecdote from Keefe (1996) demonstrated:

> An eleven-year-old friend of mine . . . has been through a traditional curriculum in both general and special education in school, but he can barely read a book written on the second-grade level, and it is obvious that reading is torture: he stumbles, he hesitates, he puts his hand on his forehead, he wrinkles his face. Outside of school, however, he pursues his interest in baseball. He reads the sports page every day to find out how his favorite team, the St. Louis Cardinals, is performing. He finds out about hits, errors, and batting averages. Perhaps he doesn't read the sports page with the same ease as non-disabled readers, but he does read purposefully and with enthusiasm. He views this activity as owner-able and do-able. (p. 14)

Evidence like this suggests that the same child we see as barely literate in an academic context may have strengths and interests outside of school that we can celebrate—perhaps even tap for further growth—if only we are able to draw on different sets of data.

A MORAL MANDATE TO HELP ALL STUDENTS BECOME LITERATE

Sometimes the kids whom teachers find most difficult to see as literate are the very ones who need literacy the most. For students with disabilities that interfere with their ability to use oral language (e.g., cerebral palsy, autism, and Down syndrome), written literacy may provide previously unavailable communication outlets (Biklen, 1993; Buckley, 1995; Kluth, 1998). In a narrative about his nephew, a boy with autism, Martin (1994) revealed the power of print for learners who cannot speak. By the age of four, Ian had achieved a certain degree of success communicating with a VOIS devise (a portable speech synthesizer), but it wasn't until he learned to type with hand-over-hand assistance several years later that he gained full membership in his school and family communities. Written literacy allowed him to suggest useful adjustments to his carefully maintained schedule, invent playful Native-American names for his family members, and express himself at school through narratives like the following:

> ONCE THERRE WASZ A BOY WHO LIKED TO VGO TO SCHOOL. HU HADM ALOT OGFF FRIENDS. YYOUJ CPOULD NOT BELKIEVE HOW MANY FRIENDS HE HAX. ONE DAY HE CAME TO SCDHOOLL WITH A BAD XCOLD AND A;LL THE KIDCS MADE HIM FEEL BNETTER BUT HE HAD YTOO GO HOME BERCAUSE HE WAS SICK. ABOUGT A WEEK LATER HE WENTG VACK TO SCHOOLK. ALL THE KIDS WERE HUJAPPY. (p. 255; typographic errors due to Ian's issues with fine-motor control have been retained)

Similarly, Cohen (1994) documented compelling consequences of literacy in a class for deaf students learning English as a second language. Because class members often immigrated from countries where deaf education was either unavailable or inappropriate (e.g., deaf children received the same programming as students with different disabilities), many students lacked reliable ways to express themselves and test their emerging theories about English. As they developed their abilities to sign, lip read, and (in some cases) speak, students and their teacher employed what Fountas and Pinnell (1996) called "shared writing" to co-construct short texts on the chalkboard and label objects in their home languages as well as English. Without this strategy, made possible by their written literacy in their native tongue, their English vocabulary development would have been slowed considerably.

Given these powerful examples, it is easy to see how effective literacy instruction improves the quality of learning for students with disabilities, as well as the quality of their lives. What is often overlooked is the way that written literacy enables many students to contribute to others' lives as well. A notable example comes from Harris's (1994) case study of Christine Durovich, a young woman with Down syndrome who, at her own and her parents' insistence, began attending regular ninth-grade classes after years of segregated schooling. Not only did Christine's participation in a journalism class improve her literacy skills, but her eventual assumption of a weekly column in the school newspaper allowed her to share her perspectives on school and community issues with a wide audience. On one notable occasion, she used her column to speak out against the exclusion of a student with cerebral palsy from regular education classes. Without the ability to read and write in sophisticated, critical ways—not merely to decode or encode print—Christine would have been unable to raise important questions about diversity, inclusion, and fairness for her peers' consideration.

SEEING OURSELVES AS LITERACY TEACHERS FOR ALL STUDENTS

As teachers of any subject, not merely of English language arts, we have a moral responsibility to help students like Christine and Ian develop literacy in ways that allow them to shape their, and our, world. If we don't see them as worthy of our effort and able to learn, it is unlikely that we will invite and assist them to "break their silence," to borrow a phrase from Adaline Carson, the character whom I described at the beginning of this chapter. We can't afford to see this as someone else's job.

Similarly, approaches that serve the needs of literacy learners with various disabilities can also better serve the needs of a wide range of students, including those who are English language learners and those who identify with home cultures not congruent with the middle-class, mainstream discourse of most American public schools. As both Roller (1996) and Routman (1994) pointed out, the key to effective and responsive pedagogy for all students is to recognize them as individuals and to build instruction from their strengths and interests, rather than their deficits. Celebrating this variability rather than lamenting it is the first step toward meeting learners' diverse needs.

When it comes to ensuring that all students have access to high-quality literacy instruction, however, I'm convinced that how we see ourselves as teachers is just as important as how we see our students. If we do not believe we are ready to deal with diverse student needs, then we may miss signs that students themselves are ready to learn. In such cases, the deficits may be our own, rather than students'.

Making this shift is about more than changing attitudes, though. It is also about acquiring and refining a knowledge base to inform our teaching of diverse learners. If we know little about the nature of particular disabilities, for example, then we are likely to set unrealistic expectations for student learning—just as often too low as too high. If we do not understand how written literacy develops over time, then we are likely to overlook growth in students whose progress is significant, yet still well below conventional notions of "grade level." By informing ourselves about these areas, we gather new lenses with which to view our work, our students, and ourselves. Only then will we be able to challenge what Altieri (1998) called "the image of the 'other' " that prevents us from seeing all learners as literate.

For Discussion and Reflection

1. Consider the author's assertion that "how we see ourselves as teachers is just as important as how we see our students. If we do not believe we are ready to deal with diverse student needs, then we may miss signs that students themselves are ready to learn. In such cases, the deficits may be our own, rather than the students." Describe how you see yourself as a teacher. What do you see as your strengths in recognizing the signs that students are literate? What are your "deficits" or areas of need? How might you address those needs in your own professional development?
2. Where do our beliefs about literacy come from (e.g., media, our own experiences)? Where in your preservice or in-service education do you learn about diverse learners and multiple literacies?
3. The author states that "written literacy enables students to contribute to others' lives." Discuss how the cultivation of written literacy in all students could be important to the mission of an inclusive school?

In the Field

1. Schedule an interview with your school's Coordinator/Supervisor of Reading Curriculum (titles will vary by school district). Ask her or him to describe the evolution of the school's literacy curriculum. You might ask: "In what ways has the reading and writing curriculum invited more students to 'break their silence?' " and "What remains the school's greatest challenge in inviting students to do so?"
2. In this chapter, the author candidly reveals the assumptions that she held about her students' literacies. Review a lesson plan (or ask a colleague to review a plan) that you have written to teach students a particular content knowledge (e.g., science, social studies, math). Within that plan, try to identify the assumptions that you made about students' reading and writing competencies. How might you challenge these assumptions in a future lesson plan?

REFERENCES

Allen, J. (1995). *It's never too late: Leading adolescents to lifelong literacy.* Portsmouth, NH: Heinemann.

Allington, R. (1998). *Teaching struggling readers.* Newark, DE: International Reading Association.

Altieri, E. (1998). Using literacy activities to construct new understandings of disability. In T. Shanahan & F. Rodriguez-Brown (Eds.), *Forty-seventh yearbook of the National Reading Conference* (pp. 529–541). Chicago: National Reading Conference.

Alvermann, D., & Phelps, S. (1998). *Content reading and literacy: Succeeding in today's diverse classrooms* (2nd ed.). Boston: Allyn & Bacon.

Biklen, D. (1992). *Schooling without labels: Parents, educators, and inclusive education.* Philadelphia: Temple University Press.

Biklen, D. (1993). *Communication unbound: How facilitated communication is challenging traditional views of autism and ability/disability.* New York: Teachers College Press.

Brooks, J. G., & Brooks, M. G. (1993). *In search of understanding: The case for constructivist classrooms.* Alexandria, VA: Association for Supervision and Curriculum Development.

Buckley, S. (1995). Teaching children with Down syndrome to read and write. In L. Nadel & D. Rosenthal (Eds.), *Down syndrome: Living and learning in the community* (pp. 158–169). New York: Wiley.

Cohen, L. (1994). *Train go sorry: Inside a deaf world.* Boston: Houghton Mifflin.

Crawford, J. (1989). *Bilingual education: History, politics, theory, and practice.* Trenton, NJ: Crane.

Drummond, M. J. (1994). *Learning to see: Assessment through observation.* York, ME: Stenhouse.

Erickson, K., & Koppenhaver, D. (1995). Developing a literacy program for children with severe disabilities. *The Reading Teacher, 48,* 676–687.

Fine, M. (1992). *Disruptive voices: The possibilities of feminist research.* Ann Arbor: The University of Michigan Press.

Fountas, I., & Pinnell, G. S. (1996). *Guided reading: Good first teaching for all children.* Portsmouth, NH: Heinemann.

Freeman, D., & Freeman, Y. (1994). *Between two worlds: Access to second language acquisition.* Portsmouth, NH: Heinemann.

Harris, T. (1994). Christine's inclusion: An example of peers supporting one another. In J. S. Thousand, R. A. Villa, & A. I. Nevin (Eds.), *Creativity and collaborative learning: A practical guide to empowering students* (pp. 293–304). Baltimore: Brookes.

Harvey, S., & Goudvis, A. (2000). *Strategies that work: Teaching comprehension to enhance understanding.* York, ME: Stenhouse.

Hart-Hewins, L., & Wells, J. (1999). *Better books, better readers: How to choose, use, and level books for children in the primary grades.* York, ME: Stenhouse.

Henry, J. (1995). *If not now: Developmental readers in the college classroom.* Portsmouth, NH: Boynton-Cook/Heinemann.

Jorgensen, C. (1998). *Restructuring high schools for all students: Taking inclusion to the next level.* Baltimore: Brookes.

Keefe, C. (1996). *Label-free learning: Supporting learners with disabilities.* York, ME: Stenhouse.

Kinzer, C., Rieth, H., Prestidge, L., Williams Glaser, C., Peter, J. A., & Gabella, M. (1998). *An integrated curriculum and life-style knowledge approach to literacy and social studies instruction for students with mild disabilities: Final project report.* Washington, DC: U.S. Department of Education/SEP.

Kliewer, C. (1998). *Schooling children with Down syndrome: Toward an understanding of possibility.* New York: Teachers College Press.

Kluth, P. (1998). *The impact of facilitated communication on the lives of individuals with movement differences.* Unpublished manuscript. University of Wisconsin, Madison, WI.

Kucer, S., Silva, C., & Delgado-Larocco, E. (1995). *Curricular conversations: Themes in multilingual and monolingual classrooms.* York, ME: Stenhouse.

Lather, P. (1991). *Getting smart: Feminist research and pedagogy with/in the postmodern.* New York: Routledge.

Levstik, L. (1993). I wanted to be there: The impact of narrative on children's historical thinking. In M. Tunnell & R. Ammon (Eds.), *The story of ourselves.* Portsmouth, NH: Heinemann.

Lissi, M. R., & Schallert, D. (1999). A descriptive study of deaf students and their reading teacher participating in computer-networked conversations. In T. Shanahan & F. Rodriguez-Brown (Eds.), *Forty-eighth yearbook of the National Reading Conference* (pp. 365–375). Chicago: National Reading Conference.

Martin, R. (1994). *Out of silence: An autistic boy's journey into language and communication.* New York: Penguin.

McNabb, M. (1998). Using electronic books to enhance the reading comprehension of struggling readers. In T. Shanahan & F. Rodriguez-Brown (Eds.), *Forty-seventh yearbook of the National Reading Conference* (pp. 405–414). Chicago: National Reading Conference.

Meier, D. (1995). *The power of their ideas: Lessons for America from a small school in Harlem.* Boston, MA: Beacon Press.

Oberlin, K., & Shugarman, S. (1989). Implementing the reading workshop with middle school LD readers. *Journal of Reading, 32,* 682–687.

Onosko, J., & Jorgensen, C. (1998). Unit and lesson planning in the inclusive classroom: Maximizing learning opportunities for all students. In C. Jorgensen (Ed.), *Restructuring high schools for all students: Taking inclusion to the next level* (pp. 71–105). Baltimore: Brookes.

Osborne, M. P. (2000). *Adaline Falling Star.* New York: Scholastic.

Parker, D. (1997). *Jamie: A literacy story.* York, ME: Stenhouse.

Pirrone, J. (1998). Literacy lessons across the lines: E-mail exchange in English class. *Teacher Research: The Journal of Classroom Inquiry, 5,* 92–107.

Roller, C. (1996). *Variability not disability: Struggling readers in a workshop classroom.* Newark, DE: International Reading Association.

Routman, R. (1994). *Invitations: Changing as teachers and learners, K–12* (2nd ed.). Portsmouth, NH: Heinemann.

Shapiro-Barnard, S. (1998). Preparing the ground for what is to come: A rationale for inclusive high schools. In C. M. Jorgensen (Ed.), *Restructuring high schools for all students: Taking inclusion to the next level* (pp. 1–14). Baltimore: Brookes.

Short, K., Harste, J., with C. Burke. (1996). *Creating a classroom for authors and inquirers* (2nd ed.). Portsmouth, NH: Heinemann.

Sizer, T. (1992). *Horace's school.* Boston: Houghton Mifflin.

Stainback, S., & Stainback, W. (1996). *Inclusion: A guide for educators.* Baltimore: Brookes.

Vacca, R. T., & Vacca, J. L. (1999). *Content area reading: Literacy and learning across the curriculum* (6th ed.). Glenview, IL: Scott, Foresman.

Whitmore, K., & Crowell, C. (1994). *Inventing a classroom: Life in a bilingual, whole language learning community.* York, ME: Stenhouse.

Wilhelm, J., & Friedemann, P. (1998). *Hyperlearning: Where projects, inquiry, and technology meet.* York, ME: Stenhouse.

Chapter 5

Equity for All Learners of Mathematics: Is Access Enough?

Susana M. Davidenko
State University of New York at Cortland

Patricia P. Tinto
Syracuse University

In 1989, a landmark study by the National Research Council, *Everybody Counts: A Report to the Nation of the Future of Mathematics Education*, made a clear link between access to both higher education and the world of work, and opportunity to study mathematics in school. This study called for specific changes to occur so that teachers could bring about meaningful change in their mathematics classrooms. Also in 1989, the National Council of Teachers of Mathematics (NCTM) published the *Curriculum and Evaluation Standards for School Mathematics* (NCTM, 1989). One task set by NCTM was to determine what it means to be mathematically literate in the current world and to propose changes in the curriculum and classroom environment that will give opportunity for all students to become mathematically literate. The 1989 Standards state that "equity has become an economic necessity" (p. 4). The implicit assumption that mathematical literacy is bound to issues of equity in the world beyond school began to be made more explicit. *The Professional Standards for Teaching Mathematics* (NCTM, 1991) and the *Assessment Standards for School Mathematics* (NCTM, 1995) brought into the discussion the needed changes in practice to reach all students and the use of equitable assessment methods.

The major shifts in the mathematics classroom environment proposed by the *Standards* may be summarized as follows:

- toward classrooms as mathematical communities—away from classrooms as simply a collections of individuals;

- toward logic and mathematical evidence as verification—away from the teacher as the sole authority for right answers;
- toward mathematical reasoning—away from merely memorizing procedures;
- toward conjecturing, inventing, and problem solving—away from an emphasis on mechanistic answer-finding;
- toward connecting mathematics, its ideas, and its applications—away from treating mathematics as a body of isolated concepts and procedures. (NCTM, 1991, p. 3)

Numerous articles and research reports document that the United States continues to face a crisis in the number of children from diverse backgrounds that do not have an understanding of mathematics at a level useful for solving problems they may encounter in their lives. Secada (1992) asserted that this problem is most notable in children from poor communities and children from homes where standard English is not the main language. Secada stated, "the American educational system is differentially effective for students depending on their social class, race, ethnicity, language background, gender, and other demographic characteristics" (p. 623).

Recent national and international assessments (e.g., *the Third International Mathematics and Science Study, TIMSS*; *National Assessment of Educational Progress, NAEP*) indicate that not only is the level of mathematics performance of United States students lower than those from many countries but that there is also a continuing negative disparity in performance among subgroups based on socioeconomic status and race/ethnicity, favoring affluent and White students (Campbell & Silver, 1999; Mullis et al., 1994; http://timss.bc.edu/TIMss1/AboutTIMSS.html, http://nces.ed.gov/timss).

Asian-American students have been seen as a non-White minority which has performed at higher levels in mathematics especially compared with other minority groups (Secada, 1992; Silver, Smith, & Scott Nelson, 1995). However, studies on Asian-American students' performance in mathematics (Bracey, 1997; Olsen, 1997) alert us about the danger of such stereotypes and myths. Olsen (1997) claimed that as Asian Pacific American students are expected to excel, this becomes a barrier to acknowledging that many Asian Pacific American children are failing in school.

Bracey (1997) discussed the misleading construction of ethnic categories like "Asian students" which includes students from countries that have very different cultures such as Japan, Vietnam, and India. In addition, within the groups of students coming from the same Asian country, there are great differences in their academic performance. Findings from Bracey's study indicate that "the groups of Asians who score well on tests are those whose parents have the most education and the [groups with] higher proportions of kids born in this country" (U.S) (p. 330).

Campbell and Silver (1999) reported on the findings of a task force on *Mathematics Teaching and Learning in Poor Communities*, including not only inner city urban populations but also rural and migrant students as well. This report provides a view of the underlying conflicts regarding the education of children living in poverty such as the allocation of resources and unding. However, the report also describes success stories of effective mathematics education in such impoverished contexts, and proposes an agenda for attaining equitable mathematics education in poor communities. The report discusses the important role played by teachers, schools, districts, parents, and the community to accomplish systemic changes "that support educational quality and educational justice within schools and school districts that serve students who live in poverty" (p. 22).

Studies reported in *New Directions for Equity in Mathematics Education* (Secada, Fennema, & Adajian, 1995) address issues of equity at the political and socio-cultural level, as well as within the school and classroom contexts. The NCTM series, *Changing the Faces of Mathematics*, continues to explore in depth issues of diversity and equity in mathematics education. The authors of this series, *Perspectives on*, attempt to synthesize recent reports around groups such as *Asian Americans and Pacific Islanders* (NCTM, 1999a), *Latinos* (NCTM, 1999b), *African-Americans* (NCTM, 2000a), and discuss other important issues in *Gender and Multiculturalism* (NCTM, 2000b).

The Principles and Standards for School Mathematics (PSSM) (NCTM, 2000c) is a document based on the foundation of the three previous standards documents (NCTM, 1989, 1991, 1995) and on the evaluation of the past years of practice and research on mathematics education. The PSSM includes six principles—Equity, Curriculum, Teaching, Learning, Assessment, and Technology—and curriculum and process standards for school mathematics at levels PreK–12. Setting the tone of the NCTM document, the first principle is the Equity principle. It states, "Excellence in mathematics education requires equity-high expectations and strong support for all students" (NCTM, 2000c, p. 11). This principle directly challenges the belief that only some students can understand mathematics. The Equity principle argues that all students must experience worthwhile mathematics:

> Low expectations are especially problematic because students who live in poverty, students who are not native speakers of English, students with disabilities, females, and many nonwhite students have traditionally been far more likely than their counterparts in other demographic groups to be the victims of low expectations. Expectations must be raised—mathematics can and must be learned by all students. (p. 13)

Some progress has been made demonstrating that children from diverse backgrounds can learn high levels of mathematics. The program, *Toward a*

Mathematics Equity Pedagogy (TMEP) (Fuson et al., 2000) has shown that young children in Grades 1–3 from schools in poor communities can succeed mathematically. The authors of this project especially address equity noting that,

> Equity, to us, means a classroom in which each child is included and affirmed as an individual and in which access to mathematical competencies valued by the culture is provided to all children. Central to equity is setting high-level goals for all and then using various methods of learning support so that individual children can go as far as they can. (p. 200)

In ensuring classrooms where all children learn mathematics, it is interesting to note that Fuson et al. (2000) and her colleagues stated, "We found that we needed to consider affective, social, motivational, self-regulatory, and self-image aspects of learning and not just focus on building mathematical conceptions" (p. 201).

A parallel situation is seen in looking at inclusive classrooms. At its most basic definition, *inclusion* is the practice of educating students with and without disabilities together (Bley, 1994; Elliott & Garnett, 1994; Turnbull, Turnbull, Shank, & Leal, 1999). While many researchers and advocates have called for challenging academic opportunities for *all* learners in settings that are truly inclusive (Downing, 1996; Fisher, Sax, & Pumpian, 1999; Jorgensen, 1998; Kluth & Straut, 2001), in too many instances the actual implementation of inclusive schooling has impacted the places or educational environments in which students are educated more than it has their curriculum and instruction. In other words, some have been content to label a classroom "inclusive" if all children are included in the physical space and social structure of that classroom. Unfortunately, these errors in language and practice often lead to a continued reduction of goals in the content areas for many students, especially those that carry some type of label (Bradley, 1984; Oakes, 1991; Silver et al., 1995; Sau-Lim Tsang, 1984; Trafton & Claus, 1994). In this chapter, we emphasize the idea that educators who have been focusing only on the affective and environmental aspects of a student's learning in inclusive classrooms, must now also focus on the building of mathematical understanding of a rich mathematics curriculum.

IS ACCESS TO ALGEBRA ENOUGH?: A STUDY OF TWO CLASSROOMS

The ideas discussed in this chapter highlight the learning experiences of Latino ESL students mainstreamed into English-taught mathematics classes. The study is taken from a larger work by Davidenko (2000) which focused on language minority students taking algebra classes in an urban high school, within a poor community. The study looks at affective, academic, and sociocultural aspects that impact the education of ESL[1] students.

The School, The Students, and the Teachers

The research took place at an inner city high school in a medium-sized city in central New York. The school neighborhood is part of an economically depressed area and approximately 60% of the 1,100 students at Jefferson High are enrolled in a free or reduced lunch program. The school has a culturally diverse student population composed of Caucasian (48%), African American (36%), Latino (9%), Vietnamese (4%), and Native American (1%) students. The English-as-a-Second-Language (ESL) students—Latino and Vietnamese—constitute approximately 10% of the school population. These students are a minority within the school and within each mainstream classroom they attend.

Low rates of attendance affect classes throughout the school. The parents of most of the students at Jefferson High have not completed a high school level of education. According to the teachers the parents not always encourage their children to pursue higher education. From an educational perspective, Ms. Romero said:

> It's not the parents' fault. It's just that they don't have that experience, getting out of the neighborhood and getting a college degree. They don't see what the big deal is, because, I don't think they had experienced it. And this goes down to students.

It is important to point out that the students' socioeconomic status, their cultural background, or their parents academic preparation should not be considered as a justification or an explanation for the students' school performance. However, these factors should not be overlooked for they have

---

[1]The literature related to the education of students who live in the United States and whose home language is other than English, uses different labels and acronyms such as Language minority (LM), limited-English-proficient (LEP), English language learners (ELL), and English as a second language (ESL) students. ELL has become the prevalent expression (e.g., Echevarria & Graves, 1997; Doty, 1999; Moschkovich, 1999). This expression focuses on the *process* of learning English more than on a *lack of* some type of proficiency. Throughout this chapter, we refer to the Latino students who take English as a Second Language classes as "ESL students." We use the acronym ESL because it is the expression used by all people involved in the study (e.g., students, teachers, principal). We want to emphasize that we consider the label ESL as *temporary*, not as a trait of a student. "Being ESL" denotes a stage in the student's adjustment to a new culture. When working with ESL students, it is most important that researchers and educators carefully consider the particular group of students they are investigating, or is being served by a given school. See Myer (1985) for a useful classification of immigrant students that encourages educators to consider not only students' English proficiency, but their previous economic, social, and academic experiences in their native countries.

great impact on a student's education (Secada, 1992; Silver et al., 1995; Tate, 1994).

The ESL Program. The school has a team of three ESL teachers and a teacher assistant. The teacher assistant is a Puerto Rican woman who lives in the school neighborhood and knows most Latino families whose children attend the high school. The school also has tutors who help the Vietnamese students.

When the ESL program was established at Jefferson high school, the three ESL teachers had to decide which model of second language acquisition they preferred to implement. They each had experiences in other schools where the ESL students spent the entire day in self-contained classrooms, in a specially designated part of the building. They disliked that type of setting and the learning experience it created for the students.

Thus, in addition to teaching the ESL classes, the ESL teachers at Jefferson High have implemented a push-in strategy. That is, each ESL teacher pushes-into different regular classrooms to help a small group of ESL students during the lessons. Because it is not possible to support all the ESL students in all their classes, the ESL teachers mostly push-into the lower level academic classes in mathematics, science, and social studies. They felt more confident about their own knowledge in these content areas within the introductory levels of the high school courses.

This push-in strategy is based on the view that a second language should be learned in meaningful contexts and through students' social interactions (Cummins, 1986; Echevarria & Graves, 1998; Moschkovich, 1999). This strategy is analogous to the in-class model of instruction for students with disabilities, in which a special education teacher provides individualized attention to the students in the regular classroom (Greenes, Garfunkel, & DeBussey, 1994).

The Algebra Classes. Two ninth-grade algebra classes were chosen for the study because each had at least three Latino students attending class. The classes were taught by Ms. Wenger and Mr. Malvasi. Whereas Ms. Wenger was in her third year of teaching, Mr. Malvasi was a veteran teacher. Both had taught primarily at Jefferson High School and both were certified secondary mathematics teachers.

A total of nine students, some with identified learning disabilities, were interviewed for the study[2] including three students from Ms. Wenger's class

[2]The four ESL students who participated in the study, two from Puerto Rico (male and female), and two male Mexican students (brothers) had been in the United States between 8 months and 2 years. They all expressed that they understood the conversations in their classes quite well although they had some difficulties with the directions of the assignment, the new vocabulary, and expressing themselves in the second language.

and five students from Mr. Malvasi's class. An ESL student from Mexico, who was taking a college track algebra course, was also included in the study. His participation provided the opportunity to explore the experiences of an ESL student exposed to a higher level of mathematics content to learn how second language issues were manifested at that level.

A special education teacher assistant, Mr. Hints, "pushed into" Ms. Wenger's class every day to provide in-class support to six students who had learning disabilities. Mr. Hints also "traveled" with these students into their science class. The students in the special education program were integrated into Ms. Wenger's class with the other students. When walking around the room, Mr. Hints assisted any student who asked for help. On many occasions, he also collaborated with Ms. Wenger by teaching some concepts or procedures since he was a certified mathematics teacher.

An English speaking ESL teacher, Mrs. Young, pushed into Mr. Malvasi's class every day to provide English support to three ESL students. They sat at the back of the room and Mrs. Young circulated around them to clarify some words, to point at students' notes, or to repeat the teacher's directions in simplified English. When the students in the class worked on some worksheets or textbook problems, Mrs. Young would help her students follow the step-by-step algebraic procedures. This in-class support was provided during the entire year.

LOOKING FOR ACCESS: WHAT WE LEARNED

Our study illustrates that access to academics (e.g., taking an algebra course) was not enough to provide students with an equitable, worthwhile education in mathematics. In the following section we explore seven issues related to academic access and what we learned about these issues through our study of two high school classrooms.

Hidden Beliefs Underlying Mathematics Instruction

The core of the mathematics instruction took place in the algebra classrooms. Both algebra teachers taught the traditional algebra curriculum in an instrumental manner. That is, they modeled how to perform algebraic procedures (e.g., addition of two polynomials) focusing on rules but nei-

---

Two Latino non-ESL students also were selected; one Puerto Rican female student who had just exited the ESL program after participating in it for 5 years, and a male student born in the United States from Puerto Rican parents. This latter student had learning disabilities in reading and writing in both Spanish and English. Three non-ESL students were also included; an African-American male student and two Caucasian students, one male and one female.

ther explaining their meaning nor promoting student-made connections among concepts and procedures.

The teachers played a dominant role in the classroom discourse. Their questioning approaches elicited instrumental type, one word, or short phrase answers. Even when posing a why-type of question, they stay at a superficial level of the procedures. The teachers expected students to listen, observe, take notes, practice learned procedures, and answer specific questions. Open-ended questions were not part of their tools for teaching mathematics.

During class the students worked on practice dittos or textbook problems. Ms. Wenger and her teacher assistant circulated around the room to answer students' questions. Mr. Malvasi would help students, frequently while sitting at his desk. The students often worked with partners or small groups talking to each other about how to do the problems. There were almost no discussions about mathematical ideas or alternative approaches to solve problems. Although the students somewhat participated in the class, they had a passive role with respect to thinking and understanding the content.

The teachers' descriptions of their strategies, seemed to reflect they were "in transition" to reformed mathematics classes.[3] They expressed that they did a lot of questioning and group work, and had implemented some innovative strategies at the beginning of the school year. Mr. Malvasi described the difference between his teaching style at the beginning and end of the year, explaining that at the start of the school year he uses a variety of interactive strategies to help students learn. He noted that by the end of the year, "you're just reviewing procedures. . . . You need to go down to the 'nitty-gritty' stuff."

Similarly, Ms. Wenger explained that she used a lot of collaborative strategies at the beginning of the year, but found that, "toward the end, . . . like after February, I say, "Oh my god! I have this much to do and this much time" and I got up there trying to give it to them in the easiest way you can . . . because, you know, . . . not because you want to, it's just . . ." [somehow a little embarrassed].

Although the activities described by the teachers may suggest that they were in transition to creating NCTM-standards (NCTM, 1989, 1991, 2000) based mathematics classrooms, they were, instead, examples of disguised traditional practice (Cohen, 1991; Schoenfeld, 1988). A close look at teacher explanations about their teaching and their descriptions of the students reveals that the teachers held strong behavioral views about the students' learning of mathematics. Following are examples of the expressions that Ms. Wenger used to describe her students' performance:

---

[3]We refer to reformed mathematics classrooms as those where the teaching is consistent with the NCTM Standards and a constructivist approach.

> Most of the time he does his homework;
>
> Not very good at keeping his stuff organized in his notebook, it's all over his place;
>
> She always does her homework, she works hard.

Work habits and student organizational skills were of primary relevance for Ms. Wenger. She would not promote a student into a higher level course, if she considered he or she did not have good organizational skills. Ms. Wenger stated:

> They must have good work habits; they may "have it," they may be able to "do it with their thinking," but if they don't practice and they don't do the work, then they can't go on; because it's so important that you do your work in Course I. So much material and very rigorous.

For Ms. Wenger, being able to "do it with the thinking" was not so important. The expressions "understanding" or "not understanding" were not part of her vocabulary for describing her student. She would say instead, "he's good in math," "she's doing well," or "he doesn't get it." The importance given to student work habits, organization, and responsibility to practice, reflected Ms. Wenger's views of learning mathematics as acquiring instrumental knowledge; that is: listening to the teacher, taking and keeping notes, and practicing through the assigned homework.

Mr. Malvasi used the following expressions to describe his students' performance:

> He has a low self-esteem when it comes to mathematics;
>
> She can do OK but, if she focuses more, she probably can do much better;
>
> If he doesn't know he will ask me questions, he listens, he works very hard;
>
> He's way behind and he's not confident in his ability.

The message underlying Mr. Malvasi's expressions—which he made clear to the students during class—was that to do well in his class the students were supposed to listen, work hard, focus, and be responsible for their homework.

Expressions like "being able to explain their thinking," "using different approaches to problems," "understanding the meaning of the concepts" were not used by Mr. Malvasi or Ms. Wenger in relation with student performance. It appeared that meaningful understanding was not part of the teachers' expectations for these students.

This analysis makes it clear that in order to accomplish authentic changes in practice—teaching and assessing—it is not enough for teachers to try different types of activities or use the vocabulary of reform such as "cooperative grouping" and "hands-on activities." In particular, it is common that teachers believe they do "a lot of questioning during their lessons." However, the teachers' questioning strategies only elicited one word or short phrases for answers. The teachers used these answers to continue "telling" the content. Mr. Malvasi's inquiry included why-type of questions regarding the procedures (e.g., "Why do we divide?" "Why do we cancel?"). These questions, although more significant than asking for a particular number or operation, fell short in eliciting genuine thinking on the part of the students. The students became used to responding to these types of questions, which had a limited set of answers, in an automatic way.

Teachers' Expectations

Teachers' low expectations for students may create real barriers to attaining equal access and opportunities for all students (Secada, 1992; Tate, 1995). The participating teachers expressed a genuine interest in their students' success and felt they had high expectations for their students. However, a close analysis of teacher talk reveals biases and unintentionally inequitable practices. The following excerpts from an interview with Ms. Wenger illustrate this statement. In the first excerpt, she talks about solving linear equations in one variable; in the second Ms. Wenger refers to solving a system of linear equations.

Excerpt 1: The teacher refers to solving a linear equation such as $4x + 3 = 19$.

W: I wanted to make it clear that we are changing the operation, we are not changing the signs, per se. We are changing addition to subtraction, or changing multiplication to division, and vice-versa. I tried to make sure that I was consistently saying that we are changing the operation and not the sign. Because I noticed that some people were getting confused with that.

Excerpt 2: The teacher refers to solving a system of two linear equations such as $y = 3x + 2$ and $2x + 2y = 7$

W: We did it graphically and algebraically too. But only by substitution. We decided not to do the other method because the students were having so much trouble, it was so difficult for them to do it just with substitution, that we didn't even try elimination. We tried to spend more time in substitution so everyone would do well. But, they still made mistakes and didn't do very well on the test, because of all the mistakes they made.

There are a lot of ideas, the ideas we've done throughout the whole year, you know. Distribution, solving for one variable, plug-it-in, substitution, several things they have to remember, and they will do some mistakes here and there.

It is apparent that the teacher did not expect students to understand the procedures. In the first excerpt, she showed concern about "consistently saying" the same things so students, in her mind, would not get confused. In the second excerpt, she manifested her belief that simplifying a procedure and showing students only one way of solving a problem would benefit her students. Whereas, presenting multiple approaches would confuse them. When Ms. Wenger acknowledged that the students did not do well on a test because they made mistakes, she never mentioned the possibility of the student's lack of understanding, or limited knowledge base.

Following is another example in which the teacher's low expectations led to inequitable practices. Ms. Wenger described the different expectations she had for the students in two of her algebra sections: the "regular" one (observed in the study) and one that she considered had more capable students. In the following excerpt, Ms. Wenger and Mr. Hints explain their views about teaching the FOIL method to multiply two polynomials.[4]

W: The reason why I use FOIL is . . . it's something easy for all of them to remember. That's the only reason I use it. With my other groups I use distribution. But the only reason I use FOIL . . . and if we had more time I would use distribution instead, because I prefer that. With the other algebra class, where I have more advanced students, and with my Course I students, I use distribution instead, because it is consistent with everything. Whereas with this group, they need things they can remember.

R: Why do you think so?

W: Because . . . I don't know . . .

H: Well, the kids come out of middle and grade school with more or less rote cookbook recipe type of stuff so, if you can put it in a structure, they feel safe with that.

Although the FOIL method may be easier to remember for a long time and students can apply it and do the computations correctly, it is "conceptless." That is, it hides the actual use of the distributive property, which, when well understood, can be transferred to other multiplication contexts. Instead of encouraging students to make connections between concepts and procedures, the teaching of the FOIL method became a tool for meaningless

---

[4]FOIL: When multiplying two binomials, like $(a + b)(c + d)$, students are taught that F means they multiply a & c, the First terms, O means they multiply a & d, the Outer terms, I means they multiply b & c, the Inner terms, and L means they multiply b & d, the Last terms. Then, to multiply the binomials they just have to "write F+O+I+L." That is: $(a + b)(c + d)$ = FOIL = $ac + ad + bc + bd$.

teaching to the so-called "regular" class. This type of teaching leads students to learn procedures by memorizing the steps, without even being exposed to the justification of the procedures. The students are deprived from seeing meaning in mathematics and do not develop reasoning abilities. These students are not provided with true academic support and equitable opportunities to succeed in mathematics.

Conflicting Roles of Multiple Teachers in one Classroom

As previously noted, Mr. Hints was a special education teacher assistant who pushed into Ms. Wenger's class to support a group of 5 or 6 special education students. These students were scattered around the room, they were not singled out in the class. In this way, one of the goals of inclusion in the classroom, that all children are educated together (Sapon-Shevin, 1992) appeared to be accomplished.

Ms. Wenger and Mr. Hints planned the lessons together and Ms. Wenger encouraged Mr. Hints to participate during the lessons. Mr. Hints was a certified mathematics teacher and on some occasions he offered conceptual or procedural explanations to the whole class. For example, he suggested alternative procedures to solve algebraic problems. This promoted some exchange of mathematical ideas among students and teachers. Although not all students were able to see equivalence of the procedures, at least the students had the opportunity to see and compare alternative methods. In this way, Mr. Hints provided a more meaningful academic support in the mathematics class.

The second teacher in Mr. Malvasi's class was Ms. Young. She "pushed-into" the algebra class every day to assist the ESL students. An important goal of this strategy, as explained before, is that the students are included socially and culturally in the classroom while they learn English in a meaningful context. The role of the ESL teacher in the classroom is to facilitate ESL students' understanding and communication with others, by making the English input more comprehensible for the ESL students.[5]

The ESL students—Mario, Patricia, and Robert—sat in the last row next to each other, without integrating with the other students. During the entire lesson, Ms. Young moved around or sat among these students to provide assistance. While Mr. Malvasi talked to the class, she would whisper his

[5]Krashen's *input hypothesis* (1996) is very relevant in understanding how students learn in a second language. This hypothesis claims that "we acquire language by understanding messages, by obtaining comprehensible input" (p. 3). When the messages are comprehensible, the learners move a little beyond their current level of competence. The goal of the ESL teachers when teaching content matter is to provide comprehensible input to ELL students.

directions to the ESL students, explaining some words or pointing out in their notebooks the key words or information they had copied. Her role was not that of a translator, since she did not speak Spanish. Instead, she would simplify the vocabulary and give easy step-by-step directions about what to do to solve the problems.

The relationship between the ESL students and Ms. Young created a mini-context for learning mathematics within the algebra class. The ESL students greatly appreciated Ms. Young's support during the mathematics class. However, there were several problems with this strategy. The following excerpt from an interview with Mario shows his view of the role of the ESL teacher in the algebra class.

R: When you are in Mr. Malvasi's mathematics class, Ms. Young is there with you and the other ESL students. How do you find that, is it useful? What happens when some day she doesn't go? Is it different?

M: Well, when she goes it is like I feel more like . . . confident because I know that she will explain to me. But when she doesn't go, like it happened now . . .

R: Today?

M: Yes, I feel more nervous. Because, when we came, we almost did not understand the teacher at all, but after a while we had already become used to the teacher. Then she came to help us more, then we became used to her and when she doesn't come we feel nervous because we don't know some things.

R: Aha.

M: The math teacher tries to explain the meaning of some mathematics words.

R: For example?

M: The slope.

R: How does Mr. Malvasi explain what the slope is and how would Ms. Young do it?

M: The teacher and the ESL teacher say the same, except that we are not with the teacher, we are with the ESL teacher in a group. So, she listen and then she explains to us.

R: So, you don't pay attention to what the teacher says?

M: Yes, when it is time to hand in the papers and all that, but to do the equations and that, the ESL teacher explains to us how to do it and then we try. And if we can do the problems, then she lets us work alone and goes to help the other [ESL] students.

R: Do you think that if she were not there you still would be able to learn?

M: I don't know, perhaps no . . . Because it has been a long time we are not alone with the regular teacher. Maybe, I don't know.

Ms. Young's push-in strategy into Mr. Malvasi's class did not work in an inclusive manner as expected by the team of ESL teachers. The ESL students did not communicate with the rest of the students in the class, and they seldom talked to the teacher during class. They would answer Mr. Malvasi's questions if he asked them to, but the ESL students rarely directed questions to Mr. Malvasi. They would rather consult with the ESL teacher.

The students missed great parts of the teacher discourse, which is supposed to be rich in mathematics language. The mathematics teacher mostly assessed the ESL students through their written assignments and exams, missing the ongoing assessment through class participation. The relationship between these students and the mathematics teacher was, somehow, filtered by the ESL teacher.

Even if this close instruction could be appropriate at the beginning of the school year, students' understanding of the classroom discourse should be reevaluated periodically. It was apparent during the interviews that the students understood many of the teacher's messages and they could have participated more during the class. The continued support by the ESL teacher kept the ESL students isolated academically, and prevented them from developing social interactions with the rest of the students. The following excerpt from an interview with Ms. Young exposes her views of learning and teaching mathematics.

Y: Another thing I've found difficult here. When I took math, if I were doing . . . I don't know, quadratic equations, anything, perhaps solve the equations. Our teacher told us step by step. We knew what work was required of us, what needed to be on paper. I don't just go from the first step down to the answer. The teacher wants to see my work once he knows I got the answer, this is how it's supposed to look like, everybody in the class is the same thing. That's not how they do mathematics here. However you come up with the answer, great! I don't see how you got the answer . . . Oh . . . individualism! And it makes me crazy that there is no set pattern in the way that we go through a problem. So these kids are all over the place. As long as they arrived to the right answer, is not a real big deal. And that really bothers me, I wish there is a structured way that they would do it. So the kids know exactly what it is expected, you know that you follow all these steps you will arrive to the right answer and you can explain how you arrived at that answer.

R: But, in most cases you can approach math problems in different ways.

Y: Well, but . . . for example Mario, when they use . . . He teaches them that but . . . I don't know. As a teacher I would say: "Look, the first step is: you've got to write out, write out everything, because this is the first time we are doing this, write everything. So what are you multiplying and adding? Write it out. From there, now we will actually multiplying it together and get an answer . . . and put like terms together after that. So you might have as many as four lines of stuff for this problem." But Mario, he will copy the problem and in the very next line, he's got the answer. And so, when he gets the answer wrong . . .

R: Does he?

Y: Yes, sometimes he does because he does it too quickly and tries to do too much in his head. And there are times, when it is too difficult to do in your head, but he tries to do it anyway, because to him, it's really cool, if he can do the problem in just two lines. And so, when I say to him "well that's not quite right, this term is not quite right, if you had all your work there we could go back tracking and it could be easily to see where you went." Now he just erases the whole line and goes back and does the problem all over it again. I just couldn't get him into the habit, everybody was in the habit of doing step-by-step-by step. Once you got really good at it, it's no problem, leave a couple out. But, in the beginning, we are not that good at it, so let's write all this up . . . but . . . he won't, because it's not cool [she laughs].

The ESL teacher was not educated as a mathematics teacher and, as she acknowledged in the previous excerpt, she tried to teach in the way she was taught. The academic support in mathematics provided by the ESL teacher was through instrumental teaching, where the students were expected to memorize straightforward procedures without any type of reasoning. We consider that this support was not true academic support since it did not promote meaningful understanding of mathematics. In addition, as we can infer from the excerpt, the ESL teacher missed the fact that Mario was able to skip steps because he had understood the rules of distributivity in the multiplication of two polynomials. She even discouraged him from thinking on his own, being afraid that he would not get right answers.

From Mr. Malvasi's point of view, the participation of the ESL teacher was an important support for his students.

M: Some of the words I use, they don't quite connect. For example, I may say "perpendicular." Now, they won't connect the word with what that means: perpendicular lines. Then Ms. Young explains the word to them. And she does that, when I use words that they don't connect visually with what that is, Ms. Young will help with visualizing what I'm talking about [. . .] Well, the strategy works very well because of the language issue that I, obviously, have with the students. I don't understand their language, I don't speak their language. I try to get somewhere in the middle, speaking slow enough that they might pick up something. But I can't speak too slowly because I would lose other kids.

R: But, if they talk to you in English do you understand?

M: Yes I do. I don't understand if they talk Spanish too much. But the main idea is that when I'm talking to them in English, I need to "slow down," so they are able to hear and process. But I can't slow it down too

> much. That's where the ESL teacher helps tremendously. She'll fill in some words that I use and quickly give them the definition of it, which is very helpful, because . . . I might or might not know if they understood a word I used. And it hurts them for the whole meaning of the sentence.

The previous excerpt indicates an advantage for the ESL students as the ESL teacher provided comprehensible input during the lesson. As we have discussed previously, she extended her role to teach mathematics to her students during the class using an instrumental, drill and practice, approach.

Although Mr. Malvasi explained some of the algebraic procedures going through the justification of the steps, he quickly moved to reviewing the procedures at the drill and practice level, without deep reference to the meaning. Thus, the ESL teacher's approach did not differ greatly from the math teacher's approach. In this limited context, the ESL students benefited from her support to keep up with *this type* of traditional course.

Placement in Mathematics Courses

When students who are English language learners first enroll in the school district, they go through a process of placement, which includes tests on their English language proficiency, and a review of their academic transcripts. Sometimes the placements are temporary, since they are reconsidered after the complete translation of their records from the previous school. Ms. Romero, the vice principal interviewed in this study, mentioned that she revises each new ESL student's placement made by the counselors. She wants to make sure the students are not underplaced in content area courses because of their language proficiency.

> That's a battle we have here sometimes. The counselors want to put the students at a comfort level. They don't want to place ESL students in social studies, because of the vocabulary. But they might still benefit from these classes. It's a constant battle with the guidance counselors. Some of the ESL teachers want them to place the students higher, and the counselors lower, or the other way around. [. . .] These are difficult decisions and I spend a lot of time at the beginning of the year going through every ESL student's paper, Vietnamese or whoever, and looking and checking, and checking their exam scores, and saying: "Wait a minute, if this student got an 85 in algebra, why stick him in . . . consumer math?" [Laughed]. You know, and I go through, making these corrections. It's extra work for me, because *they* are supposed to do it. Anything they can do to get them out of here and graduate the students . . .

These types of incidents, however, are not limited to Jefferson High School. This is a common situation faced by English-language learners when their placement is based on their English language proficiency and not on an appropriate assessment of their mathematics knowledge (Moschkovich, 1999).

The topic of placement was also discussed during the interviews with the algebra teachers. The students who pass the algebra course, may be placed in two different mathematics sequences. The higher academic track is the college preparatory sequence; the lower track consists of completing a geometry class after the algebra course. The placement depends on the students' performance on a district test and the recommendations of the algebra teachers. As explained earlier, Ms. Wenger considered that work habits and study skills were essential to succeed in Course I, and she did not recommend any of her students to the higher level track. Mr. Malvasi did not show much interest in promoting his students for Course I; it all depended on the student's performance on the district (traditional) algebra test. In consequence, all of Ms. Wenger's students and most of Mr. Malvasi's students were placed out of the college preparatory sequence. These yearly decisions made by the teachers are another source of possible inequitable practices.

Most students at Jefferson High School come from families whose parents had not pursued higher education, or completed high school. Although in general parents may advocate for higher placement for their children, these parents may not realize whether or not their children are inappropriately placed. As a result, the children whose parents have a limited educational background face yet another barrier for attaining equity in their education.

Supportive Relationships

Jefferson High School seemed to be very supportive to students and their families during their adjustment to the new culture. The importance of having an ESL teacher assistant who shared the same language with Latino immigrant students and lived in the same neighborhood became apparent in the ESL students' interviews. This assistant had helped students and their families turning a frightening experience into a pleasant one.

The ESL teachers were very well prepared, and continually reflected on their practices. The goal of the push-in strategy aimed at ESL student inclusion and participation in mainstream classes. Although this participation was not yet accomplished in Mr. Malvasi's class, as reported earlier, the ESL teacher did support her students by providing comprehensible input during the lessons.

It was clear throughout the study that the ESL teachers usually play a significant role in the ESL students' lives. They support their students through the period of adjustment after they move from their native countries. They get to know the students and issues about their lives outside the school, and they follow students' development in English and in the content areas through more than one year. The relationship between the ESL students with the ESL teacher as "their" mathematics teacher, extended beyond the mathematics classroom. When the students needed help in mathematics for homework or tests, they arranged meetings with the ESL teacher, not with the mathematics teacher. This was also true for science and social studies. So, the ESL students have plenty of opportunities to build strong relationships with the ESL teachers who become their advocate in educational issues.

English Language Academic Proficiency

Cummins (1981) brings into the discussion about second language learning, the concepts of two types of English language proficiency to be acquired. These are, *conversational proficiency* needed for everyday interactions and *academic proficiency* required for schoolwork. The ESL students' development of academic language is key in determining whether they should continue in the ESL program or they could be exited from it and mainstreamed into all English taught classes. The ESL students interviewed acknowledged that their greatest difficulties were in science and social studies where an ample vocabulary for reading and writing was required for the assignments. However, they said they did not have major difficulties with the language in the mathematics class or on the assignments.

This fact reflects that the use of language in these traditional mathematics classrooms was limited. At most, the students needed an explanation or the translation of a few words to understand the directions of the assignments and the problems. During the interviews, the students were asked to explain their reasoning and justify their answers. In these situations, the ESL students revealed their lack of an appropriate academic language or a mathematics register to express mathematical ideas (in both languages in the case of Latino students). Although native English speakers exhibited an articulate command of conversational English, they had not developed an appropriate academic language of mathematics either. We believe that Cummins' discussion about conversational versus academic proficiency should be seen as an issue that concerns *all* learners of mathematics.

In the following excerpts Ms. Wenger reflects on her students' language proficiency:

W: Word problems are difficult for them, the vocabulary is hard. [She meant all the students in that class, not just the ESL students.]

R: What kind of vocabulary?

W: The math vocabulary or just regular vocabulary. You know, not knowing what the word "sum" means. You know, but most of it is probably the math vocabulary. They don't know it.

R: Oh.

W: If you say . . . "product" many people ask: "What is product?" This is like. . . . You assume that they are supposed to know that by now, but they don't.

R: Do you ever have them write something where they can use those words?

W: Oh yeah. More at the beginning of the year we have them writing "how to do" problems, explaining to people. . . . For example, "Explain to a friend how to do this problem" you know, but [reflecting on her teaching] . . . I guess I should do more on the vocabulary, I haven't . . . I guess I just think that they know it when they come here and I forget that they don't. And sometimes when we are in the middle of something and that one word happens to pop-up once, you know . . . and then you are just like . . . "Oh no. . . ."

R: There are words they always use but not in a math context.

W: Right, and I know they always give out worksheets in elementary school and they have "add" and they write the word "sum" there . . . then you think that somehow they get it, but no . . .

During an observation, Ms. Wenger displayed on the overhead screen a set of problems that asked for addition and subtraction of polynomials. One of the problems was the following: "From $5x^2 + 3x - 2$ subtract $2x^2 - 4x + 9$." An English-speaking student raised her hand and asked: "What does 'from' mean?" Ms. Wenger, who was walking around the room to assist the students, stopped to answer the student: " 'From' means that this one (pointing at the polynomial $5x^2 + 3x - 2$) is the one we put on top, when we subtract." The student said: "Oh, I get it." Ms. Wenger continued assisting other students.

Ms. Wenger not only missed the opportunity to encourage students to read the entire problem and try to interpret the meaning of it, but her answer suggested some type of "role" of a polynomial depending on the position it is written on the paper. The teacher's response was in agreement with her instrumental view of teaching polynomials. She provided a "technical" answer instead of eliciting some meaning for the operation.

Following is an example of how the teacher could have addressed the question about the meaning of "from" to promote students' connections with previous knowledge.

Let's say the teacher stops the class from doing the problems since all students can benefit from the discussion. Then, the teacher writes on the board the expression, "6 – 4," and asks the students to read the expression aloud in different ways. Some possible responses the students may provide are:

Six *minus* 4,

Subtraction of 6 *minus* 4,

Six *take away* 4,

Subtract 4 *from* 6, and

From 6 *subtract* 4 (the teacher can say this one if the students do not).

From their experience in arithmetic, the students *understand* subtraction of two numbers as well as the meaning of the result (2 as 6 – 4). Reading the entire expression "six minus four" or "from 6 subtract 4" will convey these meanings. By comparing these expressions with those for the polynomials the students may transfer what they know about "6 – 4" to the abstract case of subtraction of polynomials. Instead of relating the word "from" to a technical aspect of the procedure, we propose that the teacher pose questions that promote students' retrieval of their previous knowledge and elicit connections to the new situations.

It is clear that the previous argument will be valid only if the students *understand* that a polynomial could be treated as a number (for each value assigned to the variable *x*, a numerical value of the polynomial can be calculated). This was not likely to be the case of the students in Ms. Wenger's class. In any case, we want to stress the importance to take advantage of the opportunities to model the use of language in the mathematics and see it as a *tool* for conveying meaning of concepts and procedures.

Learning the English Mathematics Register in a Second Language

When analyzing the transcripts of the Latino students' interviews, it was interesting to see the appearance of some scattered English words.[6] Some examples of these words are: *keyboarding, homework, slope,* and *degree.* It is important to differentiate among these examples. The students knew both the English word, "homework," and the equivalent in Spanish (*tarea*) and used both interchangeably. They could have used expressions equivalent to keyboarding but they chose to use the English term. However, regarding the new concepts learned in the course such as slope or degree of a polynomial, the students had not learned the concepts in their native language. They *did not know* the corresponding Spanish words either. They could not translate the words and so they just used the English word learned in class. These examples show that the students had learned the *concepts* slope and degree along with their *mathematical registers in context.* The English register had become part of the student's conceptual network of that concept, as is the case for English speaking students in the classroom.

[6]The interviews with the Latino students were conducted in Spanish or English according to their preferences. Two students switched between Spanish and English within the same conversation. The other three students spoke in Spanish about 100% of the time. These students were not only more comfortable speaking in Spanish, but they were concerned about "losing" the language, so they chose to do so, without mixing the two languages.

RECOMMENDATIONS

As we did at the beginning of this chapter, we again ask ourselves: What have we learned about access to academics in the mathematics field and equitable practices in inclusive settings? And, with that knowledge, how do we ensure that all students receive an equitable education in an inclusive setting? We are just beginning to explore and understand how to effectively support students in inclusive classrooms when we hold high expectations for all students. We have seen the important role played by mathematics teachers and other teachers who may be present in mathematics classrooms. But we also found hidden teacher beliefs that lead to traditional practices that hinder opportunities for students to succeed in learning mathematics meaningfully. We may not yet know how to best support all learners in mathematics courses, but data from this study and our own experiences as teachers of mathematics suggest that helping ESL students, and perhaps all learners in inclusive classrooms means going beyond access and engaging all learners in challenging and appropriate mathematics instruction.

Posing Questions and Listening to Students

In classrooms that promote meaningful understanding, teachers pose questions that encourage students to think beyond how to find an answer. The focus is on the processes and concepts involved in the problem situations. Questions such as "Did anyone solve it another way?"; "Tell us about what was going through your mind when you were working on this problem?"; and "Can you explain how you solved it?" promote student communication and validation of their thinking. This conversation, in turn, helps promote equity in the classroom (Campbell & Langrell, 1993; Whitin & Whitin, 2000). Questions or directions using verbs such as "*explore, investigate, invent, discover, revise,* and *pretend*" (Whitin & Whitin, 2000, p. 12) encourage students to look more closely into a given problem.

For the teacher to take first steps into this inquiry style of teaching, and generate questions that promote students' thinking, requires a change in teachers' deepest beliefs about mathematics as a collection of facts and procedures, and learning as memorizing facts and applying procedures. Teachers must move toward a view of mathematics as a dynamic, culturally related field, and learning as construction of knowledge.

Simultaneous Language and Mathematics Instruction

ESL students in this study, even when their participation in the classroom discourse was limited, learned concepts and language together. This suggests that ESL students would greatly benefit from a more frequent and purposeful *use* of language to communicate in the mathematics classroom.

In reformed mathematics classrooms student talk plays an essential role in developing connections and reasoning. ESL students in these classrooms may need more complex supports than the type provided in a traditional math classroom. A purposeful use of mathematics language may bolster skills in both language and mathematics in more meaningful ways. Moschkovich (1999) claimed that most studies that have focused on ESL student difficulties in learning mathematics were related to their ability to solve word problems or translate mathematics symbols. She suggests there is a need for research on ESL students' linguistic needs in reformed-oriented classrooms in which "students are expected to write and talk about their solutions to open-ended problems, present written or oral arguments for or against conjectures, and defend their conclusions about a mathematical solution" (p. 7). We must understand that students' learning of mathematical concepts and language is contextual and that both oral and written communication including diagrams, pictures, graphs, and tables, must be encouraged.

Equitable Assessment Tools

In making placement decisions for the following year of mathematics courses, we have seen that algebra teachers did not promote their students to the highest possible placement. Their decisions were made only considering traditional, factual, procedural tests, and guided by low expectations about their students' capabilities to handle higher levels of mathematics work. We claim that a different type of assessment should be considered for placement decisions.

Reform in mathematics education not only calls for changes in curriculum and practice but also for changes in assessment of mathematics knowledge and understanding. The *Assessment Standards for School Mathematics* (NCTM, 1995) stated the need for assessment to enhance mathematics learning as well as for promoting equity. In the PSSM, the 2000 standards document, the NCTM asserts that,

> Many assessment techniques can be used by mathematics teachers, including open-ended questions, constructed-response tasks, selected response items, performance tasks, observations, conversations, journals, and portfolios. These methods can all be appropriate for classroom assessment, but some may apply more readily to particular goals. (p. 23)

We believe that these types of assessment techniques could be used within the mathematics classroom as a tool for students' learning and for teacher instructional decisions. These strategies could also be used for the placement of students who are English language learners or for students who transfer from a different educational system. In this way, fair and meaningful assessment will become a tool for equitable practices in mathematics education.

CONCLUSIONS

The study has shown us that access to academics, in this case, to a high school algebra course, was not necessarily a path for students' success in mathematics. Issues of inequitable opportunities for meaningful learning of mathematics appeared at different points in time and within different contexts that affected students' academic advancement.

Looking across the contexts we see that each student had a different way of obtaining academic support. Some fell short in that endeavor. The data revealed that most of the students who had a positive attitude toward education, had some type of academic support that helped them build that attitude. For example, students referred to their parents' interests in their education; they mentioned being tutored by the ESL teachers or by the sports coach, or meeting with friends who helped them with homework assignments.

For most of the interviewed students, however, there was a mismatch between their academic needs and the academic support in mathematics provided within the school context. The teachers' traditional approach to teaching mathematics and the teacher-centered classroom discourse did not allow for students' participation in meaningful discussions of mathematics. The instrumental teaching hindered students' understanding, leading them to view mathematics as a collection of facts and formulas to memorize. The following excerpts illustrate this point.

Stella, a Caucasian student who was taking algebra in her senior year of high school, expressed:

S: I don't understand algebra.

R: Why?

S: I don't know . . . I just was never good at math. . . . Sometimes I understand something, like graphing and stuff like that, not that slope. . . . Just when you put the points.

Patricia, an ESL Puerto Rican student, described how she saw herself as a student of algebra.

R: How are you doing in math?

P: In mathematics . . . I am bad . . . [chuckled]

R: Why?

> *P:* I don't know, like in algebra. . . . In general mathematics, add, subtract, multiply, divide, I'm fine. But in algebra . . . I see a lot of numbers and those letters and I get confused, you know? I see it and I don't know where to start.

Patricia described that the ESL teacher helped her during class:

> *P:* I don't know what to do, but Ms. Young, she is there with us. And she explains to me and now I am understanding more [. . .] When the teacher tells us we have to do some exercise, then she explains to you, in a way you understand, you know? She starts doing it with us. Then, when it is time to take the exam, then one knows more or less what to do.

We can see that Stella's and Patricia's academic need for meaningful understanding did not receive the appropriate academic support from Mr. Malvasi nor from Ms. Young. The "extra" support still accentuated the instrumental aspect that did not facilitate Patricia's understanding. An appropriate support would emphasize the connections between numbers and variables, helping students derive the algebraic structure of a word problem by using students' informal logical thinking.

Mr. Malvasi attributed Stella's and Patricia's lack of understanding to a lack of interest, saying, "Stella . . . she's very too busy with the social problems, she is a good person, good student. She can do well but she is just too occupied with her on-again, off-again boyfriend [. . .] She has . . . a low self-esteem when it comes to mathematics." About Patricia he commented, "Patricia started out real well. Then she started getting with the groups in the building . . . Groups that will skip out of the class. Leaving the building then coming back after a period [. . .] Then we got her back on track . . . and she's doing better."

Mr. Malvasi's comments did not include issues of understanding the content, skills, or concepts. He considered that students' performance was quite dependent on their attitude, mainly "hard work" and "focus." Although it may have been the case that Stella and Patricia made little effort to perform better in the class, the students' descriptions revealed a mismatch between academic needs and academic support. The students were frustrated by the gap between their previous knowledge of arithmetic and the current content of the algebra class. The fact that Patricia was confused by the numbers and letters, does not show a lack of effort but a lack of understanding. Hard work, seen as practice of procedures learned in class, would not help her to attain that understanding. In the case of Patricia and Stella, instead of looking at their poor performance due to their lack of interest, we argue that the case may be the other way around. We may infer that the lack of understanding led to a lack of interest in the course. In this case, we *can* take a different approach to the problem.

We have seen in several instances that students use informal logical and algebraic thinking. In the case of Patricia, she demonstrated proficiency with word problems when she solved them mentally and talked aloud. She struggled when asked to "do algebra" that required instrumental vocabulary. Algebra teachers should help students build on this informal thinking that is developed when students work on problems in familiar contexts, using every day language. Teachers can facilitate students' transition to a more formal algebraic reasoning. Instead, when teachers just reinforce their instrumental teaching, many students' become frustrated due to the lack of understanding and become alienated from the subject.

We have discussed earlier that there were other circumstances in which a mismatch between students' academic needs and academic support arose. These situations were originated when students were placed in lower levels of mathematics courses than the ones they might have been in.

Andrew, who had moved to New York State from another state, was quite capable in mathematics. He had demonstrated through the interviews that he had good number sense, estimation skills, and logical thinking. However he had been placed out of the college preparatory mathematics sequence because of the mismatch between the mathematics courses he had taken in his previous school and Jefferson High School required courses. When he was asked in an interview whether or not he had consulted with his counselor or anybody else to be placed in a more challenging mathematics course, Andrew explained that he felt ready to be placed in higher math, but lacked access to placement tests or parental support that would ready him for college level math.

We believe that Andrew was not provided with academic guidance to get into the appropriate classes nor support for planning a college career. He did not see his counselor as an advocate. The rules followed for placement decisions were imposed in his case without looking at Andrew's individual academic needs or at his academic abilities—knowledge and understanding—in mathematics. His misplacement shows the need for appropriate assessment tools.

We have learned that teaching and assessing only for instrumental understanding creates barriers for students' academic success even though they have had access to these algebra classroom—as in the case of Jefferson High. Educators must take a closer look at classroom routines to see whether or not students are provided with true equitable opportunities to learn mathematics with understanding. Teachers should hold high expectations, which will be reflected in their selection of engaging tasks that promote students' reasoning and problem-solving abilities.

We have learned that the teachers' beliefs about mathematics learning and the teachers' expectations for their students greatly influence their practice (Ladson-Billings, 1998; Secada, 1992; Thompson, 1992) whether in an explicit or implicit way. Teachers can only break the cycle of low expectations and low performance in the mathematics class by taking responsibility for each student's development of understanding that goes beyond performance of procedures. Teachers must see the impact that they and their teaching have for empowering students mathematically.

Kilpatrick and Silver (2000) stated that ensuring mathematics for *all* students means that we must also rethink our categorization of the capable and the incapable. Indeed, Kilpatrick and Silver note that these labels are highly unstable and shift by the context of the circumstance. However, as long as teachers, parents, and educators buy into the belief that ability to learn mathematics is a fixed property of an individual then inequities in education will exist.

If we are to move beyond access and ensure equity of education, we must educate our preservice and practicing teachers to look at both students' academic needs and the structures that support each student's success. Teachers must rethink education beyond the traditional ideas of instruction and academic success, and develop a mind set flexible enough to ensure all students equitable learning opportunities and possibilities of success.

For Discussion and Reflection

1. If you were asked to set goals for yourself as a teacher of mathematics, how would you have responded before you read this chapter? After reading this chapter? How has this chapter challenged your thinking about mathematics instruction?
2. The authors ask: "Is access enough?" In what ways does *access* fall short of serving all learners? What would it mean to go beyond access?
3. In this chapter the authors suggest that low expectations have disserved a wide range of students. How can teachers hold high expectations for students who are struggling with math content without frustrating them? What would it look like? What strategies could be used?
4. The authors of this chapter suggest that high standards are central to equity in education. How is this assertion different from recent discussions in the public arena about higher standards and expectations and "raising the bar?". How might this *political* interpretation of "high expectations" disserve some students? How can we make sure that high expectations are used in ways that truly serve all students?

In the Field

1. Review your school district's math curriculum documents. What cultural assumptions can you identify within the document? What assumptions about student learning can you find?

2. Explore your school district's practices on educating students who use English as a Second Language. How are placement decisions made? What types of supports do students receive? What kinds of roles do ESL teachers play in the school?

REFERENCES

Bley, N. S. (1994). Accommodating Special Needs. In Carol A. Thornton & N. S. Bley (Eds.), *Windows of opportunity: Mathematics for students with special needs* (pp. 137–163). Reston, VA: National Council of Teachers of Mathematics.

Bracey, G. (1997). Asian math scores: Genes, effort, or parental education? *Phi Delta Kappan, 79,* 329–330.

Bradley, C. (1984). Issues in mathematics education for Native Americans and directions for research. *Journal for Research in Mathematics Education, 15*(2), 96–106.

Campbell, P. F., & Langrall, C. (1993). Making equity a reality in classrooms. *Arithmetic Teacher, 41*(2), 110–113.

Campbell, P. F., & Silver, E. A. (1999). *Teaching and learning mathematics in poor communities.* A Report to the Board of Directors of the National Council of Teachers of Mathematics. Reston, VA: National Council of Teachers of Mathematics.

Cohen, D. (1991, Fall). Revolution in one classroom (or, then again, was it?) *American Educator.* American Federation of Teachers, pp. 16–48.

Cummins, J. (1981). The role of primary language development in promoting educational success for language minority students. In California State Department of Education (Ed.), *Schooling and language minority students: A theoretical framework* (pp. 3–49). Los Angeles: National Dissemination and Assessment Center.

Cummins, J. (1986). Empowering minority students: A framework for interventions. *Harvard Educational Review, 56,* 18–36.

Davidenko, S. (2000). *Learning mathematics in English: ESL and non-ESL students' perspectives.* Doctoral dissertation, Graduate School of Syracuse University.

Doty, R. (1999). Taking on the challenge of mathematics for all. In NCTM (Ed.), *Changing the faces of mathematics: Perspective on Latinos* (pp. 99–111). Reston, VA: The National Council of Teachers of Mathematics.

Downing, J. (1996). *Including students with severe and multiple disabilities in typical classrooms.* Baltimore: Brookes.

Echevarria, J., & Graves, A. (1998). *Sheltered content instruction: Teaching English language learners with diverse abilities.* Needham Heights, MA: Allyn & Bacon.

Elliott, P., & Garnett, C. (1994). Mathematics power for all. In C. A. Thornton & N. S. Bley (Eds.), *Windows of opportunity: Mathematics for students with special needs* (pp. 3–17). Reston, VA: National Council of Teachers of Mathematics.

Fisher, D., Sax, C., & Pumpian, I. (1999). *Inclusive high schools.* Baltimore: Brookes.

Fuson, K. C., De La Cruz, Y., Smith, S., Lo Cicero, A. M., Hudson, K., Ron, P., & Steeby, R. (2000). Blending the best of the twentieth century to achieve and mathematics equity pedagogy in the twenty-first century. In M. J. Burke & F. R. Curcio (Eds.), *Learning mathematics for a new century. Yearbook* (pp. 197–212). Reston, VA: National Council of Teachers of Mathematics.

Greenes, C., Garfunkel, F., & DeBussey, M. (1994). Planning for Instruction: The Individualized Education Plan and the Mathematics Individualized Learning Plan. In C. A. Thornton & N. S. Bley (Eds.), *Windows of opportunity: Mathematics for students with special needs* (pp. 115–135). Reston, VA: National Council of Teachers of Mathematics.

Jorgensen, C. (1998). *Restructuring high schools for all students.* Baltimore: Brookes.

Kilpatrick, J., & Silver, E. (2000). Unfinished business: Challenges for mathematics educators in the next decades. In M. J. Burke & F. R. Curcio (Eds.), *Learning mathematics for a new century. Yearbook* (pp. 223–235). Reston, VA: National Council of Teachers of Mathematics.

Kluth, P., & Straut, D. (2001, September). Standards for diverse learners. *Educational Leadership, 59,* 43–46.

Krashen, S. D. (1996). *Under attack: The case against bilingual education.* Culver City, CA: Language Education Associates.

Ladson-Billings, G. (1998). It doesn't add up: African American students' mathematics achievement. In C. Malloy & L. Brader-Araje (Eds.), *Challenges in the Mathematics Education of African American Children: Proceedings of the Benjamin Bannekier Association Leadership Conference* (pp. 7–15). Reston, VA: National Council of Teachers of Mathematics.

Moschkovich, J. (1999). Understanding the needs of Latino students in reform-oriented mathematics classrooms. In *Changing the faces of mathematics: Perspective on Latinos* (pp. 5–12). Reston, VA: The National Council of Teachers of Mathematics.

Mullis, I. V. S., Dossey, J. A., Campbell, J. R., Gentile, C. A., O'Sullivan, C., & Latham, A. S. (1994). *NAEP 1992 Trends in Academic Progress* (Report No. 23-TR-01). Washington, DC: National Center for Education Statistics.

Myer, L. (1985). *Excellence in leadership and implementation: Programs for limited English proficient students.* San Francisco, CA: San Francisco Unified School District.

National Council of Teachers of Mathematics. (1989). *Curriculum and Evaluation Standards for School Mathematics.* Reston, VA: The Council.

National Council of Teachers of Mathematics. (1991). *Professional standards for teaching mathematics.* Reston, VA: The Council.

National Council of Teachers of Mathematics. (1995). *Assessment standards for school mathematics.* Reston, VA: The Council.

National Council of Teachers of Mathematics. (1999a). *Changing the faces of mathematics: Perspectives on Asian Americans and Pacific Islanders* (Series Ed. W. Secada, Vol. Ed. C. Edwards). Reston, VA: The Council.

National Council of Teachers of Mathematics. (1999b). *Changing the faces of mathematics: Perspective on Latinos.* Reston, VA: The National Council of Teachers of Mathematics.

National Council of Teachers of Mathematics. (2000a). *Changing the faces of mathematics: Perspectives on African Americans* (Series Ed. W. Secada, Vol. Eds. M. Strutchens, M. Johnson, & W. Tate). Reston, VA: The Council.

National Council of Teachers of Mathematics. (2000b). *Changing the faces of mathematics: Perspectives on multiculturalism and gender equity* (Series and Vol. Ed. W. Secada). Reston, VA: The Council.

National Council of Teachers of Mathematics. (2000c). *Principles and standards for school mathematics.* Reston, VA: The Council.

National Research Council. (1989). *Everybody counts: A report to the nation on the future of mathematics education.* Washington, DC: National Academy Press.

Oakes, J. (1991). Tracking: Can schools take a different route? *Rethinking Schools.* March/April, pp. 12–14.

Olsen, L. (1997). *An invisible crisis: The educational needs of Asian Pacific American Youth.* ERIC NO: ED 416273.

Sapon-Shevin, M. (1992). Ability differences in the classroom: Teaching and learning in inclusive classrooms. In D. A. Byrnes & G. Kiger (Eds.), *Common bonds: Anti-bias teaching in a diverse society* (pp. 39–52). Wheaton, MD: Association for Childhood Education International.

Sau-Lim Tsang. (1984). The mathematics education of Asian Americans. *Journal for Research in Mathematics Education, 15*(2), 114–122.

Secada, W. (1992). Race, ethnicity, social class, language, and achievement in mathematics. In D. Grouws (Eds.), *Handbook of research on mathematics teaching and learning* (pp. 623–660). New York: Macmillan.

Secada, W., Fennema, E., & Adajian, L. B. (Eds.). (1995). *New directions for equity in mathematics education.* New York: Cambridge University Press.

Shoenfeld, A. H. (1988). When good teaching leads to bad results: The disasters of "well taught" mathematics courses. *Educational Psychologist, 23,* 145–166.

Shoenfeld, A. H. (1989). Problem solving in context(s). In R. I. Charles & E. A. Silver (Eds.), *The teaching and assessing of mathematics problem solving.* Reston, VA: The National Council of Teachers of Mathematics.

Silver, E. S., Smith, M., & Scott Nelson, B. (1995). The Quasar Project: Equity concerns meet mathematics education reform in the middle school. In W. G. Secada, E. Fennema, & L. B. Adajian (Eds.), *New directions for equity in mathematics education* (pp. 9–56). New York: Cambridge University Press.

Tate, W. (1994). Race, retrenchment, and the reform of school mathematics. *Phi Delta Kappan, 75,* 477–484.

Thompson, A. (1992). Teachers' beliefs and conceptions: A synthesis of the research. In D. Grouws (Ed.), *Handbook of research on mathematics teaching and learning* (pp. 127–146). New York: Macmillan.

Third International Mathematics and Science Study (TIMSS). Available at http://nces.ed.gov/TIMSS/timss95/

Trafton, P. R., & Claus, A. S. (1994). A changing curriculum for a changing age. In C. A. Thrornton & N. S. Bley (Eds.), *Windows of opportunity: Mathematics for students with special needs* (pp. 19–39). Reston, VA: National Council of Teachers of Mathematics.

Turnbull, A., Turnbull, R., Shank, M., & Leal, D. (1999). *Exceptional lives: Special education in today's schools* (2nd ed.). Englewood Cliffs, NJ: Prentice-Hall.

Whitin, P., & Whitin, D. (2000). *Math is language too: Talking and writing in the mathematics classroom.* Urbana, IL: National Council of Teachers of English.

Chapter 6

Accessing Power Through Intentional Social Studies Instruction: Every Day for Every Student

Diana M. Straut
Syracuse University

Kevin Colleary
Hunter College

Framers of the United States constitution emphasized that the vitality of a democracy depends on the education and participation of its citizens. Schools have long been charged with the task of helping students become contributing citizens who will work to improve society. However, public schools, often held up as laboratories for democratic processes, are participating in an exclusion that challenges the very democracy upon which our nation was founded. By denying students access to a comprehensive social studies curriculum, schools silence the voices that can potentially take political and social action to strengthen our country. We argue in this chapter that through intentional social studies education—social studies curriculum and instruction thoughtfully planned and implemented across the curriculum—teachers can give all students the skills and dispositions that they need to fully participate in our democratic society and to understand their role in global issues.

SOCIAL STUDIES: FROM CENTER TO MARGIN

From the first days of the republic, instruction in history, geography, and civics were vital to education efforts in the United States. In 1820, Thomas Jefferson wrote, "I know of no safe depository of the ultimate powers of the society but with the people themselves; and if we think them not enlightened enough to exercise their control with a wholesome discretion, the remedy is not to take power from them, but to inform their discretion through instruction" (cited in Carrol, 1997, p. 80). We know, of course, that the social realities of our nation's early years did not mirror the idealized goals of democracy and equality voiced in our founding documents. The pernicious institution of slavery as well as gender, cultural, and religious-based inequities were realities faced by all at the time of our nation's founding. However, the goal of a nation—"*E pluribus, Unum*"—was clearly stated, if not actualized, from our nation's very beginning.

In the earliest days of compulsory education, social studies instruction was at the very center of the curriculum. Even if not called "social studies," the curricular goals of schooling in the late 19th century were consistent with contemporary understandings of social studies instruction. Influential educators viewed the common school as central in promoting social harmony and ensuring that the republic would be guided by an intelligent moral citizenry.

Social studies as a discrete content area has always borne special responsibility for inculcating the citizenry with moral values and for readying students to assume adult roles in our democratic republic. Particularly in elementary schools, social studies is relegated to "second string" status after literacy, math, and science. The issue of access in social studies, then, is really twofold: Relatively few U.S. classrooms offer students a challenging, systematic social studies curriculum, and when social studies is taught, it is often a perfunctory coverage of events or is reduced to celebrations of heroes and holidays. How has this happened? The answers are plentiful and quite easy to understand. High-stakes testing, standardized assessments, and even local standards documents usually minimize the importance of social studies or just leave it out of the elementary school curriculum altogether.

Many K–6 classroom teachers in the nation believe that their primary responsibility is to teach children to read and to understand basic mathematical concepts. This message is underscored boldly by principals, parents, and school board members in every district in the nation. When this message is supported by the administration of high-stakes tests that focus exclusively on reading and math skills, most classroom teachers find little reason or support for taking time out of a busy elementary school day to teach social studies or any other content that won't appear on the assessment.

Another reason for the dissolving social studies instruction in the United States today is the fact that over the last decade, many scholars have argued that the classic "widening horizons" or "expanding environment" (me→ family→neighborhood→community→ state/region→nation→world) social studies curriculum has become too weak and outdated (Maxim, 1999, p. 21). This has fueled a debate about what constitutes social studies instruction and how topics as benign as "neighborhood" can teach important historical and social concepts. Many have written about the need for more history or more geography starting at the earliest grades to shore up an otherwise boring and redundant primary social studies curriculum about family and neighborhoods (Ravitch, 2000; Nash, Crabtree, & Dunn, 1997; National Center for History in the Schools, 1994).

This problem has been further complicated by the proliferation of standards documents in the social sciences published in the past decade. Whereas reading and math discussions and debates focus mainly on *pedagogy* (whole language vs. phonics, arithmetic vs. constructivist math, etc.) only social studies has major academic and research organizations and lobbies fighting over the focus of *content* that should be taught to our students. Note, for example, that standards documents (many in multivolume works) in world history, U.S. history, geography, economics, civics AND in social studies have been published since 1990. How can we expect elementary curriculum developers and teachers to deal with all these documents and the expectations they assume? In some cases the standards have helped classroom teachers and local curriculum developers define a scope and sequence for instruction but more often they have caused confusion at the local level. Some educators may simply choose to avoid the confusion by avoiding the teaching of social studies altogether.

Another reason why social studies has not been enthusiastically embraced in schools is because the teaching profession and the nation it reflects have not always welcomed multiple points of view. The attempt to create a national (or even local) social studies curriculum has ignited a rhetorical battle between "traditionalists" and "multiculturalists" (Hitchens, 1998). Traditionalists tend to advocate for content informed by historical events and tied closely to social science disciplines like geography, economics, and anthropology. Multiculturalists call for presenting historical information from many points of view that emphasize ethics, values, and social issues. The focus in traditional social studies instruction on military and economic themes has been challenged by a call to balance these themes with social history. For example, texts are likely to focus on World War II strategies, losses and gains, but not on the ethics of Japanese Internment Camps. Or students are taught that the internment camps were a necessary strategy of war, needed for U.S. protection. Consequently, students learn "that the world is shaped by social and economic trends that are beyond anyone's control . . ." (Ravitch, 1998, p. 503); a message that condones passivity in the learning of and response to history.

A nearly exclusive focus on dead, White, European males has meant that a majority of students have been disconnected from social studies content (Loewen, 1996). Social studies curriculum has often ignored the contributions of people with disabilities, members of various religious and ethnic groups, immigrant families, gays and lesbians, and women and girls. Examples of these exclusions are found in traditional studies of labor movements, which depict children working in turn of the century factories but don't address the working conditions of contemporary migrant farmers or sweatshops in Thailand; or in studies of exploration that focus on men (e.g., Lewis and Clark or Neil Armstrong) but minimize the contributions of women (like Sacajawea or Mae Jemison). When students don't see their own faces represented in history, it's easy for them to see themselves as passive recipients of historical knowledge, rather than as activists who can challenge, critique, and work for social change (Ladson-Billings, 1997).

BARRIERS TO INCLUSIVE SOCIAL STUDIES INSTRUCTION

A routine, unscientific survey of the preservice teachers in an undergraduate social studies methods course reveals the same finding semester after semester. When asked, "How much social studies did you observe during your first 4 weeks of field work in an elementary classroom?" Well over 50% of the students will report "little to none." As the students embark on their second field experience—another 4 weeks in an elementary classroom—they are armed with a new mission. They are encouraged to ask the host teacher to identify times when they (the preservice teachers) will be able to observe social studies instruction. Consistently, the students return from the field confused and frustrated. Representative of their comments are statements such as, "My host teacher said she doesn't teach social studies. She doesn't have time because she's getting the students ready for the English/Language Arts exam," or "My host teacher said he taught social studies in the beginning of the year. He doesn't do it after the Winter Break," or "My host teachers told me that I could watch social studies being taught last Tuesday afternoon, but there was an unplanned assembly that day and now they don't know when they'll get to their unit on Africa." Within these honest and well-intentioned responses from classroom teachers we find pervasive assumptions that have historically relegated social studies education to the bottom of the curriculum priority list. Consider the barriers, both real and perceived, that inhibit meaningful social studies education.

"I'm So Busy Teaching Other Subjects": Content Compartmentalization

Many teachers still view social studies as a discrete subject to be taught at a certain time of day. This compartmentalization of social studies has meant that students are not making connections to "the big picture." They are not able to see historical or economic events as connected to their world. They don't see the relationship between graphing skills learned in math and the ability to read U.S. census figures presented in bar graph form and they don't see how the life cycle and habitat of a Karner Blue Butterfly (a science concept) has implications for the economic development of their community.

The assumption that social studies needs its own discrete time slot leaves teachers with the seemingly impossible task of finding an "open slot" within the school day. Inasmuch as reading, language arts, and math typically fill the morning in an elementary school, the social studies curriculum is left to fill an afternoon slot. In the event that there remains unfinished business from the morning, or if there is an assembly, fire drill, or other event out of the teacher's control, social studies is often the first thing to go. Further, with students needing time for counseling, band instruction, play practice, language classes, and other "pull out" programs or services, many are lucky to receive even serendipitous social studies instruction.

"I'm Not a Historian": Lack of Comfort With the Content

When done well, social studies requires the teaching of issues and complexities that often don't have answers. This has become painfully evident since the September 11, 2001 terrorist attacks on the World Trade Center and the Pentagon. Teachers must be prepared to skillfully facilitate potentially tense discussions when considering issues such as the taking and treating prisoners of war, ethnic cleansing, religious freedom, distribution of wealth and power, treatment of youth and women, and struggles over territory throughout the world. After September 11th, many schools responded with well-intended patriotic activities but failed to help untangle the complexities of the United States' relationship with the rest of the world.

To really help students critically analyze historic and current events, teachers need both skill *and* content knowledge. Lacking confidence in their own skill or knowledge, some well-intentioned teachers resort to simplistic projects such as the "red, white, and blue button flag," the "sugar cube igloo," the "popsicle-stick Alamo," or units of study like "inventions" or "safety" that keep teachers from drifting into uncertain turf.

Ravitch (1998) observed, "we do not need historians teaching first, second, and third grade. But we should have teachers in the early grades who understand the value of biographies, myths, legends, and history stories. Sadly, due to the power of the current social studies curriculum, little kids are compelled to learn abstract or trivial ideas about families, and communities" (p. 502). The National Association for the Education of Young Children (NAEYC, 1986) takes the well-supported position that young children can learn basic social studies content, and develop "a spirit of inquiry that will enhance their understanding of their world so that they will become rational, humane, participating, effective members of a democratic society" (p. 5). This suggests that teachers must instill in all children a sense of global awareness and a yearning for historical knowledge.

"My Materials Are So Old I Don't Even Bother": Lack of Appropriate Resources

Outdated textbooks and trade book materials that focus on literacy, but give only superficial attention to history, geography, or economics, and a lack of professional development opportunities in areas such as teaching from primary and secondary source documents have limited teachers' options for offering a powerful social studies curriculum. Even in schools where resources exist, it is rare to find multiple resources that consider the same event in different ways. For example, a teacher wishing to help students understand the complexities of the revolutionary war might supplement the textbook with primary source documents such as old letters, diaries, and photos, or with contemporary tradebooks such as *My Brother Sam Is Dead.* With already full schedules, however, teachers don't have a lot of time to mine relevant and accurate social studies resources.

The issue of appropriate resources becomes even more complex when one considers the political and economic factors influencing the creation of social studies textbooks. Even in schools where the textbooks are current, the material within those texts has limitations. In the interest of economic survival, textbook publishers shy away from controversial or potentially unsettling images. In the absence of up-to-date materials that portray diverse experiences, many students don't find their histories or perspectives represented within social studies instruction. Thus, the invisibility of already marginalized students is reinforced by social studies materials.

SO, DOES IT MATTER IF WE TEACH SOCIAL STUDIES?

The casual dismissal of social studies aids and abets a serious crisis in the education of our citizenry. United States Census statistics indicate that in the November 1996 election (a presidential election year) 32.4% of registered voters between 18 and 24 reported voting. This represents a decrease of more than 10% from the 1992 election. In that same age group in the 1996 election, 16.5% of voters between the ages of 18 and 24 cited "lack of interest" as their reason for not voting (www.census.gov). Throughout the census data of the past few decades, there is an identifiable trend of a lack of representation among 18 to 24 year-olds in the United States. There is some indication that African American voters are defying this trend. However, Hispanics, Asians, and Pacific Islanders continue to vote at lower levels

(44% and 45%, respectively) than Whites (61%) and African Americans (53%) (U.S. Department of Commerce, 2000).

Onerous statistics aside, one need not look farther than the "Jay Walking" segments of NBC's *Tonight Show* to find evidence of ignorance. During these segments, late-night talk-show host Jay Leno queries people on the street, to suggest that Americans have big gaps in their understanding of such basic topics as the structure of our government, the geography of our nation, or the names of the most influential policymakers in Congress. Although election statistics and trite media segments should hardly stand as an indictment of social studies teachers, they do raise questions about where and when students in our schools can expect to learn about themselves as members of a democratic republic. Arguably, young (or any other group of) Americans may not register or vote as an expression of their discontent, and certainly any number of reasons can confound statistical data, but there is substantial evidence that Americans lack basic knowledge about history and an ability to think critically about their role in a democratic republic.

The 1994 National Assessment of Education Progress (NAEP) in history indicated that a majority of fourth graders didn't know why the Pilgrims and Puritans first voyaged to America (Hitchens, 1998). Fifty-seven percent of high-school seniors scored "below basic" in American history (Ravitch, 1998). Some political pundits have interpreted these statistics to mean that youth aren't historically literate, civic-minded, or that they just don't care to be involved in their government. The prevailing notion is that youth have chosen not to be involved.

Others contend that there is a fraying of community in our nation that is supported by a curriculum that promotes individualistic thinking. In *Bowling Alone*, Putnam (2000) challenged us to better understand the deep changes in society that have occurred since the end of World War II. These changes have effected each of us as members of families, neighborhoods, and communities. Throughout the book, the author contends that civic participation is on the decline, pointing out that Americans today sign fewer petitions, belong to fewer organizations that meet, know their neighbors less, meet with friends less frequently, and participate less in civic causes than they have in past years. According to Putnam, we're even bowling alone.

The breakdown of a traditionally understood communal sensibility in the nation as a whole could have dire consequences for our future. As technology allows us to do more as individuals, the concepts of "neighbor," "democracy," "community" and "technology" will be continually re-defined. This reality alone is enough to suggest that social studies—or at least the purposeful study of our roles as citizens—still has an important place in U.S. schools.

When we look at schools as potential laboratories for democratic processes, we wonder: In what ways have schools taught students to participate in their community? Society? Government? And, how many students haven't been given opportunities to participate? What messages have students received about who is allowed or empowered to participate? What is "desirable" participation? The social studies have the potential to equip students with a historical knowledge that helps them understand the present and prepare for the future. They begin to understand their relationship to other people, as well as to social and political institutions. Students can analyze the complexities of our government, face their own histories, build tolerance for others, analyze how the actions of Americans impact other nations, and learn ways to take action to change their world. These important foundations for life may not naturally occur in other curricular areas. To present such ideas, teachers must offer explicit and intentional social studies instruction for all students.

IT DOES MATTER: POWER THROUGH SOCIAL STUDIES INSTRUCTION

How can schools help all students understand their role as citizens in a democracy? This question has relevance for all teachers. However, when we look specifically at students who have been marginalized from important curriculum the issue becomes even more significant. Students of color, students with disabilities, or students with economic disadvantages are rarely seen at the center of any curriculum. Rarely are learning opportunities built around them or their experiences. When teachers do take steps to open their classrooms to multiple perspectives, controversial issues, and challenging and accessible content, they begin to reach a wide range of learners.

A curriculum devoid of opportunities for participation and engagement breeds apathy. Students can become indifferent to social justice issues, not seeing the importance of undertaking civic action, not seeing themselves as responsible for social action, lacking a sense of obligation or responsibility for righting social wrongs. So, what would it look like if all students had access to an empowering social studies education? What matters in the delivery of a powerful social studies experience for all students?

Curriculum Matters

Powerful social studies education is grounded in challenging content that is specified in national or state learning standards and up-to-date curriculum guides. We believe that curriculum supports powerful social studies instruction when it is systematically designed and explicitly articulated, and challenging and relevant for students. Districts need to align their own curricular scope and sequence with national or state level standards and ensure that the content pushes students beyond "heroes and holidays" (Lee, Menkhart, & Okazawa-Rey, 1998). Relevant curriculum draws on the knowledge and experiences of students. It helps them see the complexity of issues, and it is socially transformative, in that it helps students develop "individual and collective agency" to work for change (Lee et al., 1998, p. viii).

In articulating a challenging and relevant set of curricular frameworks, schools let teachers and parents know what is expected of them. Likewise, teachers and parents can know what was taught at the previous level, and what they can expect in terms of foundational social studies knowledge and skill. In the absence of such a framework, teachers understandably resort to teaching the content that they know best, or the same units that they've done for years. Challenging and relevant curriculum presents each student with information and skill that is connected to the student's life. It pushes students to analyze, explain, and apply new information.

Traditionally, the social studies curriculum has not expected much of learners in the earliest grades. In many schools the Grade-1 curriculum scope and sequence suggests that students will study community and the people in their community. This is often translated into a unit on careers (e.g., teaching children what the postal carrier does and that the police officer helps students stay safe). Although no one would dispute the import of this information, we believe that most students come to grade school with this knowledge or that the information can be infused into curriculum without dedicating to it a full school year. For example, a relevant and challenging community unit would help students understand and navigate their own community. Students in an inclusive classroom might study the community's approach to accessibility. In a small village in upstate New York, the community is embroiled in a debate over whether or not to "tamper with" the historical authenticity of the town and place ramps at the entrance to every business on the main street. Imagine the power of helping students analyze the issues, interview their peers, and write letters to community leaders about the issues.

A graduate student in a course taught by one of the authors recently undertook a unit that taught first graders in an urban school how to read a map, identify landmarks, and follow bus routes in their community. Students created simple maps showing routes to the local shopping center, then took walking fieldtrips using their maps. In another community unit, an undergraduate preservice teacher helped students interview important community figures (including a police officer and juvenile peace officer) and create a map of community "favorites" (pizza parlor, ice cream stand) to be included in a welcome guide for new students. The curriculum in both examples was meaningful in that it taught real-life skills to be used in the students' community, and it was challenging, as the students had little prior experience with mapping. Students developed pride in their community as they learned about it from local figures and tried to explain it in a brochure to newcomers. Additionally, the unit taught students basic skills to use in future years when they learn more sophisticated geographical concepts.

As we suggest throughout this chapter, the social studies curriculum may be integrated with other curricular areas but it requires that teachers know what constitutes their social studies curriculum at each grade level. A systematic and clearly articulated set of guidelines will help teachers plan instruction and ensure that social studies isn't lost or diluted in interdisciplinary units. Teachers using a curriculum sequence that is aligned with National, State, or District level standards find ways to ensure that even those activities most sacred in the school year (e.g., holiday celebrations, school pageants, and service projects), would be linked to important social studies curriculum. All students, then, are more likely to receive important social studies instruction.

Climate Matters

Students who are empowered through social studies education should be invited, in fact expected, to grapple with difficult issues. This means that students need to learn in a climate that is tolerant, supportive, and open to multiple points of view; a climate that recognizes that "talk is inseparable from power" (Foucault, cited in Himley et al., 1997 p. 43). Students need to get involved with curriculum that forces them to think deeply and talk about historical and contemporary issues. This doesn't mean that they would find answers to tough questions, but they would find the opportunity to *grapple* with hard issues. Sizer and Sizer (1999) contended that "wise schoolpeople and parents cannot underestimate the power that they can find in young bodies, minds, and hearts. . . . We're selling our children short when we believe that grappling is beyond them. In fact, most of them are engaging in dilemmas of intense seriousness while we're looking the other way" (p. 24).

In their book, *The Students are Watching*, Sizer and Sizer (1999) described what happened when a high school student, Dave, arrived early to class and announced, "I've decided one thing. I don't want to be American. As soon as I get the chance, I'm leaving" (p. 1). Prompted by his teacher, Dave goes on to describe his dissatisfaction with American society.

> Americans think they are so great. We think we have the answers to everything. . . . I don't want to live in a place that's only thought of as rich and pow-

> erful. Especially when it's not really a democracy. . . . Other countries are better. I'll just go live in one of them. (p. 1)

The teacher asks "Do you have a country in mind?" and when Dave names a few countries, his classmates enter the discussion to suggest that those countries have problems too. The authors describe the scene that unfolds as the teacher "does not take part as various facts are traded back and forth. The clock keeps ticking. Class is about Dave" (p. 2). Through this vignette, the authors demonstrate how a student-centered climate supported rich social studies content. They present evidence that students have their own ways of knowing. Students can see the world in complex ways and, when given the opportunity, can respectfully interrogate thorny social issues—especially when the classroom climate supports this type of risk taking.

Opportunities to grapple present themselves in both historical content and contemporary events. Difficult topics present themselves every day, although they are not blatantly obvious to all students. Helping students become aware of the complexity of current events, and then creating space in the classroom to discuss those events, is a necessary precursor to creating socially aware citizens for the future. Consider, for example, the teachable moment that arose when Matthew Sheppard, a young, gay, university student was murdered in Wyoming (Straut & Sapon-Shevin, 2000). Or the teachable moments that arise when a fast food restaurant makes the news because of reports of racist behavior toward customers; or when large athletic shoe companies are accused of child labor violations; or when a wealthy entrepreneur wants to tear down an inhabited apartment complex in order to make room for a casino. Bullying, fast food, sneakers, and issues of turf are all relevant to American students. When invited into the classroom, these and other controversial issues become opportunities to translate social studies curriculum into social action.

The Playing Field Matters

Students need to participate on a level playing field, one that reduces assumptions about race, class, gender, age, ability, and other characteristics that restrict students' opportunities for full inclusion. This means giving students a variety of ways to interact with social studies materials. In recent years, social studies has been moving from a text-based (that is, reading and writing dependent) subject to one that values hands-on interaction with the content. Many hands-on learning activities break down the boundaries that have traditionally kept many students "out of" challenging social studies content. Through the use of role plays, simulations, rehearsed dramatic or choral readings, primary source documents, and other visual or performing arts-based activities, students can participate in curriculum without being disadvantaged by limited literacy skills.

In November 2001, as local election campaigns were underway, a kindergarten teacher we know helped her 5 and 6 year olds understand the complexities of voting. Using very simple, pictoral ballots, students voted to decide the daily snack. The teacher revealed the three snack choices (banana, goldfish crackers, or graham crackers) and gave students time to "lobby" or campaign for their favorites. Students cast secret ballots in a voting booth, and discussed what would happen in the event of a tie. The teacher gave students the option of not voting (just as they have in "real life") and discussed the pros and cons of not voting. The teacher introduced words like "majority," "ballot," "lobby" to young children with very limited literacy skills. The teacher reported, "these kids can't read or write, and they probably don't have families that are talking about politics. They come from very poor families where survival is more important than politics. I wasn't sure they could handle the lesson." But, because the teacher found a way for all students to participate, social studies instruction became accessible and relevant. Young learners were exposed to very basic, and immensely important, principles of democracy.

Allowing students to take on new roles or act in simulated events gives them license to speak and act in ways that they might not otherwise be comfortable doing. Newscasts, videotaped documentaries and oral histories allow students to step out of their own stereotypes and into opportunities for new renderings. In "Getting Off Track: Stories From an Untracked Classroom," Bill Bigelow (1994) described improvisation as another kind of "leveling" role play. He wrote:

> In a unit on US slavery and resistance to slavery, I provide students with a set of first person roles for different social groups in the South, which supplements information already gleaned from films, a slide-lecture, poetry, a simulations, readings and class discussions. They read these roles and in small groups select from a list of improvisation choices. They can also create their own improv topic or combine some of mine to form something new. The topics are bare-bones descriptions requiring lots of student initiative to plan and perform. (p. 60)

Bigelow acknowledges that there's always a risk of students resorting to stereotypes to "insulate themselves from the enormity of the subject" and/or "trivializing one of the most horrendous periods in human history." He contends, however, that it is a greater danger to allow students to stay "outside" of such powerful content. Bigelow goes on to share how students, "regardless of supposed skill levels" have risen to the challenge and produced "inner monologues" displaying passionate perspectives on the topic of slavery (p. 60). The inventive teacher levels the playing field in his or her classroom by offering multiple ways of seeing, understanding, contributing, and learning.

In the absence of activities that put the experience of marginalized groups at the center of the curriculum, students are given permission to know, but not to feel. Students who read about discrimination or intolerance, but never have the opportunity to experience it (even if that experience is simulated), run the risk of themselves being intolerant. Granted, simulation in and of itself doesn't prompt change; however, it does give students more affective experience than a text might. Moreover, simulations need to be done sensitively, intentionally, and with ample opportunity for dialogue afterward. Simulations should never reduce powerful social history to a trite "re-enactment." Rather, well-constructed simulated experiences give students data with which to "make decisions and take action" related to an issue, concept, or problem studied in a unit (Banks 1997, p. 239). The ultimate goal is to incite social action through powerful and thought-provoking learning experiences.

For example, the authors recently observed a discussion about an activity in which students simulated the lunch-counter sit-ins of the 1960s. An African-American student observed, "it was so good to see my history given so much attention in our class. It meant that students had to experience it. They couldn't just read about it. When teachers do these kinds of activities they make the black experience real." The student seemed to be deeply moved and somewhat surprised by the acknowledgment of her history.

Systems and Supports Matter

Powerful and equitable social studies instruction invites families and community members into the learning. Perhaps more accurately stated, powerful social studies takes the learning out of the classroom. It makes connections to families, institutions, and political systems. While teaching fifth grade, one of the authors of this chapter issued a call to families, seeking historical documents or artifacts that might support the Grade 5 social studies curriculum. The response was overwhelming. Ethan's mother—who had only limited (and usually discipline-related) contact with the school—spent an entire afternoon sharing her great-grandfather's diary and artifacts from his journey to California during the Gold Rush. This not only brought the Grade 5 "U.S. History" curriculum to life but it gave Ethan, who was often isolated because of his behavior, a chance to take center stage in a very positive way.

Carrie, a student who had been socially marginalized because of her physical appearance (avant-garde clothing, a unique hairstyle) became a hero of the class when her mother visited to share interesting artifacts that were discovered when the family moved into a very old house. Among the artifacts was an old family bible containing information about an unknown family's history. Small groups of children, sitting with Carrie's mother and touching the yellowed pages of a very old bible, became interested in knowing more about Carrie's attic and what it might reveal about life in the 1800s.

In a fourth-grade classroom at the same school, the local historian spent a morning in the early part of October sharing local folklore about homes in the community that were reported to be haunted. Through collaborative planning between the classroom teacher and the historian, students had fun looking at old newspaper clippings, and looking at maps to understand the local lore. In a follow-up visit to a local cemetery (which the historian organized), students looked for familiar names and evidence of plagues in the community. They then took a visit to the town office building to look at census records and meet with town officials. What began as a fun Halloween activity became a full-scale study of the local community.[1] Students learned about, and began to take pride in, their community.

At a suburban high school in central New York, several students organized to lobby local political leaders for a skateboard park. Students that were perceived by many to be radical, skateboard-riding "hoodlums" forced the community to rethink their assumptions. The students, with the help of a teacher and a counselor from the community center, composed thoughtful letters to the legislature, analyzed geographic and financial data, and proposed a workable plan for a skateboard park. The students learned about political decision-making processes, fundraising, zoning, and liability. For the students, the interest was recreational. The learning, however, was authentic, important to their lives, and done in collaboration with community officials.

Time and Place *Do Not* Matter

Social studies can be infused into just about any area of the curriculum or school. To ensure that every student receives social studies instruction every day, however, classroom teachers need to work collaboratively with other subject area teachers and support personnel. The social studies curriculum can be delivered in nontraditional areas of the school. An arts presentation on Kabuki Theatre becomes an opportunity to help students locate Japan on a map and understand the deep history of Asian cultures. A Saint Pat-

[1]NYS Learning Standard 1—Key Idea 4: The skills of historical analysis include the ability to: explain the significance of historical evidence; weigh the importance, reliability, and validity of evidence; understand the concept of multiple causation; understand the importance of changing and competing interpretations of different historical developments.

rick's Day celebration opens the possibility for teaching about Ireland and the issues of immigration, famine, and political oppression.

A Kindergarten teacher we know used the gymnasium as her classroom, during a unit designed to help students understand the National Council for the Social Studies theme of *global connectedness.* Through a variety of activities, students compared and contrasted traditions and practices from different cultures. The teacher helped students understand how practices such as schooling and recreation were carried out in cultures other than the American culture. Because she was struggling to infuse social studies into her limited classroom time, she enlisted the help of the physical education teacher. Together, the two created a week-long physical education experience called "Hopscotch around the World" (Lankford, 1996). Students played hopscotch or variants of it from 16 countries and learned geographical, historical, or facts about various cultures' versions of the game. The physical education teacher made adaptations to ensure that every student participated.

At a very basic level, the teacher's objective was to help students learn that children around the world play similar games. At a much broader level, the teacher was building a foundation for 5 year olds who would eventually need to "*understand different world cultures and civilizations focusing on their accomplishments, contributions, values, and beliefs*" (University of the State of New York, 1996. Social Studies Standard 2—World History, p. 8).

Music is another area that invites curricular integration with social studies—and invites the possibility for more students to experience social studies every day. A music teacher near Albany, New York, teaches fourth graders songs about New York State history—"15 miles on the Erie Canal" for example—as part of her regular curriculum. The music teacher, working with fourth-grade teachers, has revised her curriculum for fourth graders to, where possible, complement the topic of state and local history. This is just as easily done with music of the human rights movement or labor history, battle/war songs, many contemporary (albeit edited) rap songs and cultural music. Integrating music and social studies provides students with an opportunity to use their talents in nontraditional ways.

CONCLUSION

When done well, social studies instruction prompts students to critically examine the society in which they live—from a historical, geographical, economic, political anthropological, or sociological perspective. Students need to see social studies as connected to the big picture. It is hard for students to understand connections between or the relevance of events when those events are disconnected from students' lives, history, or culture.

In learning about the complexities of how our society came to be, students discover who has influenced change and how change has occurred throughout history. They identify values, practices, and traditions that unite (or sometimes divide) Americans. When taught well and taught intentionally, social studies stimulates a process that lets students ask critical questions. Students will get angry, inspired, idealistic, and will come to see themselves as having a role in turning around injustices. When they know others' exclusion, pain, and trials, they find that they can't be passive observers.

For a long time, the social studies curriculum has protected children from the dirt and grime of our history, an approach that Sizer and Sizer (1999, p. 1) described as the "Ain't We Americans Just Dandy" approach, or what Loewen termed "heroification" (1996, pp. 28–29). The danger of such an approach is that it sets up older students for disillusionment. Certainly, developing pride in our nation's triumphs and an understanding of the issues we currently face are important goals for teachers and students. However, understanding the complexity of history and society, both the positives and negatives, is a right that all students in America deserve. This charge can't be left to the secondary school teachers and a single high school "Participation in Government" class alone. To be effective, this work must begin at the earliest grades. As Walberg and Tsai (1983) and the National Council for the Social Studies (NCSS, 1988) have shown, those students who receive more knowledge/content earlier on are better able to understand more as they progress through school.

Any curriculum—social studies or otherwise—falls short of its potential if it promotes a citizenry that is obedient, passive, and silent (Strom, 1995). If there is something to be learned from social studies, it is that in voice there is power. Our job as social educators is to help students, especially those who have been denied access and voice in the past, to believe that they can make a difference in their world; our world. Parker (2001) reminded us that "A mind furnished with powerful concepts is indeed a fertile ground for the germination of new ideas" (p. 13).

Without a strong background in history, geography, economic principles, and systems of government, how will our students make informed decisions about local and global issues? How will they have the depth of understandings necessary to work together to re-define and re-create the communities they will need to survive? Although an exclusionary focus on reading skills and mathematical understandings might make for a literate and numerate society, will it be a compassionate or just one? Although individuals in that society may be able to access and utilize technology, to what ends will that technological knowledge be put? We can't claim that we're giving students "access to academics," much less access to power, when we offer them a watered-down curriculum that is disconnected from their lives.

The charge for educators is immense. We need to offer students *more opportunities* to participate in challenging content, and we need to offer *more students* access to power through knowledge. Without a clear understanding of the lessons of history and the civic foundations on which our society is built, how can tomorrow's citizens continue to build a "United" States that truly promotes "liberty and justice for ALL?"

For Discussion and Reflection

1. How can teachers address the barriers to inclusive social studies instruction that the authors identify?
2. Discuss your own experience with social studies instruction from your elementary school years (K–6). What were some highlights? Lowlights? How does it compare to your experience in high school social studies classes? What do these reflections suggest to you as a teacher?
3. What are the characteristics of good citizenship typically promoted by the American education system? How does the education system promote these? Problematize these? What does this suggest for social studies instruction?
4. Who are potential partners in the delivery of social studies instruction? How might you make linkages with these potential partners?

In the Field

1. Conduct a curriculum audit of the social studies documents in your school. What are the major categories of instruction? What seems to get the most emphasis? The least emphasis? How does this align with the NCSS (National Council for the Social Studies) standards?
2. If your state administers a state-wide social studies test, take the test yourself. Then analyze: What skills are needed to be successful on the test? Are these skills related to social studies? What content knowledge is required to be successful on this test? In what ways do the skills and content align with or diverge from curriculum you deem important?

REFERENCES

Banks, J. A. (1997). Approaches to multicultural curriculum reform. In J. A. Banks & C. A. McGee Banks (Eds.), *Multicultural education: Issues and perspectives* (3rd ed., pp. 229–250). Boston: Allyn & Bacon.

Bigelow, B. (1994). Getting of the track. In *Rethinking Schools*. Rethinking Schools, Ltd. Milwaukee, WI.

Carroll, A. (Ed.). (1997). *Letters of a nation.* New York: Broadway Books.

Himley, M., Larson, A., & Lefave, K. (Eds.). (1997). *Political moments in the classroom.* Portsmoth, NH: Heinemann.

Hitchens, C. (1998). Goodbye to all that: Why Americans are not taught history. *Harper's, 297*(1782), pp. 37–43.

Ladson-Billings, G. (1997). Crafting a culturally relevant social studies approach. In W. Ross (Ed.), *The social studies curriculum* (pp. 123–135). Albany, NY: SUNY Press.

Lankford, M. (1996). *Hopscotch around the world.* New York: William Morrow.

Lee, E., Menkhart, D., & Okazawa-Rey, M. (Eds.). (1998). *Beyond heroes and holidays.* Washington, DC: Network of Educators on the Americas.

Loewen, J. (1996). *Lies my teacher told me: Everything your American history textbook got wrong.* New York: Simon & Schuster.

Maxim, G. (1999). *Social studies and the elementary school child.* Upper Saddle River, NJ: Prentice-Hall.

Nash, G. Crabtree, Ch., & Dunn, R. (1997). *Culture wars and the teaching of the past.* New York: Knopf.

National Association for the Education of Young Children (NAEYC). (1986). "Position statement on developmentally appropriate practice in early childhood programs serving children from birth through age 8." *Young Children,* September, pp. 4–19.

National Council for the Social Studies (NCSS). (1988). *Social studies for early childhood and elementary school children: Preparing for the 21st century.* A report from NCSS task force on early childhood/elementary Social Studies. NCSS.org

National Center for History in the Schools (1994). *Exploring the American experience and the national standards for world history.* University of California, Los Angeles.

Parker, W. (2001). *Social studies in elementary education.* Columbus, OH: Merrill/Prentice Hall.

Putnam, R. (2000). *Bowling alone: The collapse and revival of American community.* New York: Simon & Schuster.

Ravitch, D. (1998). Who prepares our history teachers? Who should prepare our history teachers? *The History Teacher, 31,* 495–503.

Ravitch, D. (2000). *Left back: A century of failed school reforms.* New York: Simon & Schuster.

Sizer, T., & Sizer, N. (1999). *The students are watching.* Boston, MA: Beacon Press.

Straut, D., & Sapon-Shevin, M. (2000). Challenging future educators to take a powerful stand against homophobia. *Democracy & Education, 13*(3), pp. 24–27.

Strom, M. (1995). Preface in *Participating in democracy: Choosing to make a difference.* Brookline, MA: Facing History and Ourselves National Foundation, Inc.

United States Department of Commerce (2000). African Americans defy trend of plunging voter turnout, Census Bureau reports. U.S. Department of Commerce News: Washington, DC. Available [online] at http://www.census.gov/Press-Release/www/2000/cb00–114.html

University of the State of New York. (1996). The State Education Department. *Learning standards for social studies.*

Walberg, H. J., & Tsai, S. L. (1983). Matthew effects in education. *Educational Research Quarterly, 20,* 359–373.

Chapter 7

Auto Mechanics in the Physics Lab: Science Education for All

John W. Tillotson
Paula Kluth
Syracuse University

Teachers and educational leaders alike are troubled by the number of students who, each year, opt out of higher level science courses such as chemistry and physics. Despite the recent focus on success-for-all in schools, participation in science by students "in the margins"—including students of color and White females—remains significantly low (Barba, 1998, Clark, 1999, Monhardt, 2000). Some of these students take only the science classes required for graduation or college. Those who do not see graduation or postsecondary schooling as a goal may avoid taking science courses altogether.

These differences among students are important because students in advanced classes experience more active and interactive learning activities and have opportunities to engage in more enrichment activities than those in lower track classes (Oakes & Lipton, 1998). Perhaps more importantly, students taking more sophisticated courses have increased access to opportunities during and *after* secondary school.

Whereas we might ask why students seem so disinterested in science, we might also ask another equally important set of questions: Why are so few students encouraged to pursue the highest-level science courses? Why are some students marked for honors courses, others expected to complete only minimum requirements, and still others relegated to the vocational track? Are some of these decisions made based on our ideas of who students are and who they can be intellectually? How can we see abilities in students even in the midst of the competitive nature of high-school classes, assessment systems, and social structures?

In this chapter, we explore how many students who learn differently, especially those who struggle to sit and listen quietly, pay attention to the teacher, or engage in other "acceptable" classroom behaviors are excluded from the most rigorous academic classes. This phenomena can be observed across subject areas, but it is a most ironic phenomenon when it happens in science classrooms. Science, after all, is a discipline that prides itself on the hands-on aspects of research and problem solving (i.e., the "process" of generating knowledge about the natural world), yet school science often revolves around content knowledge and memorization (Hazen, 1991). This focus on facts and figures can lead to didactic teaching, which is often contrary to the learning styles of so many students who are actually skilled problem solvers with high aptitudes for being successful as practicing scientists. This paradox is damaging because many students deserving and capable of challenging academic work are being turned away from biology, chemistry, physics, and other science courses based on faulty assumptions and academic prejudices.

We suggest that teachers may need to study the greater school community, the curriculum, organization, politics, and culture of the school instead of tracking and sorting students into academic categories. According to the National Science Education Standards (1996), science education should be available for all learners:

> The Standards apply to all students, regardless of age, gender, cultural or ethnic background, disabilities, aspirations, or interest and motivation in science. Different students will achieve understanding in different ways, and different students will achieve different degrees of depth and breadth of understanding depending on interest, ability, and context. (National Research Council, 1996, p. 2)

In practice, however, there are many students who are not becoming scientifically literate. Too many students are not welcomed or encouraged to pursue scientific learning in American secondary schools.

THE PLIGHT OF SCIENCE EDUCATION TODAY: WHERE ARE THE AUTO MECHANICS?

As we visit secondary schools in the United States, we have begun to notice a need for science educators, building administrators, and guidance counselors to invite a wider range of students into science classrooms or at least into science curriculum. We were most struck by this stratification when we visited an Auto Mechanics class where students were working to restore a 1963 Ford Mustang. They were assembling the engine, crawling under the belly of the vehicle to examine the exhaust system, and discussing ways to make the car travel faster. They used a complex jargon to engage in these discussions and appeared competent and knowledgeable about the work they were doing.

Although the aforementioned learning experience was undoubtedly valuable and worthwhile for the students involved, we wondered: If students could perform so remarkably in this setting, why were they not also being formally included in a science curriculum? Clearly, their knowledge about forces, acceleration, and torque was related to a physics curriculum. However, none of the students described in this scenario were enrolled in the upper level science courses available in their high school. Yet the content they mastered during the lesson and the approaches they used to "solve the problems" of the vehicle, demonstrated how prepared these youngsters seemed to be to participate in a rigorous science curriculum.

Perhaps the most frustrating part of the "tracking scientists problem" relates to the history of the field. Traditionally, science has been a discipline where individuals with different learning needs and profiles have found success and acceptance. Einstein, for example, is "variously described as a late speaker, a dyslexic, a loner, a prodigy, a poor student, and a diamond in the rough" (Gardner, 1993, p. 90). Whether or not Einstein had a learning disability is contested (Gardner, 1993; Marlin, 2000); it is not contested, however, that he spoke late and was a quiet child (Gardner, 1993) and that he had unusual behaviors and ways of learning. Gardner reported that,

> he is supposed to have walked through the streets of Munich by himself as early as the age of three; he often played alone even when other children were around. For the most part he was quiet and thoughtful, but sometimes he exhibited powerful tantrums, including one episode when he hurled a chair at a tutor. (p. 90)

Einstein is also reported to have disliked learning that was overly structured or regimented. In fact, "He particularly disdained the subjects requiring rote learning, and he revealed his contempt by performing poorly and acting defiantly in class" (Gardner, 1993, p. 91). Despite Einstein's trouble with formal schooling, however, he was able to find a home of sorts in scientific learning. After all, in science (although not in all science classrooms), thinking "out of the box" and rejecting convention is prized.

The story of Einstein, biographical accounts of diverse learners, and stories from students we have taught and known, lead us to believe that many learners can excel in the sciences if provided with access to interesting, motivating, and relevant curriculum and instruction. Because a variety of skills are required to engage in scientific inquiry, students with a range of strengths can find a niche in the science classroom. For example, during a lab experiment activity, students who are skilled in written expression will be needed to construct lab reports; students who excel in mathematics are needed for analyzing data and calculating results; students who are strong intrapersonally can lead experiments and delegate roles for participation in activities; students who like to solve problems might enjoy troubleshooting solutions when the experiment doesn't "work"; and students who are verbal might try to explain the outcome of the experiment to peers or to the teacher. Clearly, science is not a discipline for individuals. Rather, teamwork and collaboration are the norms in all of the sciences from astrophysics to zoology. In fact, Derek De Solla Price (cited in Fort, 1990) estimated that, "on average, it takes eight people doing many separate tasks to produce a single scientific breakthrough" (p. 668).

The skills and competencies needed in science are so diverse, in fact, that having a wide range of learners in the classroom can only enrich the learning experiences for all. Fort (1990) reminded us that we need to keep this perspective of diversity in mind as we think about the labels we assign to students and the criteria we use to determine who is, for example, "gifted":

> Gifts and talents in science are as varied as science itself. The abilities needed to make a contribution in science are so wide-ranging and encompass so many fields that, in an important sense, everyone is—or could be, given the opportunity—"gifted in science." (p. 668)

SCIENCE EDUCATION FOR ALL

Clearly, steps must be taken to improve the quality of science learning experiences in our nation's secondary schools. In fact, much of the science education reform movement over the past four decades has revolved around the central mission of making science education accessible to all learners as opposed to just a select few (American Association for the Advancement of Science, 1993; National Research Council, 1996). This message is boldly conveyed in the recent report from the John Glenn Commission entitled, *Before It's Too Late: A Report to the Nation from the National Commission on Mathematics and Science Teaching for the 21st Century* (2000) in which it is noted that:

> Four important and enduring reasons underscore the need for our children to achieve competency in mathematics and science: (1) the rapid pace of change in both the increasingly interdependent global economy and in the American workplace demands widespread mathematics- and science-related knowledge and abilities; (2) our citizens need both mathematics and science for their everyday decision-making; (3) mathematics and science are inextricably linked to the nation's security interests; and (4) the deeper, intrinsic

> value of mathematical and scientific knowledge shape and define our common life, history, and culture. (p. 10)

We offer the following recommendations as a means toward achieving these goals for all learners in science.

Recommendation 1: Teach in Reverse (Use the Inquiry Process)

If you ask a scientist to describe what goes on during scientific research, he or she will likely offer an explanation depicting the dynamic series of events that lead to the generation of new information about our world. Involved in this process are activities such as reviewing the literature for information about prior studies that have been done, designing experiments to test key variables, collecting, organizing, and analyzing a variety of data, and ultimately generating hypotheses that lead to further testing. Scientists must possess the ability to think critically, solve problems, and use reasoning skills in each stage of this inquiry process.

Often, the pursuit of new knowledge in science requires extensive collaboration among individuals working on many project components, with each team member making unique contributions to the overall project. Scientists identify curiosity, creativity, and skepticism as being important traits to rely on in the research endeavor. These characteristics enable individuals to consider divergent solutions to problems that arise and to question the integrity of the data gathered and conclusions reached. The broad knowledge and skills required to do science are critical in many other professions where cooperation, communication, and strategic problem solving have become so vital in our global economy.

In spite of the wide array of knowledge and skills required to do science investigations, the learning experiences of most secondary science students are a stark contrast. The typical high school science student endures repeated lessons consisting of lengthy teacher lectures covering factual information, lab activities that have a single, predetermined answer, and countless drill and practice exercises aimed at reinforcing the content and skills judged by the teacher to be most important.

The pursuit of knowledge in science is often an exhilarating experience, yet school science is consistently rated as boring, useless, and irrelevant by a large percentage of secondary students nationwide (Hazen, 1991). Students who are able to adapt their learning styles to be successful in this rigid, didactic environment often have a false sense of their true abilities in science. When they are put in situations where they must apply their knowledge and skills to solve authentic problems, these students perform poorly

(Yager, 1991). Likewise, students with learning profiles that favor active, hands-on learning, who often suffer in traditional science classrooms, routinely excel when given tasks where they can demonstrate their talents and aptitudes for doing science (Colburn, 1998; Lorsbach & Tobin, 1992).

If schools are really committed to providing science education for all, then changes must be made in order for school science learning to better model scientific inquiry. Inquiry is generally used to define the active processes involved in scientific thinking, investigation, and the generation of knowledge as scientists attempt to better understand the objects and events in the world around them (Chiappetta, Koballa, & Collette, 1998). There are a number of steps science educators can take to establish a science inquiry learning environment. First, teachers must be willing to teach science in reverse. Or put another way, they must modify their instructional approach to begin with an active, investigatory learning experience prior to a formal introduction to the concepts and formulas. This pedagogical approach, referred to as the Learning Cycle, has been developed into a variety of instructional models (Atkin & Karplus, 1962; Barman, 1997; Blank, 2000; Good, 1989; Lavoie, 1992; Lawson, 1995; Lawson, Abraham, & Renner, 1989). The most fundamental Learning Cycle model begins with an exploration in which science students have an immediate opportunity to investigate the concepts that are important within the science unit being studied. The emphasis here is for students to generate as many ideas as possible about what variables are playing a role, what relationships exist between variables, and what additional information is required to fully understand the concept.

Once a "need to know" situation has been established, the teacher and students enter the next phase of the Learning Cycle known as concept introduction or invention. Here the teacher may use a variety of instructional methods to introduce students to the essential concepts. This stage may involve interactive lectures, direct instruction, question and answer sessions, independent student research, or various forms of cooperative group work.

Armed with this new scientific information, students move on to the application phase where they are given multiple opportunities to demonstrate their ability to apply the concepts in new and unique situations. This stage allows the teacher to accurately determine the level of student comprehension and skill development beyond simple rote learning (which is typically the benchmark in most traditional classroom settings).

The Learning Cycle approach to teaching science as an inquiry process has many advantages for all science learners. Extensive research carried out over a number of years has demonstrated that this approach results in greater achievement in science, better retention of concepts, improved attitudes toward science and science learning, improved reasoning skills, and stronger process skills when compared to traditional instructional methods

(Abraham & Renner, 1986; McComas, 1992). The success of the Learning Cycle can be attributed to the fact that it capitalizes on students' natural curiosity at the start of the lesson or unit and provides them with a common, shared experience that the teacher can then use to introduce difficult or abstract science concepts. The teacher can discuss these concepts by regularly connecting them to the exploration phase. The Learning Cycle provides numerous opportunities for students to collaborate and cooperate with one another. Each individual student has a chance to use his or her unique skills and talents during the process.

Teaching science in an inquiry format demonstrates to students that science does not progress by means of a single scientific method that must be strictly followed, in spite of the misleading information of this nature commonly found in science textbooks. Science teachers have traditionally relied too heavily on verification labs consisting of "recipes" that students must follow if they are to arrive at "the right answer." Students proceed through these steps with little thought as to why those steps are important or what the results mean (Hart, Mulhall, Berry, Loughran, & Gunstone, 2000). Success in these recipe lab activities becomes more a measure of a student's ability to read and follow directions than his or her understanding of concepts (Clough & Clark, 1994).

Inquiry experiences in science classrooms must prompt students to devise innovative procedures for testing their hypotheses and to seek divergent solutions to authentic science problems. The inquiry science classroom provides science teachers with a variety of opportunities to assess all students' level of understanding and skill development, not just the select few who thrive in a rote learning environment. The *National Science Education Standards* (National Research Council, 1996) reflect the role that inquiry must play in the reform of science education. These standards call for greater emphasis on understanding and responding to individual student's interests, strengths, experiences, and focusing on student understanding and use of scientific knowledge, ideas, and inquiry processes.

The heightened emphasis on inquiry-based science has resulted in the development of a number of innovative curriculum projects geared toward improving students' conceptual understanding of science. An example taken from the *Biology: A Community Context* (Leonard & Penick, 1998) curriculum illustrates how an inquiry approach can be applied to the teaching of key biology concepts. In the unit on matter and energy for life, students begin with an initial inquiry activity on the biology of trash. Students view a brief documentary of the story of the Mobro garbage barge made famous by its 5-month trek along the coast of North America in search of a dumping site. Students are encouraged to brainstorm as many questions as possible about the Mobro voyage and the various energy relationships that might be involved in the decay of trash.

Students then participate in a series of guided inquiry activities. These activities provide opportunities for students to seek answers to their list of questions and learn about the key concepts of energy systems set in real-life contexts. One of the guided inquiry options in the Leonard and Penick (1998) curriculum includes conducting a trash audit where students monitor their garbage production at home and in school over a specified period of time. In another guided inquiry the teacher relates the concept of energy to biological systems as students create compost columns in the classroom using plastic 2-liter soda bottles. Throughout each of the guided inquiry activities, the science teacher has numerous opportunities to use a wide variety of instructional methods to teach important concepts. The flexibility of an inquiry curriculum such as this one enables a teacher to easily make lesson accommodations that support the specialized learning needs of all students in the class. These inquiry activities can involve a combination of individual and small cooperative group work depending on the goals and preferences of the teacher. This type of collaboration prompts learners to support each other. Diverse learners will also profit from the different types of lesson format—watching a film, engaging in group discussion, participating in experiential projects—involved in an inquiry unit.

As students progress through the unit, the guided inquiry activities increase in their level of scientific sophistication with regard to the concepts introduced and the methodologies employed by students. The energy cycle involved in living systems is explored in depth, but always within the context of practical applications from students' everyday life experiences. At the close of the guided inquiry section, students complete a self-check working in small groups to answer important conceptual questions related to the material in the unit.

The unit then moves to what Leonard and Penick (1998) referred to as a conference where students work together to decide what they do and don't know about the major concepts covered in the unit through the construction and presentation of a written abstract. This abstract then shapes the nature and extent of students' work during the next phase of the inquiry process where they complete extended inquiry projects.

In the extended inquiry component, students must apply their knowledge of the concepts in novel situations on topics such as composting, landfill use, sewage treatment, incineration, and recycling as they apply locally in the community. Each of these extended inquiry project options emphasizes the scientific research process and prepares students to present their research to their peers following the extended inquiry period.

Students must then also complete another self-check before the culmination of the inquiry unit that features a "congress" and a "forum" event sequence (Leonard & Penick, 1998). Here students prepare for and carry out a role-playing simulation of a town council meeting focused on debating the diverse issues surrounding the proper disposal of local wastes. The role-playing activities require students to synthesize all of the knowledge and skills they have developed during the inquiry unit in order to prepare for the formal debate exercise. In doing so, students experience firsthand the governmental and political process involved in dealing with these real-life scientific applications in their own community.

Leonard and Penick's (1998) inquiry-based biology curriculum engages all learners, regardless of their educational needs and preferred learning styles, in meaningful scientific investigations of key concepts. The science teacher is afforded tremendous flexibility in selecting both instructional methods and assessment tasks. Students take responsibility for their own learning and that of their peers in the cooperative group. They are challenged to build on their own experiences and use scientific information in solving interesting and authentic scientific problems.

Teaching through inquiry helps teachers to reinforce the idea that "taking chances and trying out new ideas is a good thing" (Pushkin, 1998, p. 195). In inquiry-based classrooms, the teacher is often surprised and dazzled by students' thoughts and actions. Just as the Auto Mechanics teacher we observed was constantly amazed by student creativity and ingenuity in the construction of the Mustang, a good science teacher will be open to new ways of approaching and solving problems. The teacher will also clearly communicate how he or she is learning from the student's approach to a problem.

Learning any type of information is enhanced when students are able to give examples of it, recognize it under various circumstances, state its converse or opposite, see connections between it and other facts or ideas and *make use of it in various ways* (emphasis added; Holt, 1967). In other words, students have to move, talk, and get "intellectually messy" in order to learn. As Pushkin (1998) stated: "No educator can teach a student how to contextualize a problem by doing the problem simply for the class to watch on a chalkboard" (p. 195). Teachers can, however, coach, guide, and encourage as students wrestle through the inquiry process, thus supporting the learner as she creates her own schema for understanding scientific phenomena.

Recommendation 2: Learn About Students and Teach to Their Experiences

One of the most serious mistakes a science teacher can make is to ignore the out-of-school science experiences that all students bring to the classroom. From the time they are born, human beings attempt to make sense of the natural world around them (Brooks & Brooks, 1993). Young children posit why a stick of wood floats when tossed in a stream while a rock of much smaller size sinks. Students struggle to create cognitive explanations for the phenomena they observe. Brooks and Brooks (1993) noted that

> Each of us makes sense of our world by synthesizing new experiences into what we have previously come to understand. Often, we encounter an object, an idea, a relationship, or a phenomenon that doesn't quite make sense to us. When confronted with such initially discrepant data or perceptions, we either interpret what we see to conform to our present set of rules for explaining and ordering the world, or we generate a new set of rules that better accounts for what we perceive to be occurring. Either way, our perceptions and rules are constantly engaged in a grand dance that shapes our understandings. (p. 4)

We suggest that teachers consider what Schubert (cited in Brown, Mir, & Warner, 1996) has called the out-of-school curriculum or outside curriculum. Schubert, a leader in curriculum studies, suggested that we need a more "ecological" view of curriculum and instruction. One "that incorporates not only the curriculum of the school, but also the curriculum of the family, the home, the peer group, the nonschool organizations, the mass media, and so on" (p. 343).

If teachers are to be effective in providing meaningful science education for all learners, then they must take into consideration the powerful role experiential learning plays in the construction of knowledge (Colburn, 1998; Driver, 1989; Lorsbach & Tobin, 1992). Too often, science teachers launch into a new unit of instruction with little or no effort to determine students' prior knowledge and experiences related to a concept. In doing so, they communicate that students' prior experiences are unimportant. In reality, however, students come to science class with ideas already formed about why certain events occur (Osborne & Wittrock, 1983; Tasker, 1981). These ideas, firmly rooted in past experiences, can be extremely resistant to change and traditional, didactic methods of science instruction have been found to be particularly ineffective in causing students to abandon their initial, naive conceptions (Posner, Strike, Hewson, & Gertzog, 1982; Yager, 1991).

Watson and Konicek (1990) offered a rich example illustrating the impact that students' prior experiences can have on their science learning in school. They give an account of an elementary teacher preparing to begin a lesson on the insulating properties of different materials with her New England fourth graders. In her initial efforts to assess students' experiences with insulators, she discovered that many of them held the naïve belief that their ability to survive the cold winter weather was determined by the warmth of the sweater they wore. In other words, the students believed that the garment itself had the ability to generate its own heat as opposed to providing insulation against the elements. Using this valuable information, the teacher went on to provide students with a number of learning experiences where students set up their own experiments to test the "warmth factor" of various coats, sweaters, and hats that they brought in to class. The students' beliefs about heat-generating sweaters were so firmly entrenched that some students even reported seeing actual temperature jumps when a thermometer was stuck in between the layers of one type of garment vs. another. Eventually, students' frustrations with their inability to consistently support their hypotheses opened the door for the teacher to introduce the concept of insulators. The students then went on to test a variety of types of insulators and eventually reached the conclusion that sweaters are a type of insulator and lack the ability to generate their own heat.

Had this teacher started her unit without any regard for the previous science experiences of her students, she could have easily created more confusion than understanding about the concepts. Too many science teachers fail to take the time to uncover students' experiences and knowledge they bring to science class. Thus, the science learning experiences and the explanations offered by the teacher, as opposed to those generated by students during and outside of class, form the basis of the facts to be memorized for the test and later purged from a student's memory (Osborne & Wittrock, 1983). Research suggests that students may develop two sets of mutually exclusive explanations about science phenomena, one set that applies to their everyday world, while the other applies only in science class for the sole purpose of doing well on teacher-administered exams and quizzes (Brooks & Brooks, 1993; Pushkin, 1998; Tasker, 1981).

Constructivist theory recognizes the role that experiential learning plays in an individual's overall cognitive growth and development. Constructivism is a theory about knowledge development that is used to explain "how we know what we know"; teachers use this theoretical framework as a referent for making instructional decisions (Lorsbach & Tobin, 1992). This theory vastly differs from the traditional objectivist beliefs that are so pervasive in American education. Objectivism is based on the assumption that knowledge exists outside our bodies, independent of thinking human beings. Science then becomes a search for objective truths and discovering laws and theories associated with reality. Science learners are taught to view nature with an objective point of view, avoiding the potential influences of imagination, values, beliefs, and intuition.

Constructivism, on the other hand, asserts that the knower must rely on his or her senses and experiences to interpret the world around them. This theory holds that knowledge cannot be transferred intact from the brain of the teacher to the minds of students ignoring the role of experiences (Lorsbach & Tobin, 1992). Constructivists also understand the substantial role that other individuals play in a student's learning process. Thus, when using constructivism as a referent for teaching science, cooperative learning becomes a key instructional method allowing students the chance to check their understanding of the world with others and share ideas. Thus, when using a constructivist perspective, "Teaching science becomes more like the science that scientists do. It is an active, social process of making sense of experiences, as opposed to what we now call 'school science' " (Lorsbach & Tobin, 1992, p. 2).

Schubert (cited in Brown et al., 1996) proposed that teachers become familiar with the diversities that students bring to class. Through examining student differences, teachers may be able to locate spaces to teach from—specifically, educators may begin to understand what kinds of assumptions students hold and what kind of knowledge they already possess. Schubert suggests that educators "think about the influence of different levels of socioeconomic class, race, gender, and ableness on access to knowledge in the world" (p. 347). He posits that most teachers "interpret educational needs and problems and needs through middle-class lenses and without much empathy for people 'on the boundaries' " (p. 347). Therefore, it is imperative that educators acquaint themselves with all of the differences students bring to the classroom, while being conscious of their own biases, perspectives, and approach to learning.

Recommendation 3: Make It Meaningful

One of the biggest criticisms of secondary science courses cited by students is the lack of relevance the curriculum has to their everyday lives (Mullis & Jenkins, 1988). This statement is astonishing when one considers how inextricable science is from everyday experiences. Perhaps this perceived lack of relevance is the reason students claim science class is boring or too difficult. The answer becomes clearer when you consider the evolutionary aspects of science curricula from the elementary grades up through the secondary level. Because the majority of elementary teachers lack an extensive science background, science is taught far less often than other subjects like reading and mathematics unless high stakes science exams and state curriculum mandates dictate otherwise. When science is taught, the curriculum at the early grade levels—when students' curiosity and interest are at peak levels—tends to place greater emphasis on fun activities as opposed to dealing with significant amounts of content information.

Students take their growing interest in science with them to the middle grades where they begin to experience the science disciplines broken out into life and physical science courses. Here an increased curricular emphasis is placed on content learning and the lab activities are more structured than in the lower elementary grades. The teacher plays the major role in the design of the course and the selection of topics to be addressed is typically dictated by the textbook used. By the end of the middle grades, much of the curiosity about the natural world that students entered with has been replaced by the false notion that science is merely a large body of information to be memorized. Lab experiments are thought of as a series of rigid procedures that must be followed rather than opportunities to creatively solve problems (see Berry, Mulhall, Loughran, & Gunstone, 1999; Edmondson & Novak, 1993; Hart et al., 2000).

When these same students enter high-school science, they begin to characterize science as being a difficult, abstract subject that lacks any meaningful application to their everyday lives. Content acquisition, devoid of any relevance to students, becomes the sole focus of the learning experiences. This results in widespread student disdain for science courses, which leads them to choose instead, subjects they perceive to be more practical and interesting. More disturbing is the fact that students who are unable to adapt their learning style to be successful in this content-driven environment are tracked out of science, with little or no consideration of the vast array of talents they may posses that make them ideal candidates for success in an authentic science context (Hazen, 1991; Leyden, 1984; Pike, 1992).

If we are to achieve true scientific literacy for all learners, science teachers must strive to develop curriculum materials where important content is embedded within a relevant context. By replacing verification lab activities with real-world science problems, for example, students begin to make connections between the science concepts they study and their applications to everyday life. The guided and extended inquiry experiences described earlier in reference to the *Biology: A Community Context* curriculum (Leonard & Penick, 1998) vividly illustrate this type of curricular focus.

There are a number of ways to rethink science curriculum development in order to satisfy the need for relevance. The Science-Technology-Society (STS) movement has strongly advocated the value of using student-generated topics as a basis for curriculum development. In STS classrooms, the science problems and issues selected for investigation have local significance within the community and the learning experiences tied to the investigation endeavor to tease out the scientific, technological, and societal connections involved (National Science Teachers Association, [1992–1993]; Yager & Roy, 1993). For example, students living in an urban area might be interested in learning about the relationship between pollution and asthma while students in California may want to investigate the history of earthquakes in their county or city. Students in one high school we visited worked with the local homeless population to design low-cost tents that were portable and warm enough to use during the winter months in the midwestern United States.

In classes where relevant science curriculum materials are employed, students with diverse learning profiles can find multiple opportunities to contribute to the overall science learning experience as the problems chosen for study typically require the use of a broad spectrum of thinking, reasoning, and problem-solving skills. Our earlier auto mechanics example provides an excellent illustration of how engaging a relevant science curriculum can be for all students. Using the restoration of the 1963 Mustang as a context, a science teacher could easily challenge students to articulate and demonstrate their understanding of important concepts by relating them to the functioning of various systems within the car. For example, some engine bolts must be precisely tightened. The physics teacher can introduce the concept of torque and show students how the torque wrench works and how it can be used to produce the recommended tightness on various bolts. After the car is restored and running, the teacher could address the horsepower of the engine and work with students experimenting to determine the energy efficiency and acceleration of the car. In these scenarios, students would be required to apply their physics knowledge and problem-solving skills in a meaningful and interesting learning scenario.

A savvy science teacher might even approach teachers in Auto Mechanics, Architecture, Industrial Arts, or Computer Science to collaborate on curriculum related to authentic problems, situations, and needs. Educators might co-teach classes and co-design curriculum. One of us worked with two teachers who did construct such a plan—a Computer-Aided Design teacher collaborated with a Biology teacher to educate students about the construction of the Brooklyn Bridge. All students in both courses learned about design and construction of the suspension bridge (including information on calculating maximum wind speed and learning about dead loads vs. live loads). They also received instruction on caisson disease (now known as the "bends") as several of the builders of the bridge and its designer became ill and died as a result of working underwater on the bridge and repeatedly coming up from the excavation chambers. Students—in mixed groups from both classes—then worked together on inquiry projects related to the bridge and specifically studied the dangers and risks of being a pioneer in any scientific enterprise.

Recommendation 4: Assess What You Teach

We live in an era where many believe the solution to improving our educational system is higher standards and high-stakes achievement tests. The assumption is that American schools are performing poorly because we haven't made schools challenging enough or had high enough expectations for students. Although it would be difficult to argue against higher student achievement, the negative fallout associated with the standards and testing movement should not be overlooked.

With high standards come high-stakes assessment exams for science students. These exams are intended to provide an accurate assessment of student achievement in science, yet many educators argue they simply test a student's literacy skills and their ability to recall the factual information presented in the course. That is, exam scores are only a superficial marker of a student's ability in science (Leyden, 1984; National Research Council, 1996). As Fort (1990) pointed out these assessments often communicate little about a student's science-related abilities.

> Because science involves such a variety of skills, not all of them encompassed by academic disciplines or amenable to measurement on traditional instruments, the definition of gifted in relation to science is as slippery and as broad as science itself. Certainly scores on tests of I.Q. are unacceptable as a guide. (p. 668)

A reliance on standardized tests or the use of only a few different types of assessment is keeping many students from accessing academic content and skills as many educational decisions are made by evaluating student test scores. We argue that science teachers must adopt a more encompassing view of classroom assessment, one that that considers all forms of achievement and performance.

Historically, schools have been guilty of promoting the view that assessment is an event that occurs at the conclusion of a unit of instruction. We argue, instead, that assessment measures must permeate all phases of science instruction. Science teachers must assess students' prior knowledge and experiences related to the content if they are to carefully plan a coherent set of learning exercises (Veronesi, 2000). Without this assessment information, teachers proceed haphazardly through the unit and risk spending too much or too little time on certain topics further compounding the problems associated with content coverage and instructional time. Preassessment measures provide science teachers with vital information about student strengths and weaknesses to assist the teaching in charting the most effective set of pedagogical practices and curriculum materials to employ.

The assessment of students in science must also be firmly embedded within the learning process. Overreliance on summative assessments administered at the close of a unit does little to help the teacher modify his or her instructional approach until it's already too late to benefit struggling students. Both formative and summative assessment techniques used in science must move beyond testing for knowledge recall. Using more authentic, performance-based assessments (e.g., having students perform an experiment, asking learners to submit a portfolio of their best class work) offers students with diverse skills and abilities a chance to show academic and intellectual growth in science (National Research Council, 1996). We argue that assessment episodes should themselves be an opportunity for science students to gauge areas of personal strengths and weaknesses, as well as a chance to reflect on their own unique learning profiles. For instance, a student who is assessed on his participation in building a simple machine in a cooperative group is likely to have many opportunities to demonstrate knowledge and get useful feedback. Conversely, the student who takes a series of tests and quizzes on the same topic is unlikely to experience the assessment procedure itself as educational or meaningful.

Recommendation 5: Teach Science as Preparation for Life, Not College

Ask most high-school science teachers what purpose their course serves and you will likely get a response that addresses the perceived need to prepare students for the next level of science (Hazen, 1991; Leyden, 1984). In some cases the next level refers to a subsequent high-school science course to be taken the next school year. In other instances, the teacher is referring to the preparation of students for college-level science courses. This overwhelming desire to prepare students to move on in science is not without some merit. But, we argue that an overemphasis on college preparation can easily cause a secondary science teacher to experience academic tunnel vision.

In their quest to train students for the next level, content learning often becomes of paramount importance. What is lost in this pursuit is meaningful, practical science learning that empowers all students to be better problem solvers, develop better reasoning skills, and make more informed decisions in their lives about scientific issues (Yager, 1991). In our discussions with college science faculty from around the country, they routinely tell us that what they most desire in freshman science learners is the ability to think and to solve problems, noting that they reteach much of the high-school science content over again.

High-school science teachers often feel compelled to cover as much science content material in their course as possible in order for students to be ready for college, especially when state syllabi and exams governing these courses overemphasize exhaustive coverage (Hazen, 1991). The thought is that in order to be successful in college, science students need rigorous and in-depth science courses at the secondary level. Using high-school drop-out rates, college attendance and graduation figures, and justice department data, Leyden (1984) offered a sobering perspective on the perceived need to teach science as preparation for college. He notes that, "One thing is certain—8 years after you teach those [high school] freshman, there is a good chance that more of them will have been in jail or state prison than the 1.2 percent who will have a degree in science" (p. 28).

This rapid coverage of information opens up a Pandora's box of associated problems. In trying to cover as much material as possible in the school year, teachers often rely on very traditional teaching practices. What's absent is time for project-oriented learning activities, in-depth classroom discussions, long-term conceptual understanding, and the opportunity for teachers to engage in reflection about their pedagogy. Although some science learners have the ability to adapt their learning styles to accommodate a narrow pedagogical approach, others struggle to conceptualize the often abstract and cursory presentation of scientific information. Thus, many of the students who are tracked as future scientists are really those who have persisted in the field, not so much because of the science education they received, but rather in spite of it. Hazen (1991) wrote, "Year by year, class by class across America, the number of students who persevere in science education shrinks" (p. 7).

The Third International Mathematics and Science Study (TIMMS) (Martin et al., 1999) provides ample evidence of how our tendency to focus on content coverage can negatively impact student performance in science. This international comparison of science and mathematics achievement in schools examined a broad spectrum of variables in an attempt to understand key differences in educational practices across nations. The outcomes of this vast study showed that elementary and middle-school students in the United States performed well in relation to their international counterparts in science, yet the ranking of our secondary science students was dismal. The TIMSS report suggests that one possible reason for the sharp decline in U.S. science achievement at the secondary level could be the differing emphasis on content breadth. While American high schools tend to promote exhaustive coverage of a wide array of science concepts, high-achieving countries have schools where teachers cover fewer science topics in a school year, but study each one in greater depth than their American counterparts (Martin et al., 1999).

During our visits to classrooms we routinely hear science teachers make statements like, "We can't spend any more time on this topic. We need to move on or we are not going to cover all the material that will be on the standardized exam." The implied message here is that by "covering" all of the content outlined in the state syllabus students will automatically be prepared for the high-stakes exam at the end of the year.

Content coverage also becomes a matter of efficiency in teaching. Clearly the most expedient way to expose students to all of the content in the state syllabus is through lecturing and drill and practice worksheets. In their rush to cover all the content, teachers tend to rely heavily on the textbook as the sole source of curriculum (Lorsbach & Tobin, 1992). In fact, Yager and Penick (1983) argued that 90% of all science teachers use the textbook 95% of the time as their primary source of curriculum.

Getting to the end of the textbook or assigning all of the worksheets may relieve the stress of a busy teacher, but it does little for the students in the classroom who are struggling with concepts presented in Chapter One. Only a select few students have learning styles or preferences that enable them to be successful in this type of educational environment. Rote learners tend to excel in science classrooms, while active learners seldom have opportunities to learn content in a fashion that capitalizes on their true academic potential. Even rote learners, however, are shortchanged by the science teacher focused on covering content, because those who are able to absorb some of the material for the purposes of testing, are likely to have only a superficial understanding of concepts studied. They may be successful in the science classroom, but know little about science. As one student in the Auto Mechanics class joked: "If your car breaks down on a dark road, who do you want there to fix it? Me or a kid in [the science class]?"

CONCLUSIONS

Science teachers may face questions and concerns from a variety of educational stakeholders when expanding their curriculum and instructional strategies to meet the needs of all students. First, science teachers must be prepared to deal with students who express frustration when challenged to think critically and use reasoning skills in class. Many students are firmly entrenched in a passive learning model where the teacher is responsible for deciding what is taught, what is tested, and what students focus on in science class (Herreid, 1998). Switching to an inquiry-based approach where students are required to actively learn concepts requires time and patience on the part of the science teacher as learners struggle to make sense of a classroom environment where they assume more responsibility for their own learning (Brooks & Brooks, 1993).

Science teachers must also prepare themselves for questions from families when they implement these recommended changes. Students' families often use their own school experiences as a basis for making judgments about what ought to be going on in schools. Thus, the traditional teacher-led science classroom is one that is both familiar and comfortable to parents. Some may, at first, express grave concerns about their son or daughter's readiness for college in a science classroom where exhaustive content coverage is not the norm. Some families may need to be informed and educated about teaching methods that are unfamiliar.

These challenges, however, will be tempered by the feedback from other families who will express their gratitude for offering their son or daughter a chance to be successful as a science learner for the first time. Many families will be grateful when they see an educator giving their child a chance to display his or her unique strengths in science, instead of continuing to make that child feel inadequate because he or she has a learning style that favors teaching methods other than the lecture format.

A science teacher attempting to make his or her classroom more student centered and inquiry based may also receive warnings from peer teachers who will attempt to discourage anything but the status quo. Peer teachers will cite the need to cover the content in order to prepare students for the standardized exam and warn of the danger of spending too much time on project-based learning where depth of understanding is the goal. What many of these teachers are really implying is that the test scores are ultimately more important than the means by which a teacher helps students achieve them. Given the arbitrary ways in which these test results are used to rate teacher performance it is no wonder that any educator fears experimenting with anything other than standard routines in their teaching.

Finally, science teachers must be prepared to deal with the "organized chaos" that will no doubt appear when they move toward using an inquiry approach where not all students are working on the same task simultaneously. Teachers must be ready to handle the problems that may initially surface when students are given the freedom to learn in multiple modes. These might include students having difficulty working collaboratively in group activities, using problem-solving strategies when all of the procedures for a lab investigation aren't spoon fed to them, or grappling with the task of using a variety of resources other than a single textbook as the source of scientific information.

When a science teacher turns his or her classroom into a place where all students can learn science through active and engaging inquiry experiences, he or she must be prepared to be pleasantly surprised and to acknowledge that students who were previously thought to be low achievers in science may in fact be excellent problem solvers and critical thinkers. Students thought to be incapable or uninterested in science curricula may emerge as scientists—inventors, investigators, and innovators. Further, teachers may find that those learners thought to be strong in science are more skilled with paper and pencil tasks than with real-world problems and exploration. Both groups of students will benefit when teachers see them focusing on "real science" and learning in a wider range of situations.

When teachers design lessons using inquiry, attend to student experiences, make teaching and learning meaningful, connect assessment to classroom learning, and teach science as preparation for life, a wider range of students can demonstrate complexity and be successful. When this framework is implemented, we will have auto mechanics in the physics lab (or physics curriculum in the auto shop) and teachers will move closer toward achieving the goal of science education for all learners.

For Discussion and Reflection

1. How can the use of the Inquiry Process enhance learning for all students?

2. How can teachers learn enough about students to bring relevant experiences into the science classroom?

3. What assumptions do teachers and administrators make about teaching and learning when they make tracking decisions?

In the Field

1. What kind of language is used to describe students in different academic tracks in schools today? How do students respond to tracking? Explore these questions in your school by examining school documents (e.g., course catalogs, policy statements) and listening to conversations in the hallways, in the staff lounge, and at school board meetings.

2. Compare the curriculum across academic tracks in your school's science program (e.g., vocational, advanced placement). Does curriculum and instruction differ across these tracks? Consider materials, activities, assessments, class size, complexity of lessons.

3. Interview a student in an honors or advanced placement science class. Ask the student about himself or herself as a science learner. Ask this student about science placement in the school. How does this student understand his or her placement in this course? What assumptions does she or he hold about science learning?

4. Interview a student in a "non-college oriented" science class? Ask this student about himself or herself as a learner. Ask this student about science placement in the school. How does this student understand his or her placement in this course? What assumptions does he or she hold about science learning?

REFERENCES

Abraham, M. R., & Renner, J. W. (1986). The sequence of learning cycle activities in high school chemistry. *Journal of Research in Science Teaching, 23*(2), 121–143.

American Association for the Advancement of Science. (1993). *Benchmarks for scientific literacy.* New York: Oxford University Press.

Atkin, J. M., & Karplus, R. (1962). Discovery or invention? *The Science Teacher, 29*(5), 45–51.

Barba, R. H. (1998). *Science in the multicultural classroom.* Boston: Allyn & Bacon.

Barman, C. (1997). *The learning cycle revisited: A modification of an effective teaching model. Monograph 6.* Washington, DC: Council for Elementary Science International.

Berry, A., Mulhall, P., Loughran, J. J., & Gunstone, R. F. (1999). Helping students learn from laboratory work. *Australian Science Teachers' Journal, 45*(1), 27–31.

Blank, L. M. (2000). A metacognitive learning cycle: A better warranty for student understanding? *Science Education, 84*, 486–506.

Brooks, J., & Brooks, M. (1993). *In search of understanding: The case for constructivist classrooms.* Arlington, VA: Association for Supervision and Curriculum Development.

Brown, S. C., Mir, C. J., & Warner, M. J. (1996). Improving teacher practice utilizing curriculum theory: A conversation with William H. Schubert. *The Educational Forum, 60*, 343–348.

Chiappetta, E. L., Koballa, T. R., & Collette, A. T. (1998). *Science instruction in the middle and secondary school (4th ed.).* Columbus, OH: Merrill.

Clark, J. V. (1999). Minorities in science and mathematics: A challenge for change. *ERIC review K–8 science and mathematics education 2*(6), 40–42. Washington, DC: U.S. Department of Education, Education Resources Information Center.

Clough, M. P., & Clark, R. (1994). Cookbooks and constructivism. *The Science Teacher, 61*(2), 34–37.

Colburn, A. (1998). *Constructivism and science teaching.* Bloomington, IN: Phi Delta Kappa Educational Foundation.

Driver, R. (1989). Changing conceptions. In P. Adey, J. Bliss, J. Head, & M. Shayer (Eds.), *Adolescent development and school science* (pp. 79–104). London: The Falmer Press.

Edmondson, K. M., & Novak, J. D. (1993). The interplay of scientific epistemological views, learning strategies, and attitudes of college students. *Journal of Research in Science Teaching, 30*(6), 547–559.

Fort, D. (1990). From gifts to talents in science. *Phi Delta Kappan, 71*, 664–671.

Gardner, H. (1993). *Creating minds.* New York: Basic Books.

Good, R. G. (1989, April). *Toward a unified conception of thinking: Prediction within a cognitive science perspective.* Paper presented at the annual meeting of the National Association for Research in Science Teaching, San Francisco, CA.

Hart, C., Mulhall, P., Berry, A., Loughran, J., & Gunstone, R. (2000). What is the purpose of this experiment? Or can students learn something from doing experiments? *Journal of Research in Science Teaching, 37*, 655–675.

Hazen, R. M. (1991). Why my kids hate science. *Newsweek*, February 25, p. 7.

Herreid, C. F. (1998). Why isn't cooperative learning used to teach science? *BioScience, 48*, 553–559.

Holt, J. (1967). *How children learn.* New York: Pitman.

John Glenn Commission. (2000). *Before it's too late: A report to the nation from the National Commission on Mathematics and Science Teaching for the 21st Century.* Washington, DC.

Lavoie, D. (1992). *The effects of adding a prediction/discussion phase to a science learning cycle.* Paper presented at the annual meeting of the National Association for Research in Science Teaching, Boston, MA.

Lawson, A. (1995). *Science teaching and the development of thinking.* Belmont, CA: Wadsworth.

Lawson, A. E., Abraham, M. R., & Renner, J. W. (1989). *A theory of instruction: Using the Learning Cycle to teach science concepts and thinking skills (Monograph Number 1).* Kansas State University, Manhattan, KS. National Association for Research in Science Teaching.

Leonard, W. H., & Penick, J. E. (1998). *Biology: A community context.* Cincinnati, OH: South-Western Publishing.

Leyden, M. B. (1984). You graduate more criminals than you do scientists. *The Science Teacher, 51*(3), 26–30.

Lorsbach, A., & Tobin, K. (1992). Constructivism as a referent for science teaching. *Research Matters . . . to the Science Teacher.* National Association for Research in Science Teaching.

Marlin, T. (2000). Albert Einstein and LD: An evaluation of the evidence. *Journal of Learning Disabilities, 33*(2), 149–157.

Martin, M., Mullis, I., Gonzalez, E., Gregory, K., Smith, T., Chrostowski, S., Garden, K., & O'Connor, K. (1999). *The Third International Mathematics and Science Study (TIMSS) 1999 International Science Report.* Boston, MA: Boston College.

McComas III, W. F. (1992). *The nature of exemplary practice in secondary school science laboratory instruction: A case study approach* (Doctoral Dissertation, University of Iowa, 1991). Dissertation Abstracts International.

Monhardt, R. (2000). The evolving game of secondary science education: Every student a winner. *The Clearing House, 74*(1), 9–54.

Mullis, I., & Jenkins, L. (Eds.). (1988). *The science report card: Elements of risk and recovery.* Princeton, NJ: NAEP Educational Testing Service.

National Research Council. (1996). *National Science Education Standards.* Washington, DC: National Academy Press.

National Science Teachers Association. (1992–1993). *In National Science Teachers Association Handbook,* 1992–1993 (pp. 168–169). Washington, DC: Author.

Oakes, J., & Lipton, M. (1998). *Teaching to change the world.* New York: McGraw Hill.

Osborne, R. J., & Wittrock, M. C. (1983). Learning science: A generative process. *Science Education, 67*(4), 489–508.

Pike, B. (1992). Why I teach my children at home. *Phi Delta Kappa, 73*(1), 564–565.

Posner, G., Strike, K., Hewson, P., & Gertzog, W. (1982). Accommodation of a scientific conception: Toward a theory of conceptual change. *Science Education, 66,* 680–685.

Pushkin, D. B. (1998). Teacher says, Simon says: Dualism in science teaching. In J. L. Kincheloe & S. R. Steinberg (Eds.), *Unauthorized methods: Strategies for critical teaching* (pp. 185–198). New York: Routledge.

Tasker, C. R. (1981). Children's view and classroom experiences. *Australian Science Teachers' Journal, 27*(3), 51–57.

Veronesi, P. D. (2000). Testing and assessment in science education: Looking past the scoreboard. *The Clearing House, 74*(1), 27–30.

Watson, B., & Konicek, R. (1990). Teaching for conceptual change: Confronting children's experience. *Phi Delta Kappa, 71*(9), 680–685.

Yager, R. E. (1991). The constructivist learning model. *The Science Teacher, 58*(6), 52–57.

Yager, R. E., & Penick, J. E. (1983). School science in crisis. *Curriculum Review, 22*(3), 67–70.

Yager, R. E., & Roy, R. (1993). STS: Most pervasive and most radical of reform approaches to "science" education. In R. E. Yager (Ed.), *The science technology society movement* (pp. 7–13). Washington, DC: National Science Teachers Association.

Chapter 8

Providing Access to Arts Education: An Illustration Through Music

Katia Madsen
Syracuse University

Providing an arts education for *all* learners is a value that appears to be axiomatic among arts educators across the nation. The Consortium of National Arts Education Associations stated, "All students deserve access to the rich education and understanding that the arts provide, regardless of their background, talents, or disabilities" (National Standards for Arts Education, 1994, p. 7). The arts—dance, music, theatre, and the visual arts—often contribute to a valuable part of a student's education for those who have access to them. Each of the arts provides unique experiences exclusive to its own subject matter, and it is through participation in the arts that some students find the most reward, significance, and joy in their daily lives.

Unfortunately, the barriers that may keep a student from accessing an arts education can be numerous. Cultural, financial, and learning differences, to name a few, can function as barriers when appropriate practices for access are not used or understood. The purpose of this chapter is to provide ideas for accessing an arts education using music education as an example. Although this chapter focuses on music education, the reader is encouraged to make transfers of the material to the other arts and disciplines outside the arts when possible.

The Housewright Declaration, a product of a nationwide collaborative effort to express a vision for the future of music education, states in its first of twelve agreements that "All persons, regardless of age, cultural heritage, ability, venue, or financial circumstance deserve to participate fully in the best music experiences possible" (Madsen, 2000, p. 219). The diversity among humans in our society challenges educators with the responsibility to recognize differences in the ways that students process knowledge, approach learning tasks, perceive stimuli—experience life.

That music is ubiquitously intrinsic of every human culture may suggest that humans value music as a unique and necessary part of the human condition. Music is an art form that serves to enrich the human experience in unique ways and it is also an academic subject full of rich concepts to be learned—and to be learned by all. Music is a necessary part of every student's education and the music classroom is a place where all learners, regardless of diversities, can acquire both musical and nonmusical values to enrich their existence as human beings.

THE MUSICAL AND NONMUSICAL VALUES OF MUSIC

The idea that experiencing a music education can instill the learning of both musical and nonmusical values is one that is often expressed by music educators. *Musical values are products that are exclusive to music—ones that can only be gained through actively experiencing music itself.* For example, if a student who learns to create musical compositions by organizing sounds in knowledgeable and meaningful ways *and* as a product of these experiences gains a greater appreciation for the compositional elements of music, then he or she has achieved a musical value in his or her life. For even though the act of creativity alone is not exclusive to music, the act of creating *music* is—serving to instill within the student a value for qualities intrinsic of the music itself.

Nonmusical values in music education are desired values that are products of actively experiencing music, but are not necessarily exclusive to music. For instance, if the same student mentioned in our first example acquires a stronger sense for independent learning and a higher sense of self-esteem as a result of composing music, then he or she has achieved nonmusical values (i.e., self-independence; self-esteem) in addition to the primary musical value (i.e., appreciation and value for compositional elements inherent within music through the process of creating music). As an extension of this example, *if* creating music fosters motivation for the same student to create something other than music (e.g., a science project), then creativity and/or the desire to create outside of music is considered to be a nonmusical value achieved as a positive outcome of actively experiencing music.

The musical and nonmusical values to be achieved in the music classroom are limitless. According to both Reimer (2000) and Hoffer (1993) it is important that music educators advocate the study of music primarily for its own sake, rather than advocating music for its accessibility to instill nonmusical values such as commitment, discipline, team work, respect for others, and respect for self—these are values that can be achieved in areas other than music. However, as music teachers who are invested in the comprehensive welfare of all students, the nonmusical benefits that are achieved as a result of music participation must be valued as well. This is especially important to consider when teaching in inclusive settings.

With further regard to nonmusical values, inclusive music education sometimes requires that the teacher actually "use" music as a means to achieve nonmusical goals; this concept differs from the idea of achieving nonmusical values as natural consequences of music participation. Alley (1979), a music therapist who has had experience in educational settings, encourages the fusion of nonmusical and musical objectives to teach diverse students who are in need of developing behaviors that are nonmusical, yet are essential to the quality of their lives. Alley cited extended research studies to suggest that music used therapeutically in education settings may:

1. enhance academic skills in reading and mathematics;
2. decrease severely inappropriate social behaviors;
3. increase on-task social and academic behaviors;
4. increase "physical responses such as self-help skills, imitative behavior, [and] activity level" (p. 118);
5. enhance language skills;
6. enhance social skills; and
7. improve perceptual-motor skills.

Some music researchers and educators also support the idea that achieving nonmusical values through music participation can in turn enable learning, including *music learning*, in diverse students. In his introductory article included within a special focus edition of the *Music Educators Journal* regarding music and students considered at risk, Shuler (1991) summarized the contributions of the other authors who offered articles within this special edition in terms of how music enables and motivates students to learn.

In Shuler's summary of these articles, it was suggested that music has the ability to *enable student learning* because it provides enriching environments where diverse learners can function with success as they utilize multisensory modes of learning (i.e., aural, kinetic, and visual/sensory), develop their musical intelligence, collaborate with other students toward shared musical goals, achieve self-discipline and attending skills, and foster self-esteem through successful performance. Shuler (1991) also offered in summary that music has the ability to *motivate student learning* because it provides opportunities for "intriguing and invigorating" experiences that draw students to school. This includes solving "inherently interesting problems" via projects or tasks, creating or performing musical compositions, experiencing intrinsically rewarding subject matter, expressing one's self, enhancing communication and insuring comfort (p. 24).

Although these offered views of how music education can enhance learning and motivation in students were products of assessing strategies specifically geared for students considered at risk, Shuler (1991) summarized these ideas within a context that includes—and is applicable to—all learners. Ultimately, music teachers of diverse learners should incorporate the teaching of both musical and nonmusical values in their classrooms to facilitate a more appropriate and comprehensive scope toward the access of learning for every student.

VARIETIES OF MUSIC EDUCATION SETTINGS

The classroom music teachers that facilitate the learning of music and its subject matter do so within a variety of music settings. In many elementary schools, general music classes are required of all grade levels with beginning elementary bands, choirs, and orchestras existing at some schools. In some middle and junior high schools, general music is required for at least one grade level and elective music courses such as band, chorus, or orchestra are traditionally offered to those interested as part of the music curriculum. At the high-school level, schools usually offer a general music class as an option for students who must select a course to fulfill a fine arts credit requirement, and band, choir, or orchestra are traditionally offered for those students interested in pursuing music ensemble experience. Music curricula in high schools may also include small ensemble experiences such as, but not limited to, show choir or jazz band, and courses such as keyboard, guitar, music theory, and music composition.

MAKING MUSIC EDUCATION ACCESSIBLE TO ALL LEARNERS

When music programs such as general music, band, orchestra, and chorus, are offered in the schools, teachers and administrators must evaluate: whether all students have access to existing music programs; and whether all students participating in music programs are accessing the music content being taught in the classroom. If an educator embraces music as a subject worthy of study in the schools and concurrently chooses to value an "access-to-academics" philosophy, he or she must be sensitive to possible existing barriers regarding scheduling of curriculum, financial, cultural, and diversity issues.

One barrier that affects a student's access to music education, particularly at the high-school level, involves the scheduling of curriculum. For the past two decades, a student's choice for pursuing elective coursework has become increasingly limited due to an increase of required courses in secondary schools' curriculums as mandated by the state, and as necessary for college-bound candidates. However, if a student wants to participate in music or one of the other arts such as dance, theatre, or the visual arts, he or she should have access. Developing workable solutions regarding curriculum and sensitive scheduling demands that would help students gain access to music and arts education as part of their curriculum is the responsibility of the school, and a commitment to education that should be encouraged.

Financial obstacles occur when students are unable to participate in music ensembles, or are unable to participate at full capacity, due to their lack of ability to incur costs required of the music programs. Examples of these obstacles may include music ensemble requirements for all students to purchase or rent such items as a band or choral uniform, or a musical instrument. Consider an extension of this example—think about the student who may have enough money to purchase or rent a musical instrument, but who may lack the means or support to pay for private lessons outside of school. Ultimately, the student may feel discouraged because his or her musicianship may not progress at the same rate as another student who can afford to pay for private instruction. The acquisition of resources to help students in need of financial assistance to access music ensemble experience may include funding from the school district, fundraising efforts, building partnerships with community businesses, and grant writing.

Even if financial assistance is provided to music students with needs for these services, music teachers must also be sensitive to issues that arise as a result of financial barriers that extend beyond the classroom setting. For instance, participation in music ensembles usually requires students to participate in rehearsals and concerts conducted on- and off-campus that extend beyond traditional school hours. Consequently, students who have no access to transportation other than taking the school bus to and from school may need a teacher's support in arranging transportation services to insure their full participation in music activities that take place outside of the regular school day.

In addition to scheduling and financial concerns, existing barriers regarding cultural diversity are sometimes imposed—perhaps unknowingly. For instance, if a choral music educator teaches at a school with students representing rich cultural diversity, yet his or her choir population does not adequately reflect this diversity, this alone can create a barrier for students of diverse cultural heritages from selecting to participate in the choir. In this case, it is the responsibility of the music teacher to recruit appropriately to insure that all students feel welcome and encouraged to participate.

Another barrier that may surface as a result of cultural diversity is a language or communication barrier. Consider the student who is learning English as a second language and chooses to participate in the choral program, yet is unable to access the written musical literature that is presented in English text (i.e., words of the song). The chorus teacher, rather than referring to the problem as a language barrier that cannot be overcome until the student learns to read and understand English adequately, should create adaptive strategies for helping the student access the choral repertoire. This may be done via temporary iconic representations of the text to use in class and translation study guides of the text to use outside of music class with the help of the student's regular English teacher. The music teacher might also select a piece of choral repertoire that uses a text in the student's native language and allow the student to teach the authentic pronunciations of the poetic verse to the class. By doing this, the teacher creates a forum that may contribute to the student's value of self, while contributing to the other students' learning as they experience an authentically produced representation of the text.

Diverse learners, especially students with disabilities, will need adaptations with regard to music materials, activities, and instruction to successfully access musical concepts. For example, an elementary general music teacher may teach the concept of binary form, where music is composed of two distinctly contrasting sections, represented as A and B. This activity can be structured in a variety of ways to include the use of singing, guided listening, playing of melodic and percussive classroom instruments (e.g., xylophones, rhythm sticks, hand drums), moving to, improvising, and creating music to allow for diversity in performance approaches that may facilitate access for diverse learners to learn the musical concept.

More specifically, a child with a learning disability may be most successful learning the concept of binary form through movement activities and demonstrating accurate musical responses kinesthetically to indicate the B section of the music. A peer with a significant physical disability who is learning the same musical concept in the same class may also respond to the B section kinesthetically, however, the instruction may need to be adapted to allow for different types and ranges of movement accessible to the student.

That music is extremely accessible, can be taught and learned in diverse ways, can be responded to intellectually and emotionally, and can bring meaning to students' lives, is the beauty of music as an art and an academic subject. It is the responsibility of the schools' teachers and administrators to provide supportive and adaptive environments for students with diverse needs to insure the success of all students experiencing music education and to insure that all students who desire a music education receive one.

APPROPRIATE AND CHALLENGING EXPECTATIONS FOR LEARNERS

For all the many values educators are responsible for instilling in their students, the value of providing appropriate and challenging expectations for learners must be included within each teacher's inherent value system. Educators, regardless of their specialized fields of study, should be actively engaging in the continuous process of developing appropriate expectations for all learners. The music classroom provides an arena where diverse learners can thrive, but if not challenged appropriately by their teachers, the potential for learning suffers (Darrow, 1990; Thompson, 1990).

Providing appropriate and challenging expectations for all learners is probably one of the most difficult things to embrace as a music teacher, especially for a teacher who has had limited training in how to teach music within inclusive settings that are extremely diverse. Unfortunately, too many music teachers operate with inadequate perceptions and expectations of what their students are able to learn in their classrooms, especially with regard to students who defy what has been traditionally accepted as standard performance. For instance, some music teachers think that if a learner with significant disabilities is at least participating in music, then the student is being included, and this is not necessarily—and not usually—the case. Even students with significant multiple disabilities are capable of learning and responding to music in a variety of ways, even if perhaps the ways in which they learn and respond to music *seem* extremely limited. A music teacher must not be content to merely allow the student with significant disabilities to play adaptive instruments with no instruction or expectation for rhythmic learning, nor should the teacher be afraid to encourage singing in the student for fear of it being too loud or out of tune. Only when a teacher encourages musical responses from students, will he or she know where to begin the teaching process to adapt specifically to a particular student's musical, social, and aesthetic needs. A music teacher must believe that even learners with the most significant disabilities deserve more than mere opportunities to participate with music—they deserve opportunities to *learn* about music through participation—and at a level that is appropriate and challenging.

Students who have been recognized as musically gifted, also need to be provided with musical opportunities that will maximize their musical potential. Mark (1996) offered the familiar philosophy of gifted students feeling frustrated or becoming bored when not appropriately challenged. Select "giftedness" for music may emerge in students with a range of needs and abilities including those who are seen as "struggling learners" in other academic areas. By providing rich instruction and allowing students to be expressive in multiple ways, skilled music teachers often create a context where students will evidence gifted qualities specific to music.

What surprises some educators is that the gifted musical learner may be the student who cannot read or the young man with behavior problems or the child who is viewed by others as unmotivated. However, unless teachers hold high expectations for all learners, the likeliness that one of the aforementioned students would thrive musically is not likely. One can only imagine how many learners' potentials for highly sophisticated musical experiences are denied when music teachers do not assume appropriate expectations, or provide appropriately diverse teaching strategies and activities that encourage musical growth in every student.

Schock (1990) offered a success story regarding her experiences as a teacher working with a fifth grader with cerebral palsy and other disabilities:

> This boy is exuberant and has a tendency to be very loud. I have worked with him on the concepts of loud and soft and "stopping with the group." He has toned down his speaking voice, and he recently sang "America the Beautiful" with the class—on pitch, at the correct dynamic level, and using the correct rhythm. (p. 51)

This is an example of how diverse learners can succeed in achieving both musical and nonmusical objectives through responsive and respectful instruction. The music teacher in this scenario expected a student with a disability to learn music subject matter as exhibited by accurate performance of musical concepts—and he did.

Another lesson related to expectations comes from a high-school music teacher I know. Recently, this teacher related an experience to me regarding a student who had challenged his approach to teaching and learning and prompted him to think of all students as academic learners of music:

> One of the students in my middle school choir, Curtis, caught my attention on the first day of class. The student was loud and disruptive during class and never seemed to pay attention to daily lessons. I didn't think he really belonged in my class. A few weeks into the school year, I went into the cafeteria during the lunch hour and spotted Curtis standing on a chair, performing for the entire room. He was good—REALLY good. His face was shining; he was rapping, singing, dancing, and smiling. He looked like a different kid! He waved and grinned when he saw me. Later in the day I found out that Curtis had written that song himself. I realized then and there—I needed to teach better and expect more. I needed to know kids and teach to their experi-

ences. I was embarrassed—his own music teacher didn't know that he could sing and compose.

ACCESS THROUGH COLLABORATION

The idea of forming effective partnerships between music teachers and other educators to promote appropriate comprehensive support for diverse learners across all content areas is evident among music education professionals. As part of this collaborative concept, many music educators have asked that music teachers be seen as collaborative partners in broader ways. For example, music teachers might work with individual teachers to enhance classroom curriculum or help school leaders plan cultural events. Additionally, many researchers agree that it is particularly imperative that music teachers work with IEP[1] teams to plan goals and curricular adaptations for students with disabilities (Alley, 1979; Cassidy, 1990; Darrow, 1990; Hock, Hasazi, & Patten, 1990; Thompson, 1990).

Although it is apparent that many music educators desire collaborative bonds between themselves and other educators regarding mutually taught diverse learners, partnerships are not always formed. The potential risk for a dearth of needed connections between music teachers and other teachers in the school can be assuaged if an effort is made by all teachers to form agreements toward more effective communication and inclusion of one another in the process of meeting the needs of all learners.

To more effectively support the learning of diverse students, the following set of guidelines is offered to assist inclusive nonmusic teachers in the process of forming collaborative partnerships with inclusive music teachers, and vise versa:

- Establish a rapport with one another that allows for communication. The music teacher should be viewed as a valued team member with skills and a knowledge base that might be helpful in the design of curriculum and instruction, in supporting challenging behaviors, and in providing enrichment for students with particular talents and gifts.
- Be sensitive to each other's schedules so that all inclusive teachers, including the music teacher(s), will be able to meet and serve as equal members of school teams and committees (e.g., parent–teacher conferences, IEP meetings, curriculum committee).
- Recognize each other as professionals to be valued equally in the decision-making process. Invite music teachers into conversations about

[1]An Individualized Education Program (IEP) is a document developed for students identified as having disabilities. The IEP outlines the student's educational program.

how diverse learners' needs would best be served. This includes supporting one another in making placement decisions concerning which class or which music ensemble would be most appropriate for individual students.

- Support one another in a mutual effort for developing materials and acquiring resources. Music educators can suggest materials that might benefit all learners in diverse schools. For example, adaptations that would be useful to some students with disabilities might include large print music for those with vision impairments, coded music for students with learning disabilities, adaptive instruments for those with physical disabilities, and visual cue cards for the deaf and hard of hearing (Darrow, 1990). For students with limited resources, music educators can facilitate community connections that might offer access to instruments or a band uniform. Teachers can creatively work together to counter anything that denies access to a rich music curriculum.
- Agree to value all subject areas by not "pulling" students from each other's classrooms for special studying, testing, or practicing time unless there is mutual agreement that it is in the best interest of a particular learner. This commitment to preserving music education for all communicates to students and parents alike that the faculty values music and sees it as an important academic area.
- Agree to interdisciplinary approaches that will insure music's integrity as an art and the integrity of other content areas for their academic value. Teachers might also consider working in teams to plan integrated curriculum. For example, as long as the accuracy of the historical/cultural information and the quality of the musical experience is preserved, a social studies teacher might work with the music teacher to teach students about the music of the 1920s or to introduce learners to authentic musical instruments commonly used in Mexico.

CONCLUSIONS

As school environments nationwide become increasingly diverse, educators have a responsibility to value the diversity of human existence and expect social equality within this existence. Internalizing this principle is an essential prerequisite to acquiring the motivation to develop and utilize effective teaching strategies that will successfully meet the needs of all learners, no matter how challenging or diverse. How then, does one provide optimal learning experiences that will insure desired academic and social outcomes for *every* student? It is a question that all educators must strive to answer, and it is one in which the answer will account for as much diversity as the learners it is intended to serve.

Reimer (2000) wrote, "All humans are, at the same time, like all other humans, like some other humans, and like no other humans" (p. 45). If we choose to value this inclusive statement, we will be reminded to embrace our "oneness" as a species, our similarities as humans, and perhaps most importantly, our differences as individuals as we pursue meaningful experiences through life and hopefully—through the arts.

For Discussion and Reflection

1. How can music become a more central part of schooling in the United States? How might we change, adapt, or enhance the curriculum and instruction in grades K–12 to incorporate musical thinking?

In the Field

1. Consider the last musical performance or concert in your school: Who participated? Who did not participate? Was participation encouraged? Did students need to compete to participate? How might the event have been designed to be more inclusive?
2. Does the music curriculum in your school meet the needs of a wide range of students? Is it multicultural? Available to all?

REFERENCES

Alley, J. M. (1979). Music in the IEP: Therapy/education. *Journal of Music Therapy, 16*(3), 111–127.

Cassidy, J. W. (1990, April). Managing the mainstreamed classroom. *Music Educators Journal, 76*(8), 41–43.

Darrow, A. (1990, April). Beyond mainstreaming: Dealing with diversity. *Music Educators Journal, 76*(8), 36–39.

Hock, M., Hasazi, S. B., & Patten, A. (1990, April). Collaboration for learning: Strategies for program success. *Music Educators Journal, 76*(8), 44–48.

Hoffer, C. R. (1993). Introduction to music education (2nd ed.). Belmont, CA: Wadsworth.

Madsen, C. K. (Ed.). (2000). *Vision 2020.* Reston, VA: MENC—The National Association for Music Education.

Mark, M. L. (1996). *Contemporary music education* (3rd ed.). New York: Schirmer Books.

National Standards for Arts Education. (1994). Reston, VA: Music Educators National Conference.

Reimer, B. (2000). Why do humans value music? In C. K. Madsen (Ed.), *Vision 2020* (pp. 25–48). Reston, VA: MENC—The National Association for Music Education.

Schock, K. L. (1990, April). In point of view: How well does mainstreaming work? *Music Educators Journal, 76*(8), 51.

Shuler, S. C. (1991, November). Music, at-risk students, and the missing piece. *Music Educators Journal, 78*(3), 21–29.

Thompson, K. P. (1990, April). Working toward solutions in mainstreaming. *Music Educators Journal, 76*(8), 30–35.

Chapter 9

In the Pool, On the Stage, and at the Concert: Access to Academics Beyond Classroom Walls

Mara Sapon-Shevin
Paula Kluth
Syracuse University

In 2000, Saskatoon's Mount Royal Collegiate, a secondary school in Saskatchewan, Canada, all but abandoned after-school activities. Due to increased demands on teacher time and lack of extra funding for coaches and activity supervisors, the school was forced to temporarily halt all extracurricular activity. Students and their families were outraged (Schofield, 2000). Research suggests that the Saskatoon community has good reason to be concerned. Studies consistently show that students who participate in extracurricular sports and clubs have better grades and attendance rates, stronger feelings of attachment to school, and higher rates of college attainment (Galley, 2000; Juarez, 1996; Women's Sports Foundation, 1989).

Students who lose access to extracurricular clubs, games, and activities also miss important social opportunities. Students who play, practice, and work together develop important social skills. Students participating in extracurricular activities make new friends, learn recreation skills, and often connect with students outside their typical social circles. Group membership may also help children and adolescents form their identities and become more self-aware. Consider the potential for social support and skill development on a cheerleading team: The team members go away to a 2-week summer clinic to practice skills, work for hours after school to develop new routines, and ride together on bus trips to football games, basketball tournaments, and wrestling matches. These activities leave plenty of time for talking, sharing, connecting, and developing friendships. Typically, students in these situations find opportunities to give and get support and build community with classmates.

EXTRACURRICULAR ACTIVITIES AND ACADEMICS

One of the most important reasons to pay attention to access to extracurricular activities is related to academics. Students engaged in extracurricular activities may be more successful and academically advantaged than those who do not participate in clubs, teams, organizations, and groups, as many extracurricular activities are based on academic work. Students participating in poetry club, math Olympics, and National Honor Society clearly have opportunities to practice and develop academic skills. Few educators would argue that students participating in a sign language club learn skills of expression and communication. They will also acquire new vocabulary and be introduced to issues of discourse and audience. Likewise, students on the staff of the school newspaper practice expository writing, learn about perspective and style, and explore the politics of publishing.

Other school-based extracurricular options, such as participation in sports, may seem at first glance to be less educationally focused, but may, in fact, be just as critical to students' academic growth. In addition to learning about their own bodies, learners engaged in athletics often grow intellectually through the acquisition of new skills and the mastery of rules and strategies; students engaged in dance are learning about movement and art while students learning to play baseball learn to read visual communication (signals) and calculate and organize data (batting average, on-base percentage).

Access to extracurricular activities during school also opens doors to future academic options. Many colleges require participation in extracurricular activities for admission, and many scholarships are based on students' level of participation during high school. In the same way that not taking calculus narrows a student's college options, not being able or encouraged to participate in extracurricular activities throughout one's school years can limit future opportunities.

WHY DO STUDENTS GET EXCLUDED?

Students of all ages learn facts and skills and gain knowledge through academic societies, athletic teams, music activities, social groups and clubs, theatrical productions, and leadership and political organizations. Unfortunately, some students do not have access to these activities. For some, access is restricted due to rules, structures, perceptions, and assumptions that are in some way exclusive. That is, some students are explicitly or implicitly rejected when they express interest in or attempt to join extracurricular activities. Other students never make it to the first meetings; they may simply feel unwelcome due to past experiences of exclusion or lack of familiarity with school activities.

Although thousands of students across the country are accessing school and community clubs, organizations, teams, lessons, activities, and groups, countless others—including those marginalized because of social class, students with disabilities, and students with limited financial resources—are finding barriers to participation in extracurricular opportunities. What keeps students from learning and participating in life outside of school? We suggest that students are excluded from participation in extracurricular activities for a variety of reasons. Although each reason does not apply to every student, an examination of some of the barriers to full participation can illuminate the issue for exclusion and possible solutions for inclusion.

"But what would a student like Victoria do in the chess club? She just wouldn't get anything out of it."

An inability to conceptualize activities as inclusive and multilevel often impedes the full involvement of a wide variety of students. If one conceives of the orchestra as being only for students who can read music and play an instrument, then it becomes difficult to think about the myriad of ways in which a nonmusician could participate in that activity. If being on the volleyball team is only for those whose skills are competitive in setting and spiking, then it becomes difficult to imagine the participation of a student who is blind or has a significant physical disability.

The assumptions educators make about who can benefit from participation in a particular activity are often based on inadequate information, stereotypes, and misconceptions about the nature of participation. Assumptions about who students are and the various identities they hold may make educators reluctant to involve a wide range of students. It might be assumed, for example, that a student who is just learning English as a second language couldn't participate in a forensic competition. Or that a female student couldn't wrestle. Or that a student who uses a wheelchair couldn't play soccer.

"We can't just let anyone into the jazz band—we have high standards here."

In many schools, extracurricular activities are part of a competitive ideology that separates and sorts students. Participation in extracurricular activities is seen as the right or privilege of high-achieving students, as a ticket to a better college, and as a way of preparing students for participation in competitive, societal forms of a particular activity. Thus, being on the football team is seen as a way of training a few excellent athletes who may go on to play college football; being in the school play or chorus is a way of providing high level theatrical and musical experiences for students who excel in that area who then might pursue these activities in institutions of higher learning or as community members.

In one school, for example, participation in the foreign language program is limited to students whose reading proficiency is "at grade level." Thus, the wide range of extracurricular activities available to students who are taking French, Spanish, or Latin is also closed to many students. The field trip to Montreal, an activity of the French club, is not open to any student not taking French; participation in the Olympics (with chariot races) is not accessible to anyone not taking Latin.

"Malcolm is having too much trouble in his regular classes—there's no time for extras."

Some educators assume that participation in extracurricular activities is reserved for those students who are making satisfactory progress in their academic classes. Because educators may not perceive the embedded academic and intellectual skills within extracurricular activities, they may limit those activities in favor of the "real work" of schooling.

In some cases, this belief becomes enacted as an eligibility requirement—you can't be on the rugby team unless you are doing well in your academic work. Because students often enjoy participation in extracurricular activities, withholding such participation becomes a form of punishment, intended to enhance school performance. Although meant to keep students focused on their academic progress and accountable for learning, the result of such requirements may be to exclude the struggling learner from the *only place* he or she is learning successfully and feeling competent.

Even when not enacted as a policy, the perception that extracurricular activities are frills or (as their name implies) "extra," may keep students from participating. A mother of a young girl who was experiencing significant delays in learning how to read was advised that she should pull her daughter out of the gymnastics program in which she was participating (and excelling!). The teachers advised that all of the girl's free time should be devoted to reading tutorials and extra classes. The mother wisely argued that it was important for her daughter to remain engaged in an activity in which she experienced considerable success. Not surprisingly, when the girl's self-esteem and confidence improved, she responded more positively to the extra literacy instruction she was receiving and became a more fluent reader.

"Todd can't play hockey because parents are required to drive players to the early-morning Saturday games and his mother works all weekend!"

For many students, technical and logistical impediments may stand in the way of their participation in a wide range of school activities.

- The ski club costs money and you have to have the right winter clothes and equipment to join.
- Participation in the debate team involves trips out of town and parents must be involved in transportation.
- Students are expected to practice for the crew team every day after school and on Saturday afternoons, therefore, the coach encourages them not to get a part-time job.

Some students do not have money that can be spent on uniforms and special equipment and even when a student's family has a car, they may not have extra money for fuel. Other students (and their families) may have jobs and responsibilities that would prevent them from taking a weekend trip. Making student participation contingent upon having parents who can afford to be fiscally and emotionally supportive precludes the participation of a wide range of students.

"We offer lots of activities—if kids don't sign up for them, it's not our fault."

Although a range of extracurricular options may be offered at a school, all students may not avail themselves of those opportunities. Some students do not see themselves as represented in the offerings. Perhaps they perceive (and are correct) that participation in the swing choir requires the "right clothes" or membership in particular socioeconomic or ethnic groups. The school offerings may not reflect their own communities or represent valued activities within their own family or culture. Students may not feel welcome based on differences; in many high schools, certain sports are considered "White" and others "Black." For instance, in some schools there are often no (or few) Whites on the basketball team and few students of color on the swimming team. These existing patterns of segregation according to race or class often become reinforced and reified through extracurricular activities.

Some students literally don't know what is available or do not know how to access what is offered. If you can't read the sign that says "Field Hockey Try-Outs" or don't know what it means to "try out" for something, it is unlikely you will appear at the gym at 3:00 to compete for a spot on the team. In some schools, participation in specific extracurricular activities is closely related to specific classes (e.g., only students in the vocal music class are eligible for or aware about the school musical or only students in business education classes know about the activities of the Future Business Leaders Organization). Students may be aware of the cliquishness of particular activities and feel functionally excluded; if they do go once, they may not feel welcomed or included. Some students require concrete support and encouragement for participation; they may need someone to review their options with them, help them to select something, and then need a friend or other support person to help them make their entrée into the new group or community.

VISIONS OF INCLUSIVE EXTRACURRICULAR ACTIVITIES

In responding to the foregoing barriers, we articulate here our vision of what inclusive extracurricular activities could be like:

It would be recognized and accepted that there are many valuable benefits to participation in extracurricular activities, and that all students can learn something from participating.

One need not be able to follow every choreographed step to benefit from the aerobics club, nor does one need to excel in physics, chemistry, or biology to appreciate the creativity, problem solving, and interaction that takes place at the science fair. In schools that value the participation and success of all students, activities will be designed and cultivated that are available to all. The yearbook staff will be open to any student wanting to participate. Students might be asked to sell advertising, plan marketing strategies, take and develop photographs, design graphics for the cover or inside pages, engage in financial planning, or write copy. Every one of these roles is academic, interesting, meaningful, and necessary. As some roles require more skill or specialized knowledge than others, adult advisors can offer any student a role that will challenge and engage him or her. A student who really wants to learn more about darkroom technology can do so, whereas another student can make an equally important contribution by helping to select photos for various sections of the book.

Students who cannot physically engage in the game of basketball can still serve as a team manager, statistician, game photographer, motivational coach, or free-throw expert. Any student participating as part of such a team will undoubtedly learn about scoring, rules, teamwork, and how groups work together to achieve a common goal.

When one of us (Mara) was in high school, the Audio-Visual Club provided an opportunity for students of very different groups to meet and get to know one another. Although some activities seemed clearly segregated by race, class, or academic skill, the AV Club attracted a wide range of student types and important friendships developed there. In addition, students who were in the AV club learned to operate and repair audiovisual equipment, important skills for the future.

The goal of extracurricular activities would be to involve as many students as possible, rather than to serve as a vehicle for sorting and selection.

Schools are educational institutions. They exist to support the growth, development, and learning of *all* students. Why then are so many extracurricular groups focused on competition and winning? Most schools make "cuts" when forming their sports teams, drama productions, music groups, and, even their academic groups. How does this type of policy further the educational experience of any student? It does not and cannot; especially since these types of judgments about students are incredibly subjective and, sometimes, even biased by teachers' impressions of students' families, academic abilities, and behavior.

Take for example a typical day of try-outs or auditions in a high school. The coach, teacher, or advisor observes the skills and abilities of a student as he or she performs in some way for the adult. When the student is done performing, the adult decides whether or not the student will be permitted to participate in the organization, team, or group. Thus, the adult also decides—fairly arbitrarily, in most cases—who will have an opportunity to further develop skills and who will be dismissed from future learning opportunities. How is it that we permit this "assessment without instruction" approach in schools? And how does this pervasive model fit within diverse, inclusive schools? If schools are about teaching and learning, then we must provide students with opportunities to experience both.

Instead of counting the number of trophies in the glass cases, touting the number of "all-state" or "all-conference" musicians the school has cultivated, and advertising the number of years the school has been invited to the math decathlon, educators might congratulate themselves on how many students are joining and participating in school-sponsored activities. They might boast about the number of students who joined a club for the first time or collect data on how many hours the average student spends learning at school beyond school hours.

Participation in extracurricular activities would be viewed as a student right, and not as a privilege to be earned or made contingent on other areas of performance.

How many adults would continue to go to work each day if they were unsuccessful at everything they were asked to do? Most of us choose work that makes us feel useful, competent, and skilled in some way. Students who face only difficulty and frustration during the school day, have little incentive to show up at school at all. One way to scare students away from school (and, therefore, from academic learning) is to take away activities they love and eliminate work they enjoy. When schools treat extracurricular activities as a privilege and take them away from the students who struggle the most, they are wasting a powerful educational tool. Inasmuch as participation in extracurricular activities may actually increase the attendance of struggling students and boost their performance in the classroom, we need to do everything possible to *keep* students engaged in them.

In fact, extracurricular activity might be used as a way to support struggling students in their academics. A teacher we know once taught a frustrated math student about arc and angles during games of one-on-one basketball. The student slowly started to make the connection from basketball to geometry during these sessions. This kind of creativity can be a catalyst for designing more appropriate classroom supports for learners. If teachers examine contexts in which students are successful (when drawing, during athletic contests, through speech writing), they can bring these experiences into weekly lessons while continuing to enhance skills and knowledge through extracurricular experiences.

Participation in extracurricular activities would be separated from individual or family resources so that all students could participate fully in all activities.

Creativity is key for schools looking to tackle extracurricular logistical barriers. Scheduling must be examined; how can transportation be provided for all students? The school might engineer transportation partnerships between families and students or provide some students with passes for the city bus. Teachers and administrators might consider changing the location of some school-sanctioned activities. Is the school the most convenient place for every group to meet? Some clubs might well meet in community centers or area libraries. When is the best time for the group to meet? Perhaps some groups could assemble before school so that students with after-school jobs could still participate. Schools might even pursue the possibilities of holding extracurricular activities during the school day. Perhaps some groups can meet during lunch period or free study time. This may be an attractive option for schools with challenging transportation problems (e.g., those who serve students from rural areas or students who are bussed to a nonneighborhood school). Educational leaders should examine all logistical barriers related to student participation in extracurricular activities. Several specific questions should be considered:

- Do students need uniforms? Can teams, groups, or clubs dress in like colors or similar outfits as an alternative?
- How far are students traveling to compete or participate in activities? How could schools and school districts design competitions or gatherings so that travel across town or out of town is limited and students and their families are traveling primarily within their own communities?
- Can costs be minimized for activities? Can grants or school-wide fundraising cover activity costs for all students? Can community fundraising be used to alleviate financial demands on individual students and their families?

Schools would expand extracurricular options to include a wide range of interests and needs and to respond to the unique needs of individual students.

If a student cannot find an extracurricular home in his or her school, he or she is left to find social opportunities elsewhere. Whereas some students may be successful in finding after-school activities that are appropriate, others may turn to unsafe or otherwise inappropriate options. At Webb Middle School in Austin, Texas, for example, many of the students who did not feel connected to their school joined neighborhood gangs (Juarez, 1996). The principal decided to create more extracurricular options in the hopes of drawing the students into the school and getting them interested in something meaningful. Because many gang members struggle with issues of identity (Vigil, 1988), the principal formed the groups, in part, to provide students with opportunities to develop self-awareness through memberships that were school sanctioned. The school began to offer a wide range of extracurricular opportunities. Students who might have previously struggled to find an extracurricular match could now choose from more than 50 clubs and activities including walking, Tejano dance, ultimate frisbee, Create Your Own Futures, ham radio, and Macintosh (Juarez, 1996). School leaders were thrilled not only with the numbers of students who ended up participating, but also with the kinds of learning and excitement that resulted from the new extracurricular offerings.

INCLUSIVE EXTRACURRICULAR OPTIONS: SOME EXAMPLES

Sports

Through physical activities, students acquire information about their bodies, positionality, and directionality. Through participation in sports (in which there are rules), they learn about categorization and the ways in which examples either fit or don't fit the rule. Any kind of scoring involves learning about numbers, record keeping, and so on. Through participation in football, for instance, students can learn about symbol systems and spatial relationships as they memorize a variety of potential offensive plays.

Many physical activities can be structured in ways that allow for a wide range of participation options. The track and field team needs sprinters, long-distance runners, pole-vaulters, high jumpers, hurdlers, and relay team members; this is a model of inclusion—all are necessary, but not all do the same thing. A gymnastics team also needs members with diverse abilities. Students need not be strong in every aspect of the sport to participate;

some may be skilled at floor exercises, while others may choose to focus on the vault or rings. Within these activities, students with different abilities can work on different skills and at an individual pace. Students who are perfecting back handsprings can work alongside a student who is struggling to learn a cartwheel.

Most students in U.S. schools will not become professional athletes. Many of them will, however, want to play in a corporate or community softball tournament, join an occasional tennis game with friends, or take a jog every once in a while. Educators should, therefore, be developing the skills, abilities, and athletic capacities of all students. In fact, a task force on girls and sports sponsored by the Feminist Majority Foundation (1995), suggested that schools focus on "sports for all, not just a few" and that educators emphasize the teaching of lifetime sports (such as walking, jogging, golf, folk-dancing, and horseback riding) to all learners so that every student can experience sport and exercise.

Indeed, schools and teachers should be promoting life-long health and fitness, not just in physical education classes, but in our extracurricular activities, as well. The marker of success for the coach of the cross-country team should not be how many races his runners have won, but how many of his former team members continue to run, enjoy the sport, and increase their skills as adults. Although it is certainly important to facilitate the development of all students and to encourage them to fulfill their potential, this should not occur at the expense of other students with less athletic prowess. Skilled coaches are able to see the skill and ability in all students and pride themselves on bringing out the best in all.

In junior-high school, one of us (Paula) had a softball coach with a cooperative philosophy. Unlike other coaches in this softball league, Mr. Johnson wanted players to learn and enjoy the game—winning was not a primary objective. All of the young women on the team were expected to play in every game, even when the game was close, even when putting the second-string players in the game meant that the team might lose. All of the young women were expected to improve skills and develop new ones. Those with exceptional talents were encouraged and shown how to improve bat speed, increase hitting distance, and execute a bunt, while those just beginning to learn the sport received tips on how to catch a high fly ball and how to make contact without "popping up" when at bat.

Consider how such a model could be used for developing a high-school pompon squad. Instead of asking students to audition for a spot on the squad, all of the young women (and men) interested are welcome to join. Because the school can only afford uniforms for 20, partial uniforms are purchased for all—matching sweaters or jackets for 40 instead of full uniforms for 20. Or the students work with a Family and Consumer Education Class to design and create costumes for all. Or students put together unique makeshift outfits for the different dance routines they perform (jeans and t-shirts for a 1950s rock and roll song).

Issues of gender also must be considered if we are to push traditional boundaries related to extracurricular activities. At Lincoln High School in Los Angeles, Luisana Cruz, a player on her school's varsity football team is challenging what it means to be a fullback (Lopez, 1999). Luisana and three other young women are all on the Lincoln team and although none of them are starters, they have all seen action on the field. Luisana and her teammates might help educators reconsider gender boundaries in many sports. Schools might consider ways to make students feel welcome to cross traditional borders—boys on the figure skating, dance, or synchronized swimming teams and girls on the hockey, weight-lifting, or rugby teams.

Schools wanting to include all students in extracurricular options might evaluate the types of options that are offered. Are all of the activities competitive? Skill intense? Students who struggle with weight; those with physical disabilities; and those who are not interested in competition might appreciate offerings that are more individualistic and self-paced in nature such as power walking, water aerobics, yoga, or karate.

Music

There are many things students can learn from engaging in musical activities. Research suggests, in fact, that learning music helps students to enhance reading and math skills and to improve spatial-temporal reasoning (Rausher et al., 1997). Multicultural music can help students learn about different cultures, religions, and people (e.g., Why are some African songs written in French? What different songs are appropriate for Kwanza, Passover, or the Chinese New Year?). Music can be organized and taught so that many people at different skill levels can participate. If there are multiple parts, stronger singers can be given the more complex parts. Many songs have repetitive choruses that most people can learn. Instrumental music usually has multiple parts, and not everyone plays the same instrument or the same part. For instance, in a drumming ensemble, some drummers play the steady bass beat while others perform the fast, complex patterns. Together the sound is outstanding—all the parts are needed, and the sound is enriched by the active participation of many musicians.

To create inclusive music experiences, attention must be given to logistical support: Does everyone have transportation to the choir rehearsals and concert? Can all parents afford to attend (if there is a charge)? Are costly uniforms or costumes required for participation? Is the concert scheduled with sensitivity to the family and religious requirements of all families (i.e., not having a Friday night concert that excludes Jewish students)?

Making music inclusive also means being thoughtful about what music is selected and performed. Making sure that music is not Christian-dominated increases the possibilities of participation for a wider range of students and also helps all learners understand the diversities of their classmates and the world. Music can be used as a tool to teach about diversity and promote inclusion; learning music from different cultures, and representing various ethnic and racial groups can be an educational experience for both the performers and the audience. Learning to sing the National Anthem from South Africa can provide powerful learning experiences and discussions about apartheid, racial justice, and political change. Having students learn and perform music about the oppression of gays and lesbians (e.g., Fred Small's 1983 song, "Scott and Jamie" about two gay men who adopt two little boys) can provide an opening for exploring issues of sexual harassment and the importance of building and becoming allies.

For the last several years, one of us (Mara) has led workshops on Making Music Accessible to All. This workshop has included songs without words, songs with sign language, songs with different parts, rounds (in which some people need only learn a tiny segment of a longer piece) and songs which are done as "call and response." Each type of music has particular characteristics allowing for full (not partial) participation by all members. It is important to state that full participation does not mean that every person is doing the same thing at the same time. Full participation means that everyone has an active role (not just holding up the applause sign at the end!).

We have worked with a middle-school music educator who had an incredibly diverse choir group. This educator did not require students to qualify for the group, instead she invited in all students and voices. She provided instruction to all participating students and pushed each of them to work harder and do more. When asked why she organized her groups in this way, the teacher explained that she didn't necessarily expect her choir to be the best in the county or state, although she certainly provided them with a challenging curriculum that moved them all toward excellence. She did expect, however, to make each student a better performer, singer, and artist.

The Syracuse Community Choir provides another model of an inclusive music activity. The choir is open to all community members without auditions; the only requirement is a desire to participate. The group was started by Karen Mihalyi, a community organizer and activist. Mihalyi recalls how she initially assembled the group:

> We had some mailings that I organized. I had a committee of people, but I am the one who got it started. We did a lot of recruiting, put out notices everywhere: "This is a choir for everyone. You can say you don't know how to sing, but try out. There is a place for you in the choir."

> I had some background thinking about inclusion. The women's movement more than any other movement that grew out of the 1960s began to address the issue of inclusiveness. It was painful. People were confronted by each other: by the whiteness of the movement, by its middle classness, by the lack of sisters who were disabled. The movement inspired my intention to do something about class, race, disability, gender, and homophobia issues. (Bogdan, 1995, p. 144)

True to Mihalyi's vision, the choir has members of all racial groups, many religions, many ages and includes a significant number of people with significant disabilities, including blindness, and emotional and behavioral challenges (Bogdan, 1995).

The choir performs music that is accessible to all. The music is often four parts, and section leaders in each group help people who require it. The section leader or another strong singer will often sit next to a person who needs help staying on pitch. Other section members sit next to and support people who require other kinds of help. Tashara, for example, might sit next to Helene and help her turn the pages of her music. Peter may sit next to Ted and help him to stay seated and calm if he gets agitated or nervous at some point.

What kinds of resources are needed to include diverse learners in this choir? Some of the needed resources are physical: Braille music, large print music, music stands for those who can't hold music, and so on. Most of the resources are human; there must be sufficient numbers of able-bodied singers to support those requiring physical assistance and enough emotional support for those who require a gentle touch or a soft word in order to remain engaged and participating. Each year, the choir holds workshops to help all choir members understand differences and disabilities and to help choir members develop the skills necessary to support each other.

Drama

Students who are not fluent readers can enjoy and learn from a Shakespeare production as well as those who have studied the play and its historical context. Learning about how to identify with an audience, delighting in the music and artistry of theater, and recognizing that printed text can be experienced as a story—these are all potential learning experiences from participating in a play.

There are many academic skills embedded in all aspects of theater. Students have opportunities to improve their reading, to learn about modes of expression, inflection, body language, and nonverbal cues. Participating in a play involves coordinating your actions with others and learning about timing and collaboration. The selection of the play itself can involve students in learning about different literary genres and discourse styles.

The school play provides a wonderful example of an extracurricular activity in which everyone can be involved. To put on a successful play, the following tasks are necessary:

- Finding or writing the script
- Casting the show
- Painting scenery
- Designing and sewing costumes
- Finding props for the play
- Serving as a prompter (off stage with a script, helping those who forget their lines)
- Preparing publicity for the show, including designing and coloring posters, distributing flyers, calling local media and placing ads, posting signs, etc.
- Selling tickets, both before and during the show
- Planning, preparing and selling refreshments
- Ushering the show, passing out programs

It is impossible to read this list without finding an appropriate job for every student; each task is a necessary part of the play and each provides learning experiences.

For students who are acting in the play, flexibility should also be the rule. Participation for some students may involve the challenging of traditional ideas about casting. Does a female student need to play Little Red Riding Hood? Does a White student need to play Helen Keller in "The Miracle Worker"? Can a student who doesn't speak, but uses a communication device have a "speaking part" in the play? When Bob Blue, a teacher and children's musician from Western Massachusetts, was casting school plays, he made sure that every child who wanted to participate was included. When Bob put on *Alice in Wonderland*, 10 little girls all wanted to be Alice. Rather than choosing one (and devastating 9 others), Bob had a different solution. There was a different Alice in each scene, and students shared the spotlight. The audience had no trouble telling who was Alice—she was always the one wearing the white dress with the blue apron.

Another elementary music and drama teacher included everyone in the school play by allowing students to write their own parts. The play started out with a basic script, which students changed as they rehearsed. Students who felt more comfortable as rehearsals went on were allowed to add lines for themselves and embellish their parts. Students could make adjustments to the script until the week before the play; after that point the students worked on memorizing the final collaborative script. This cooperative work increased the participation of students; those who were reluctant at the beginning to say anything often felt more willing to participate as rehearsals continued.

Teachers can also increase the range of students who are involved in theater activities by being thoughtful in their selection of the dramatic activity being produced. Is the selection sensitive to the population of the school? Do students feel that the play "speaks to them" or do they feel excluded by the format and topic? One teacher we know allowed students to perform short plays that they selected, thereby covering a wide range of genres. All students were able to find something that appealed to them and made them comfortable with their participation.

CONCLUSIONS

As teachers move toward building schools and school communities that are more responsive to a wider range of learners, the broader curriculum of the school—including extracurricular activities—should be examined: Are all students actively invited to participate in extracurricular activities? Is there something for everyone? Do extracurricular options exist that will appeal to any student?

Being a full member of one's school community is an important precursor to being a full member of the greater community and society. With commitment and imagination, extracurricular activities can be conceptualized, supported, and implemented in ways that allow all students to actively participate. This becomes critical not only because of the benefits of participation to students during their school years but beyond as well. It is through participation in school extracurricular activities that many people learn who they are and what they enjoy, identities on which they build after they leave school. The student who participates in Spanish Club may be more likely to volunteer in a neighborhood tutoring program for Spanish-speaking adults, a student who serves on the student council may continue to pursue political work by running for the local school board, and students who learn to golf or practice kick boxing on a high-school team may be more likely to keep active with such activities as adults.

There are almost as many extracurricular possibilities as there are students in schools. Schools interested in including and responding to all learners can take on the challenge of crafting and offering "something for everyone" not only to build school community and support the social development of students but also to increase academic opportunities, success, and access for every student in the school.

For Discussion and Reflection

1. How can extracurricular access for all enhance academic success in schools?

2. Do competitive extracurricular activities serve as a barrier to inclusive education? What is the relationship between competition and inclusion? How can schools offer competitive activities (e.g., sports and music competitions) and still meet the needs of all learners? How can schools hold high standards in extracurricular programs while still including all students in extracurricular activities?

3. Think about your own experience (positive or negative) in extracurricular activities. What social and academic skills did you learn in these activities, if any? In what ways have these experiences shaped or influenced your adult life?

In the Field

1. Are there students or groups of students who are excluded from extracurricular activities? What steps could the school take to include a wider range of students into extracurricular activities (consider gender, sexual orientation, athletic ability, socioeconomic status, language abilities, communication skills)?

2. How many students in your school participate in extracurricular activities? Talk to students in your school about their participation. What are the reasons students do and do not participate in extracurricular activities?

3. Pick an extracurricular activity in your school and brainstorm ways in which it can be made more inclusive.

4. List all of the extracurricular activities in your school. Categorize them by type of activity (e.g., school leadership, sports, academic clubs) and consider: How many are competitive? How many have admission criteria? How many require good academic standing? How many meet in the evening or on weekends? With a group of students, review the list and determine if opportunities are appropriate for every learner in the school. If not, brainstorm about extracurricular activities that might be added to the school.

REFERENCES

Bogdan, B. (1995). Singing for an inclusive society: The community choir. In S. Taylor, B. Bodgdan, & Z. M. Lutfiyya (Eds.), *The variety of community experience: Qualitative studies of family and community life* (pp. 141–154). Baltimore: Brookes.

Feminist Majority Foundation (1995). *Empowering women in sports, The Empowering women series, No. 4*; A Publication of the Feminist Majority Foundation.

Galley, M. (2000). Extra benefits tied to extracurriculars. *Education Week, 20*(7), 8.

Juarez, T. (1996). Where homeboys feel at home in school. *Educational Leadership, 53,* 30–32.

Lopez, S. (1999) A fullback picks her gown. *Time, 154*(20), p. 6.

Rausher, F. H., Shaw, G. L., Levine, L. J., Wright, E. L., Dennis, W. R., & Newcomb, R. (1997). Music training causes long-term enhancement of preschool children's spatial-temporal reasoning. *Neurological Research, 19,* 2–8.

Schofield, J. (2000). After-school boycott. *Maclean's, 113*(39), 54–56.

Small, F. (1983). Scott and Jamie. On *I will stand fast.* Flying Fish Records.

Vigil, J. D. (1988). *Barrio gangs: Street life and identity in southern California.* Austin: University of Texas Press.

Women's Sports Foundation (1989). *Minorities in sports: The effect of varsity sports participation on the social, educational, and career mobility of minority students.* New York: Women's Sports Foundation.

Chapter **10**

Academics, Access, and Action

Douglas P. Biklen
Diana M. Straut
Paula Kluth
Syracuse University

In the opening of our book, we put forth a new vision for comprehensive school reform that is concerned with every learner in the school. The text goes on to critique schooling as we know it and proposes new ways to view and teach students in our diverse schools and to identify frameworks, approaches, and strategies that foster access to academic curricula. In this chapter we move beyond sharing ideas and discussing possibilities and address *approaches* and *actions* that might be taken to move schools closer to an inclusive *access-to-academics* agenda.

A CALL TO ACTION

Lest this become a rhetorical book that offers ideas but fails to inspire change we issue in this concluding chapter a "Call to Action." We ask readers to consider the deed, dispositions, and acts that they may need to pursue in order to give learners *access to academics.* In doing so responsibly, we need first to acknowledge the risk involved for readers who take up (or have taken up) this charge. We could fill another volume with stories of "revolutionaries" who, acting upon their vision of inclusive or equitable schooling have experienced significant political, financial, and personal reproach. Consider, for example, the experience of one of our colleagues who attempted to enact an *access to academics* approach when hired to teach in a self-contained middle school special education classroom. Among her requests: that less money be spent on toys and games that were not age-appropriate (e.g., stacking blocks, lacing cards) and that her classroom budget be spent on maps, hands-on science equipment, trade books, and bean bag chairs for a reading corner; that uninspiring posters about classroom behavior and rules be removed to make space for the display of student work; that students with and without disabilities be allowed to work and learn in this renovated classroom/learning center; that "her" students be moved into more inclusive educational environments; and that the special education teachers be included in the general education teachers' weekly staff meetings. The initial result: A set of performance reviews that questioned her commitment to being a "team player" among the special education staff, and a notation that she was "insubordinate" in suggesting that her school needed to rethink the curriculum and placements offered to students with disabilities. However, committed to her ideals and constantly questioning her own theories and actions, the teacher continued to advocate and build alliances with parents and other staff. Change came slowly; but it came. Students began to see themselves as learners; parents began to insist on academic instruction for their children; staff throughout the building started to find opportunities for collaboration; and the teacher knew, at the end of the day, that she was doing the right thing for students.

Other teachers have taken risks to give students access to academics . . . the English teacher who leads a literature circle to discuss the book, *Deliver us from Evie,* about a young adolescent's struggles with her sexuality; the social studies teacher who presents information about the public lynchings of African Americans or the riots at Stonewall; the teacher who refuses to give traditional grades and instead uses performance outcomes, all know the risks of being a change agent. One need not look far into the annals of school desegregration, civil rights, and women's history to find tales of struggles against the educational system, fueled by a commitment to social justice yet riddled with risk and retribution.

Our call to action is issued in full recognition of the dogmas and doctrines—implicit and explicit—that work against change in education. We recognize that no one in education works in isolation. The actions of one person can ripple throughout the system, a very political system at that, sometimes with profound consequences. Additionally, educators have always been "building the airplane while flying it," thus increasing the stakes when changes are enacted. In spite of these high-risk circumstances, we believe it necessary for educators to think deeply about their "espoused theories" (what they say they believe about learners and learning) and their "theories in action" (what they're actually doing in their classroom to act upon their beliefs; Argyris & Schon, 1974). When contradictions arise between our actions and our theories, there is opportunity for powerful learning and change. The focus is as much inward as it is outward; Asking ourselves, "What do I believe about this learner?" "What assumptions am I making?" "What are alternative explanations for the conclusions I've drawn?" and at the same time asking, "What does this learner bring to the classroom?" "How does she make meaning of the world?" In the absence of reflection that promotes learning and change, we ourselves become perpetrators and victims of policies that marginalize students. When we view schooling, and our actions, through a critical frame and seek action, we can shift from perpetrator and victim to ally and advocate. We suggest here three strategies for taking action that promote learning and change.

Investigate Assumptions

There are many, many instances to draw on to illustrate the point that taken-for-granted assumptions are not always "correct." The assumptions or interpretations that one person makes about an incident are not necessarily shared by others who experience the same event. One place where we see the inherent dangers of making assumptions about others' behaviors and others' intentions is in regard to the issue of school failure. School failure or what is routinely called "dropping out" might equally be thought of us "school leaving" or even as "being pushed out." In turning our attention to this topic we can reveal a number of conflicting interpretations of school failure—within the interpretations of the students and those of their teachers and school administrators. In considering student views, it becomes clear that the students' interpretations of their own situations also involve them in interpreting or "reading" their teachers and school administrators. So the conflict of perspectives becomes even more complicated.

In her book, *Framing Dropouts,* Fine (1991) described how educators' assumptions about why high-school students leave school are frequently at odds with how students themselves understand their own behavior. She describes ways that teachers and administrators in a school explained school leaving. She characterizes one set of explanations under the heading "Things can't change":

> Voiced with the greatest repetition, this belief blended two political strains. Educators who might be considered conservative contended that "the culture of poverty," "the underclass," "babies having babies," and "no one cares about education in these homes" were sufficient to explain absolute educational failure. They felt it unfair to hold schools accountable for problems that schools didn't create. (p. 155)

The other side of the political equation in this "things can't change" stance was taken up by teachers who blamed racism, capitalism, and sexism which had so "eroded the social fabric of" the urban center that it was "naïve to presume that schools could interrupt these overwhelming social forces." Other assumptions of educators that Fine describes include the "discipline view" where problems are defined as located in students, such then when problems arise, the solution is to get rid of the problems (p. 156); the "work with the survivors" view, which holds that most students have given up on school and that best a teacher can hope for is to help the survivors—the ones who still care about education and believe school is for them—to keep surviving (p. 156); the "educational bureaucracy obstructs progressive public education" model, which blames the school bureaucracy for keeping "low students" in classes that do not teach critical thinking, and for keeping teachers from feeling empowered to design their own educational practice (p. 156); and the "I do the best I can in my classroom."

Students' understandings about how they experienced school, which was related to why they ended up leaving school, bear little resemblance to the teachers' assumptions. A student with a learning disability explained that he felt teachers treated him as if he were hindering the class and that they "wanted me out of the way. I was being alienated from everyone else" (Fine, 1991, p. 72). Another student spoke of the cultural gulf between teachers and students:

> I'm not knocking them but I felt the teachers . . . don't understand Blacks and Puerto Ricans because in a way that they look down on them. Like "I live on Columbus Avenue and I give you an example from Columbus Avenue." He's not talking about an example up here. You got to take the example the way he said it and then imagine [if it] happened up here. . . . You have to translate into Harlem. (p. 72)

And another student talked about the social isolation of being out of sequence with her age peers:

> That's what really put me down, being older than the others. I'm older than all the kids in fifth, imagine how I feel in sixth! It's more than hurt. . . .
>
> The other kids are able to do that work, and they at such a young age, and you sittin' up there and you're not doing anything' at all.
>
> I'd be embarrassed going back now, so that's why I quit. (p. 73)

Fine (1991) also reported on a student who had a baby and who wanted to stay in school, but found herself counseled out:

> The man in the attendance office said I'm better off trying for my GED course. I kept telling him well let's see how I do this term. But he was like you know, you're not going to do good. . . . It's best you hurry up and leave while you're still young and see if you can make something of yourself. I was think-

ing, well, I don't want none of this. People keep pressuring me, I think I'll just try another school. (p. 78)

Clearly, all of the students in these particular accounts express a desire to be in school. Each expresses some remorse at being out of school or at having left school. These accounts are at odds with teachers' sense that little could have been done to enable them to stay in school. If in reading these accounts we are drawn to lend more sympathy to the students accounts than to the teachers, it may be because the students are the ones losing out on education, but also it may be because at least a proportion of the teachers' commentaries on school leaving involve them in making assumptions about students' intentions and desires; judging from the accounts that Fine reports, in this instance, that is a dangerous enterprise. It is also plainly obvious that there is a difference of character between the students' personal stories and the more distanced-sounding explanations of teachers and administrators about how students approach and experience school. From our access-to-academics viewpoint, it is crucial that educators work at *not making assumptions about how students experience school.*

One aspect of a logical strategy for interrogating taken-for-granted assumptions is to consider the multiple voices heard in schools that may interpret events and processes of schools in diverse ways. The example of school dropouts/pushouts—perhaps it is best just to call it school leaving, allowing the question of responsibility to be an open one—illustrates the value of hearing multiple perspectives.

There are many "givens" of schooling we contend should be considered or challenged from multiple perspectives. What constitutes "participation" in class, for example? The system seems to value verbal, active participation in class, rewarding students who contribute to class discussion in "acceptable" ways and marginalizing those whose participation is "nontraditional." Students who are quiet, pensive, or shy, students who value listening over speaking, and students who bring cultural norms to the classroom may participate in ways not accepted in American culture.

One of the authors of this chapter experienced the impact of cultural norms when a young woman from a middle eastern country joined the author's fifth-grade classroom. The student, although performing well on written assignments, rarely participated in class discussions. When assigned a role as an attorney in a mock trial, the student quietly asked for a different role. She explained to the teacher, "I should not be debating and giving my opinion. It is not right." Another example of cultural influence on participation occurred during a brainstorming exercise. The teacher asked students to brainstorm "best case" and "worst case" scenarios or solutions to an environmental problem—overuse of natural resources. At the conclusion of the exercise, a student in her class who is Hopi Indian expressed frustration at her classmates' inability to think in grand and positive terms. She said, "In my culture, we do not think about the negative. We see possibilities. It's hard for me to imagine worst case, but I can dream big about the best case."

The assumption that all students will participate in the same way or with the same level of comfort may drive educators to put in place highly structured, very basic, functional curricula that do not involve much academics and instead focus on self-help skills or the like for students who participate in nontraditional ways. By not checking our assumptions about practices of schooling, we risk assimilating students into existing structures. As a result, the "assimilated students" may be denied opportunities to demonstrate their gifts and talents. Our point is that unless educators have found a way for all students to communicate equitably, it is probably *not* necessarily a good assumption to assume low interest or low intellectual ability.

Examine Language and Signs

Studying representation is a useful tool for understanding the idea of access to academics. The way to study representation is to look at particular uses of language and other signs within a cultural setting and to ask what their meanings are for the people who use them. Granted, most signs get "used" unconsciously and may be taken as "natural" or "objective"; uncovering and exploring them is difficult and necessarily ongoing.

Consider, for example social relations in schools. As Sapon-Shevin and Kluth discussed in chapter 9, activities "beyond classroom walls" and the informal rules that govern them (e.g., parents must be available to drive students to practices) may signify who can and cannot participate in particular activities. Likewise, sports teams that hold tryouts for the purpose of excluding those perceived as less skilled send the message that winning is more important than participating and as Madsen emphasized in chapter 8, musical programs in schools that emphasize particular religious holidays over others can be signs of what groups of students are privileged in the school.

The way in which schools allocate time can also signify privilege and lack of privilege. For instance, in chapter 6, Straut and Colleary warn that students lose skills, knowledge, and power when certain types of content are ignored. They suggest that teachers think more critically about finding ways to teach issues of democracy, social justice, and other issues of social studies and that they think carefully about what content is taught and how it is presented. They suggest for instance, that teachers reach beyond "heroes and holidays" for social studies content and that they continuously explore silences and privilege across topics.

Privilege and lack thereof is also evident in how time is used in schools. For many students with disabilities, time is a central concern. For the student who types to communicate, other students may not engage in conversation with that student once they perceive that response time is delayed. Unless teachers model the value of taking the time to listen and to respond, the person who is slow to communicate will be silenced. A student who uses a wheelchair may take longer than other students to get from class to class or to get organized for classroom work. A student who does not use English as a first language may need more time to process verbal conversations and, therefore, may need a teacher to talk slower or to provide "wait time" after asking questions of the class.

Not adjusting uses of time becomes a signal that a student doesn't belong, or that the student is welcome so long as he or she can comply with standard ways of using and allocating time. Standard definitions of and acceptable uses of time disserve students with disabilities, students who work to carefully construct a thought before sharing it (e.g., English language learners) and students who hold their own norms about order and privilege in speaking (e.g., those from cultures where women don't speak up, or Native American students who may view the passage of time differently than European American students). Thus time, as teachers and students construct its use in schools, can be a sign of inclusion or exclusion.

We can make the same case for space in schools. The classroom that is disorganized, where the location of classroom materials shifts regularly, will not serve the student who has low vision or is blind; disorganization in such a situation becomes a sign of exclusion. Student seating also has representational meaning. A teacher who has students select their own seats may find that the students recreate patterns of association that are linked to socioeconomic patterns outside the school. The student with a disability often can be observed on the edge of the classroom, working with a teaching assistant. Here the metaphor of marginalization becomes real.

There are many hegemonic norms of schooling that go unquestioned. We challenge readers to consider the diverse learners who are served or disserved by these "norms." Practices such as lesson planning, resource allocation, even classroom decorations and stimuli symbolize what is valued in schooling. We encourage readers to take stock of these signs and symbols; question them; consider them from multiple perspectives; and ask others to interpret them.

Shift Orientations: Learning and Systems

As we have suggested throughout this chapter, the pursuit of an access-to-academics agenda requires an appreciation for complexity. Access to academics is a vision or an orientation, not a specific end that is ever achieved in a concrete moment. In fact, we have come to challenge our own orientation—one that originally articulated the "Access" agenda as a school *reform.* We believe that change, as an orientation, may be misdirected. To suggest that schools need to "reform" means that we are tinkering around the edges of an existing system. "School *reform*" implies amendments or corrections without the possibility of radical, revolutionary change. We engage in what Argyris calls "single loop" actions; that is, actions that do little more than make superficial changes. School reform gets done—new programs get implemented, teams get formed, reports get delivered. We challenge readers to shed the orientation of *reform* or implementation, and adopt instead the orientations of *learning* and *systems.*

An Orientation of Learning. In the book, *Schools that Learn,* Peter Senge and his colleagues (2000) suggested ways that schools can use a critical pedagogy to enact a learning culture; one where practitioners "hold deep conversations about their purpose, the nature of their organizations, their shared values and goals," and where teams undertake "serious attempts to identify and critically question mental models about the political and social forces that shape their system" (p. 209). In such a culture, practitioners are not so much committed to change for the sake of change or reform or compliance, but they are committed to learning; engaging in a constant cycle of reflection on and in action (Argyris & Schon, 1974). Senge (2000) pointed out that "practioners and proponents of critical pedagogy . . . continually ask questions that provoke people to focus on the purpose of schooling: What? Why? How? To what end? For whom? Against whom? By whom? In favor of whom? In favor of what?" (p. 212). Such questions are powerful, messy, and as Senge and his coauthors suggested, "uncomfortable." Thus is the nature of a *learning* orientation. Every action is influenced by reflection on and learning from previous actions. One is never comfortable, never content, never done.

In this final strategy of "shifting orientations" we suggest a shift in thinking that promotes the development and revision of theses to guide practice. This is a variation on the constant comparative method first explained by Glaser and Strauss (1967) for qualitative researchers. The basic thrust of the method is for the researcher (in this case the educator) to collect observational data such as interviews, observations, personal journal, examples of student work and the like, to code the data with topics the researcher–educator considers possibly relevant to understanding the topic at hand (in this case it is access to academics) and to then develop theme statements that may suggest ways of understanding and enacting the access-to-academics agenda.

One elementary school adopted a learning orientation as they set about creating a "Bias Free School Zone." As stakeholders assessed biased practices that disserved students within the district, they pointed to report cards that used traditional letter grades and offered very little space for teacher or parent comment. The school was shifting its assessment practices to be more performance based, and teachers desired a new report card format that reflected both the new assessment practices and their desire for more collaboration with parents. The school's shared decision-making team created a narrative report card that utilized only teacher comments and allowed space for parent response. No letter grades would be reported, but teachers would comment on benchmarks and individual student progress or achievement. As the school implemented the new narrative report cards, they launched an action research project, where they collected data from stakeholders (parents, teachers, administrators) and continually reflected on whether or not the change in the reporting system was accomplishing what they hoped it would. Theirs was a learning orientation, where they continuously sought and used feedback. Their main goal was to learn whether or not their action was in fact serving their vision.

A Systems Orientation. Given the complex nature of a learning orientation, the educator's role is that of an investigator and critical analyst, operating on multiple levels. Thus, practitioners must also adopt a 'systems' orientation—considering the multiple and interdependent levels of schooling. Change occurs at various levels—personal, classroom, school or district, and community wide. Thus, practitioners must be constantly "scanning" their environment to understand how their action, or inaction, impacts the system. In adopting a systems orientation, educators share both the responsibility and the resources for enacting an *access to academics* vision.

One example of systems thinking comes from a middle school where teachers were seeking common planning time as they implemented a team teaching approach. Teachers desired more time to coordinate curriculum and plan, across disciplines (all content areas and physical education, music, art, and library/media). The teachers came up with a plan that would shave student travel time between classes during the day, and give teachers 20 minutes of common planning time at the end of the school day. The teachers considered who was impacted by their plan, and met with cafeteria workers (as lunch would have to start earlier), bus drivers (as the middle schoolers would have to be picked up *before* the high school students), and parents and administrators in charge of the after-school program (as students would be dismissed 20 minutes early, posing potential child care problems for parents). Teachers explained their vision of cross-curricular planning, and sought help from those in the system impacted by the change in schedule. The change was embraced by most stakeholders and implemented with few glitches. Most importantly, students benefited from the creative planning and new initiatives that developed during the common planning time.

CONCLUSIONS

This book suggests a range of ways educators can broaden definitions of inclusion and consider what it means to value and successfully educate all learners. Although the idea of inclusive schooling has been associated most directly with issues of disability, there are ideological and practical reasons to expand our understandings of what it means to "include" learners and what it means to have a school that works continuously and actively *to include* and provides students with an academic education.

Inclusive schooling is about: building supportive schools; promoting relationships between students; facilitating connections between teachers and students; developing curriculum and instruction that is responsive to all learners; making schools comfortable for everyone; creating spaces for students to "show up" as competent; seeing student differences and similarities; and seeking gifts and talents in every student. Inclusive schooling involves supporting all learners and teachers in finding a critical frame; helping all stakeholders in education to consider school climate and to ensure that students are learning in spaces that are safe, peaceful, and healthy; examining specific practices that can be used in moving toward more challenging and rigorous curricula and instruction; and creating opportunities for social action. Inclusive schooling also involves focusing on ways in which both teachers and students have been included and excluded and how they may have participated in the inclusion or exclusion of others; inclusive schooling requires a cycle of action and reflection.

We hope that this book—covering issues of literacy, mathematics, music, science, and social studies as well as teacher, parent, and student perspectives—will intrigue the reader enough to join us in this work of inquiry and practice. We also hope that the reader will build on our ideas, develop new ones through reflection and praxis and constantly interrogate how all learners are asked, expected, and invited to learn. Above all, we hope that readers will be inspired to embrace a new, broader definition of inclusive schooling, one that considers the needs and strengths of all students and sees every learner as capable and complex.

Finally, we invite the reader to take action—small and big, local and global. How to begin this journey? As John Holt suggested (1994), we should begin by *doing*:

> Not many years ago I began to play the cello. Most people would say that what I am doing is "learning to play" the cello. But these words carry into our

minds the strange idea that there exists two very different processes; (1) learning to play the cello; and (2) playing the cello. They imply that I will do the first until I have completed it, at which point I will stop the first process and begin the second. In short, I will go on "learning to play" until I have "learned to play" and then I will begin to play. Of course, this is nonsense. There are not two processes, but one. We learn to do something by doing it. There is no other way. (p. 132)

REFERENCES

Argyris, C., & Schon, D. (1974). *Theory in practice: Increasing professional effectiveness.* San Francisco: Jossey Bass.

Fine, M. (1991). *Framing dropouts.* Albany: SUNY Press.

Glaser, B., & Strauss, A. L. (1967). *The discovery of grounded theory: Strategies for qualitative research.* Chicago: Aldine.

Holt, J. (1994). We learn by doing. In J. Canfield & M. V. Hanson (Eds.), *Chicken soup for the soul* (pp. 132). Deerfield Beach, FL: Health Communications Incorporated.

Senge, P., Camron-McCabe, N., Lucas, T., Smith, B., Dutton, J., & Kleiner, A. (2000). *Schools that learn.* New York: Doubleday.

Author Index

Subject Index